LIBRARY SERVICES IN THE KNOWLEDGE WEB

LIBRARY SERVICES IN THE KNOWLEDGE WEB

(Collection of papers in honour of Dr. Stanley Madan Kumar)

Edited by :

K. Veeranjaneyulu

Rabindra K Mahapatra

P. Visakhi

2012

New India Publishing Agency

Pitam Pura, New Delhi-110 088

Published by

Sumit Pal Jain for

New India Publishing Agency
101, Vikas Surya Plaza, CU Block, L.S.C. Mkt.,
Pitam Pura, New Delhi-110 088, (India)
Phone : 011-27341616, Fax : 011-27341717
Mobile : 09717133558
E-mail : info@nipabooks.com
Web : www.nipabooks.com

ISBN : 978-93-81450-19-2

Printed and Laser Type Setting at : Jai Bharat Printing Press, Delhi.-110032

Dr. Stanley Madan Kumar
Festchrift Volume

Dr. Stanley Madan Kumar: A Personality To Emulate

K. Veeranjaneyulu

Dr. Stanley Madan Kumar was born on 24th March 1941 at Kolar in Karnataka State. His father Late V. Shanthraj was a railway official and his mother Late Hilda was a house wife. Dr. Stanley's early education was chequered due to his father's frequent transfers. He had his high school education at National High School, Shimoga, Pre-University and College education at Sahyadri College, Shimoga. He obtained his B.Sc. degree from Mysore University in 1962. Later he did his B.Lib.Sc. (1966) and M.Lib.Sc. (1975) all from Karnataka University. He was awarded the Karnataka State Award and Cash Prize for securing First Class and First Rank in M.Lib.Sc.

Dr. Stanley began his career as a Teacher-cum-Librarian at Sainik School, Bijapur. He was one of the faculty members selected to train the students for the National Defense Academy. He served at Sainik School from 1966 to 1969.

In March 1969 he joined the University of Agricultural Sciences, Bangalore as Library Assistant. In May 1974 he was appointed as Assistant Librarian, and in February 1984 was appointed as the Deputy Librarian and posted at UAS Fisheries College, Mangalore.

With the establishment of University of Agricultural Sciences, Dharwad, he was transferred to Dharwad in May 1987 as Deputy Librarian with the additional charge as University Librarian. In July 1990 he took over as full time University Librarian till retirement in March 2001.

Dr. Stanley initiated the documentation services at UAS, Bangalore and compiled over 40 bibliographies especially for the on-going major research programmes of UAS and Summer Institutes and Training programmes sponsored by ICAR and hosted at UAS, Bangalore.

He also started Index to *Current Periodical Literature,* a bi-monthly publication indexing articles from the Agricultural Science journals received in the University Library. The mimeographed copies of the Index were distributed among the Colleges and Research Stations under UAS, Bangalore. Xerox copies of articles supplied against request from the scientists and teachers.

Dr. Stanley served as an External Expert for the selection/assessment of library staff for the following :

- Central Plantation Crops Research Institutes (CPCRI), Kasaragod
- Indian Institute of Horticulture Research (IIHR), Bangalore
- Acharya N G Ranga Agricultural University (ANGRAU), Hyderabad
- Dr. Panjabrao Deshmuk Krishi Vidyapeeth (PVK), Akola, Maharashtra.

He served as Resource Person at the Karnataka University Academic Staff College for the UGC Refresher Course in Library and Information Science and UAS Rural Home Science College (Dharwad) Workshop on Human Resource Management.

He also served as the Chairman for the Library Committee of the Indian Development Service, a well known NGO at Dharwad.

Dr. Stanley served as the Chief Editor from 1984 to 1995 for the *Indian Journal of Agricultural Library and Information Science (formerly AALDI Bulletin)* published by the Association of Agricultural Librarians and Documentalists of India.

He was the Assistant Editor to *Krishi Munnade* a quarterly Kannada journal published by UAS, Dharwad in 1987. He served as the Editor from 1988 to 1991.

He was the Editor for the *UAS Dharwad Annual Report* from 1986-87 to 1998-99. From 1999 onwards served as a Member of the Editorial Committee.

He was on the Committee for preparing the *Perspective Plan* 1990-2000 for UAS, Dharwad. Co-Chairman for the *Decennial Commemorative Volume* (1986-1996) of UAS, Dharwad. Editor for the First National Symposium on Integration of NSS with curriculum in Agricultural Universities (July 1999) held at UAS Dharwad. Dr. Stanley compiled and edited the Research Achievements of Indian Agricultural Universities : A Compendium to commemorate the Silver Jubilee Convention of Indian Agricultural Universities Association (IAUA) held at Dharwad (August 1998). He was the Editor-in-Chief for the National Conference on Knowledge Management in the Globalized Era organized by AALDI in collaboration with ICAR and IASRI in April 2010 at New Delhi.

Right from his school and college days Dr. Stanley was an active participant in all co-curricular activities. During his college days he was the General Secretary for the Natural Science Association of Sahyadri College, Shomoga and organized guest lectures, competitions and biological science exhibitions.

At UAS Dharwad, he was officially associated with the Dean of Students Welfare in all students' activities. He served as the Chairman of the Programme Committee and conducted the UAS Dharwad Inter-Collegiate Youth Festival from 1987 held biennially at Dharwad Campus.

As Co-Chairman of the Organizing Committee (Hon'ble Vice-Chancellor was the Chairman) he planned and organized the First All India Inter-Agricultural Universities Youth Festival, AGRIUNIFEST in March 1999 at UAS Dharwad.

Dr. Stanley has to his credit over 40 papers on Library and Information Science published in various journals conferences and edited publications.

He is Life Member for

- Association of Agricultural Librarians and Documentalists of India(AALDI) (Founder Member)
- Indian Association of Special Libraries and Information Centers (IASLIC)
- Indian Library Association (ILA)
- Society of Information Science (SIS)
- Karnataka Library Association (KALA)

The Indian Agricultural Library Fraternity feels proud to have such a multifarious personality as one of its senior members. We wish Dr. Stanley Madan Kumar a long, pleasant retired life and look forward for his continued guidance to younger library professionals.

❑❑❑

भा.कृ.अनु.प.
ICAR

डॉ. सी. देवाकुमार, एफ.एन.ए.ए.एस
सहायक महानिदेशक
(शिक्षा योजना एवं विकास)
Dr. C. Devakumar, FNAAS
Assistant Director General
(Education Planning & Development)

भारतीय कृषि अनुसंधान परिषद
कृषि अनुसंधान भवन–II, पूसा, नई दिल्ली 110012
INDIAN COUNCIL OF AGRICULTURAL RESEARCH
KRISHI ANUSANDHAN BHAVAN-II, PUSA, NEW DELHI - 110 012
Telefax : 91-11-25841559
E-mail : cdevakumar@gmail.com, adgepd@icar.org.in

Foreword

The library is an integral part of the society that surrounds it. It is shaped and changed by many of the same forces that shape other types of institutions. As it evolves into something that looks quite different than it did just a few decades ago, it is critical that librarians not only become aware of this evolution, but that they actively intervene to help reshape the institution in ways that are consistent with the core mission of libraries. In an era of changing institutions, libraries need to examine what their missions have been in the past, and how they can concentrate on the part of their core and unique mission. Librarians need to find the parts of their core mission that will be sustainable in a changed environment and must innovative ways and means to overcome the types of changes that threaten basic principles such as equal access to information and fair use.

The content of the book is a clear indication of the importance of library and information services in the new environment. The articles cover a wide spectrum of topics that depict the future of libraries and library services, and the mechanisms to implement such services. The information and knowledge contained in this book would be of immense value for the librarians, university administrators, users and all others involved in information handling.

I am happy to note that this special book is being brought out in honour of Dr. Stanley Madan Kumar who is well-known for his contributions in modernizing and development of agricultural libraries. I congratulate the editors, the authors and the publisher for bringing out this special festschrift volume dedicated to an eminent colleague.

(C. Devakumar) 07/7/11

PREFACE

Globalization has tremendous influence on all walks of life including library and information services. The former prime Minister of Great Britain, Tony Blair almost decade ago remarked "The biggest changes in the public libraries over coming years will arise from the development of Information Technology". To improve the quality of library services, to have greater access to the sources of Knowledge and information to reduce knowledge gap in the developing countries, the globalization of library services is need of the hour. To provide library services to the rural community at root level, the universalization of library services is must. It makes attractive opportunities and rapid growth of knowledge and innovation. Human knowledge is now growing at a pace which was indeed unthinkable two decades ago.

Most of the information sources are being published in the digital form all over the world. A digital library can revolutionize dissemination with respect to access, speed and availability. Internet has revolutionized and has brought sea change in the information storing, dissemination and retrieval *i.e.* Information handling. Internet is a global resource centre containing information on any topic includes e-Journals, e-Books, digital libraries, Institutional Repositories, Databases, Open access phenomenon, Information Networks, Social Networks *etc.*, Federated search Engine ,Web2.0 tools like Identity 2.0, Library 2.0, Law 2.0, Media 2.0, OPAC 2.0, tagging ,mashup, News Feeds, Instant Messaging, Synchronous Messaging, Blogs and Wikis, MARC 21 standard World catalogue, etc. proposes to bring revolutionary changes in libraries due to globalization. The institutional repositories are to create visibility for an institutional scholarly research material globally. Globalization and technological advances are leading to greater international interaction and cooperation amongst librarians on a worldwide scale. Through the Internet, email, large file sharing abilities, VOIP, open source software, Blogs, Messaging, and other almost immediate sources of information exchange, librarians are truly able to collaborate and have worldwide colleagues and partnerships not imaginable thirty years ago.

There are of course still proprietary and legal restraints as to what databases, journals, and other materials can be exchanged between libraries, but ever increasingly these barriers are being reduced or redefined. Some libraries even in this globalize context may feel a need to still hold onto or protect their "turf", while any other libraries are coming more and more to see the valuable of shared resources. International in person librarian conferences such as the series hosted by Globenet, have proved extremely popular with librarians from international locales. These international conferences have provided important opportunities for librarians from around the world to get together and share ideas, views and information in a face to face context. As such these are all positive indicators of closer and increased relationships of librarians and libraries on a global scale.

Now more than ever, thanks to capabilities made available by the Web and Internet, libraries are making materials available to patrons on an almost immediate basis provided those patrons have Internet access. Many journal articles are now made available online by libraries, provided patrons have the right entry id or password, these articles can now be accessed without any need to go to a physical library. The OCLC's Open Worldcat Libraries, Google Scholar, Google Book Search and Yahoo Subscriptions have also greatly expanded patrons abilities to look up books and articles they may want to have sent to their local library from another library. These sorts of globalized innovations have made it possible for students to live in one country while actually being the student of a school in another country. Many libraries are still suspicious and reluctant to offer their materials in such an open context, while other libraries feel this sort of instant patron service is a must in order to stay relevant and viable in the face of real threats such as Amazon and Google. One can conclude that we are in the golden age of easily accessible library information thanks to technology and globalization. In as much as a resident of a given community has a computer and Internet access, it can be argued that there is some legitimacy to this position. However one is remiss if they don't also consider the harsh realities of the digital divide. It is true that a large percentage of people in the Developed World have easy access to computers and the Internet. These people therefore have the ability to harvest the bounty of information now available from libraries on the Internet.

The present Festschrift volume is a humble presentation to Dr Madan Kumar Stanley by his professional colleagues and friends to mark his professional valuable contributions and service to the library & information science community, especially to Agricultural Librarianship even after his retirement. A look of contributors of this volume and over whelming response received shows the affection and respect towards his senior professional Dr M.K. Stanely. We extend our sincere thanks to the learned contributors and grateful acknowledges to their contributions.

We feel extremely happy and proud to join his well wishers and friends to wish him for his long, healthy and active life.

Editors

List of Contributors

(Smt) Sonal Singh: Reader & Head , School of Studies in Library & Information Science, Vikram University, Ujjain, Madhya Pradesh

A.A.Abbas Khan: Deputy Librarian & Incharge Librarian, Maulana Azad National Urdu University, Gachibowli, Hyderabad – 500 032, Andhra Pradesh, India

A. Omkar Murthy: Assistant Librarian, S. V. of Medical Sciences University, Tirupati, Andhra Pradesh, India

Ajay Kaundal: Research Associate, e- Granth, University Library, CSKHP Agriculture University, Palampur, Himachal Pradesh, India

Amit Dhar: Assistant Librarian, Govt. Millenium Polytechnic, Chamba, Himachal Pradesh, India

Arun Modak: Research Scholar, School of Studies in Library & Information Science, Vikram University, Ujjain, Madhya Pradesh

Ashwini P Paradkar: Librarian, SFS College, Nagpur, Maharashtra, India

Avineni Kishore: Assistant University Librarian, Dravidian University, Kuppam – 517425, Andhra Pradesh, India

C. Krishna Reddy: Library Assistant, University Library, Dravidian University, Kuppam -517 425, Andhra Pradesh, India

D R Meher: Librarian, Central Library, Orissa University of Agriculture and Technology, Bhubaneswar-751 003, Orissa, India

D. Joyson Soundrarajan: Senior Librarian, Christian Medical College, Vellore – 632 002, Andhra Pradesh, India

D. Konappa: Research Scholar, Department of Library and Information Sciences, S.V.University, Tiruathi- 517 502, Andhra Pradesh, India

Dr. D.Chandran: Professor, Department of Library & Information Science, Sri Venkteswara University, Tirupati – 517 502, Andhra Pradesh, India

Dev Walia: Co-PI-cum-JPA , e-Granth Project, University Library, CSKHP Agriculture University, Palampur, Himachal Pradesh, India

Dipak Krushnarao Bhalekar: Babasaheb Naik College of Engineering, Ta. Pusad, Dist. Yavatmal, Maharashtra, India

Doraswamy Naick: Research Scholar, Department of Library and Information Science,S. V. University, Tirupati – 517 502, Andhra Pradesh, India

K. Kumar: Research Scholar, Department of Library and Information Science, S. V. University, Tirupati – 517 502, Andhra Pradesh, India

K. Veeranjaneyulu: University Librarian, ANGR Agricultural University, Hyderabad - 500 030, Andhra Pradesh, India

L.S.R.C.V. Ramesh: Senior Assistant, Administrative office, ANGR Agricultural University, Hyderabad – 500 030, Andhra Pradesh, India

M. Anjaiah: Assistant Professor, University Library, Dravidian University, Kuppam -517 425, Andhra Pradesh, India

M. K. G. Rajev: Manager, Information Resource Centre, Sur University College, Sultanate of Oman

M. Muniya Naik: Professional Assistant, Indira Gandhi Memorial Library, University of Hyderabad, Hyderabad, Andhra Pradesh, India

M. R. Murali Prasad: Chief Librarian, Indian Institute of Public Health, Hyderabad, Andhra Pradesh, India

M. Sandhya: Assistant Librarian, Aurora Scientific Research Technological Academy, Bandlaguda, Hyderabad, Andhra Pradesh, India

M. Suresh Babu: Research Scholar, Department of Library & Information Science, Sri Venkteswara University, Tirupati – 517 502, Andhra Pradesh, India

M.Tholkaooian: Research Scholar, Department of Library and Information Science, S. V. University, Tirupati – 517 502, Andhra Pradesh, India

Md. Nurul Islam: Librarian, DNC College, Murshidabad, West Bengal, India

Mohd. Vali Hussain: Junior Library Assistant, ANGR Agricultural University, Rajendranagar, Hyderabad – 500 030, Andhra Pradesh, India

Monisha Mishra: Librarian, Central Library, Orissa University of Agriculture & Technology, Bhubaneswar- 751 003, Orissa, India

N K Wadhwa: Knowledge Resource Centre, National Physical Laboratory, Dr K S Krishnan Road, New Delhi-110 012, India

N. P. Ravi Kumar: Assistant Librarian, ANGR Agricultural University, Hyderabad - 500 030, Andhra Pradesh, India

N. Subramanian: University Librarian, Periyar University, Salem, Tamil Nadu, India

P. Govinda Reddy: Department of Anthropology, University of Madras, Chennai - 600 005, Tamil Nadu, India

Prabhu B. Gaddimani: Assistant Librarian, Tata Institute of Social Sciences, P.B.No. 8313, Deonar, Mumbai - 400 088, Maharashtra, India

Prashant P. Deshmukh: Librarian, Phulshing Naik Mahavidyalaya, Ta.Pusad, Dist. Yavatmal, Maharashtra, India

Prof. B. Ramesh Babu: Professor, Department of Library and Information Science, University of Madras, Chennai – 600 005, Tamil Nadu, India

R. Jeyshankar: Assistant Professor, Department of Library and Information Science, Alagappa University, Karaikudi - 630 003, Tamil Nadu, India

R. Pommal Rao: Assistant Librarian, Indira Gandhi Memorial Library, University of Hyderabad, Hyderabad, Andhra Pradesh, India

Rabindra K. Mahapatra: Chief Librarian, Central Library, Orissa University of Agriculture & Technology, Bhubneshwar 751 003, Orissa, India

Rajpal Walke: Knowledge Resource Centre, National Physical Laboratory, Dr K S Krishnan Road, New Delhi-110 012, India

Ramdas Lihitkar: Librarian, Government Institute of Science, Nagpur, Maharashtra, India

Dr. S. M. Rokade: Librarian, Anand Niketan College of Agriculture, Anandwan, Warora, Dist. Chandrapur 442 914, Maharashtra, India

Satish Kanamadi: Deputy Librarian, Tata Institute of Social Sciences, P.B.No. 8313, Deonar, Mumbai - 400 088, Maharashtra, India

Shalini R Lihitkar: Assistant Professor & Head, Department of Library & Information Science, RTM Nagpur University, Nagpur, Maharashtra, India

Shriram Venkatraman: Department of Anthropology, University of Madras, Chennai - 600 005, Tamil Nadu, India

Sunil Kumar Satpathy: Deputy Librarian, Central Library, National Institute of Technology, Raipur-492 010, Chattisgarh, India

T. Sreenivasa Rao : Assistant Librarian, S.V. Agricultural College, Tirupati – 517 502, Andhra Pradesh, India

Usha M Dangre: Librarian, PIG College of Engineering, Nagpur, Maharashtra, India

V. Nireekshan Babu: Associate Professor, Potti Sreeramulu Telugu University, Hyderabad, Andhra Pradesh, India

V. Seetha Lakshmi : Department of Anthropology, University of Madras, Chennai - 600 005, Tamil Nadu, India

V. Shailaja: SRF, NAIP e-Granth Project, Central Library, ANGR Agricultural University, Hyderabad, Andhra Pradesh, India

Y. Uma Devi: Assistant Librarian & Co-PI, NAIP e-Granth Project, Central Library, ANGR Agricultural University, Hyderabad, Andhra Pradesh, India

CONTENTS

Chapter – 1

Gigantic Role of E-Books: An Overview of Future Libraries

K. Veeranjaneyulu and L.S.R.C.V. Ramesh

INTRODUCTION

Electronic books are one way to enhance the digital library with global 24X7 access to authoritative information, and they enable users access specific research material easily, quickly and effectively. Library users are also able to remotely search, locate and check out e-books from the libraries using online public access catalogs (OPACS). As with any new opportunity new challenges emerge and utilizing the internet to deliver book content is no exception. Integrating e-books into the digital library has created challenges and opportunities for LIS professionals; publishers and e-books providers.

E-BOOKS

An e-book is based both on emulating the basic characteristics of traditional books in an electronic format, as well as leveraging internet technology to make access to e-books easy and efficient to use.

Electronic books offer creative possibilities for extending access as well as changing learning behavior and academic research. Content can always be accessible regardless of time or place, to be read on Pc or on portable book readers, books need never go out of print and new editions can be easily created. One can carry several times at once on a portable reader and over time build a personal library, features such as full text searching, changeable font size, mark up, citation creation and note taking will enhance usability. Print text can be integrated with multi dimensional object, sound to create a whole new kind of monographic work.

Despite the considered pronounce of e-books, our text force contacted that all the element that world make the e-book market viable are not quite in place. Element that we consider important to story regarding academic use of e-books.

1. Content
2. Software and Hardware standards and protocols.
3. Digital rights management
4. Access
5. Archiving
6. Privacy
7. The market and pricing
8. Enhancement and Ideal e-book futures.

Content

Academic readers need to rely on authority and integrity of content. E-books content should match any print version and include all its elements text groups and illustration. We anticipate that academics will increasingly incorporate information, that can only be presented as non-print media, content needs to be separated from the transferable in a non proprietary format, into a variety of software and hardware readers, both to offer readers a choice of additional features, and to make it possible for libraries to loan e-book content.

Software and Hardware standards and protocols

(i). Software

Non commercial monographic electronic text for scholarly exchange have been available on the internet since that early year of UNIX file exchange, file transfer, gopher and finally type text transfer protocols.

Currently there is no established standard for an interoperable e-book format for commercially produced e-books that address publishers needs to support commercial end user distribution and that also enables world value for the consumer.

(ii). Hardware

A pragmatic factor in using e-books is the reading and using them, yet e-books hardware devices are still not quite practical or cost effective enough to progress very deeply into the market. A variety of devices are being developed to replicate some of the virtues of printed monographs, including portability and network independence, so that e-books themselves will function on a variety of platforms. The two basic kinds of e-book readers on the market to-day are the full sized and the palm sized reader. Currently all readers use proprietary file formats.

Digital right management

One of the most critical element in the development of electronic publishing that will impact libraries involves digital right management still being developed. DRMS are either hardware or software that enforce control over intellectual property, such as limit by user time, fee, and for extent of content.

Access

In addition to standards allowing interoperability and ownership through digital night management issues of access include user awareness and the ability to accommodate simultaneous users. So that researches can readily identify e-books, libraries must be able to integrate with other format in catalogs and integrated library systems, in standardized forms of bibliographic information and in metadata such as MARC and other appropriate metadata.

Archiving and long term Access

Two of the roles collection of academic libraries are building research level collectors and acting as archiving of research information. Currently e-books vendor purchase models allow some flexibility such as a premium price for perpetual access versus more modest pricing for annual access to a revolving group of lines.

Privacy

Some e-book vendors are creating individual user account to track how many times an individual has changed on, and to create my library type features. The individual account on the vendor's web site may infringe on privacy, since it would, be possible for vendors to report exactly what an individual had accessed regarding the vendor's system.

The market and pricing

The demand for simultaneous access to individual e-book times should not regime libraries to purchase multiple copies of e-book and pricing models should be developed that permit same level of access.

Enhancement and Ideal future

This functionality may be varied a inclusion of multimedia information.

Full text searching mark-up citation formatting, reference linking conventions portability, interoperability on a variety of devices, availability in advance of print, advantages one pricing and the ability to share or hour information, given the variety of user needs, non-proprietary interoperability of e-book content will be needed.

ADVANTAGES OF E-BOOKS

a. The biggest advantage is the so called every hoariness of an e-book. In a similar fashion, a student away from any research library can access that library's honoring via a computer attached to a medium.

b. A large state or ration can medium their enhance on multiple copies of a book and instead make available the text as an e-book.

c. The e-book can be made available as a CD-ROM and occupy a fraction of the space of a paper volume of the same title.

d. The e-book either in the online or CD-ROM form may contain animation and live-action illustrations not possible in printed books.

E-BOOK OPPORTUNITY

The internet had sensed an emotion in the book publishing industry with the emergence of the e-book.

- Easy access to content.
- On demand availability.
- Prevention from being lost, stolen, or damaged.
- Capability to search within a book and across a coalition of books.
- Acridity to be linked to other resources including deaconries and the saurian
- Absence of physical space management
- Device independence for accessing the content.
- Access to content using standard web browsers
- Customizable search interfaces.
- Easy transportation and
- Access from any where and any time

E-BOOKS AND FUTURE OF LIBRARIES

In spite of many challenges, progress has been made in the production and distribution of e-books during the last two years. Libraries, publishers, e-book providers and integrated library system vendors have worked together to implement and integrate equations systems, text version collection development strategies propose and adopt new revised and combined standards provide new e-book hardware and software identify and test new indexing methods for full text e-books test new access and usage models; and interact archiving policies and procedures for e-books.

CONCLUSION

The role of e-book in academic libraries is still not clear, and there is considerable development of standards technologies and pricing model needed to make the market for e-books viable and sustainable. Technologies for reading and using e-books are not yet convenient enough for the longer text format to have made much market panoramas.

Print has many rights and powers that e-books don't. We like e-books but we must not allow ourselves to be look into technology or legal/ social paradigms that impair our patch discourse of our community.

REFERENCE

1. Carty, Susan (2000). The digital text book is coming. Information Searcher 1/01, pp. 123-127.
2. Crawford, Walter (2000). Wine models, one name : Untangling the e-book, muddle. American libraries, pp. 56-59.
3. Dillon, Danni's (2000). Digital books; making them, work for publishers and Libraries. College and research libraries 61, pp. 391-393.
4. Dillon, Dennis (2000). "E-books; the UT-Aushri Experience. Texas Library Journal 76, pp. 112-115.
5. Gibbons, Susan 2001. E-books; some concerns and surprises; Portal; Libraries; and the Academy 1, pp. 71-75.
6. Hawkins, Donald T (2000). E-books; A Major publishing revolution part I; General considerations and issues; online 24, pp. 14-28.
7. Halter, Donnie Small (2000). e-Books in Libraries : Some early experience and reaction, Searcher 8, pp. 63-5.
8. Lynch, Clifford (1999). Electrifying the book. Library Journal 124, pp. 3-6.

❑❑❑

Chapter – 2

Electronic Resources Collection Development: Policies and Practices in University Libraries

Avineni Kishore

INTRODUCTION

The goal of the libraries is to provide an effective combination of print, non-print and electronic resources, and the integration of the use of these resources in support of teaching, learning and research at the university. Electronic resources, however, pose challenges not encountered with the acquisitions of traditional library materials, such as access, interface, technical support and licensing. The libraries therefore need to formulate separate Electronic Resources Collection Development policy to address these issues. The purpose of this policy is to provide guidelines in choosing appropriate electronic resources and to establish consistency and priorities in managing this important part of the libraries' collection.

ELECTRONIC RESOURCES

"Electronic resources" refer to those materials that require computer access, whether through microcomputer, mainframe, or other types of computers, and that may either be locally mounted or accessed remotely via the Internet. These resources cover both free Internet resources and electronic resources purchased or licensed by the libraries from a commercial source, a non-profit organization, a professional organization or any external institution.

DEFINITIONS OF ELECTRONIC RESOURCES

The phrase "electronic resources", has broadly been defined as information accessed by a computer, may be useful as bibliographic guides to potential sources but, as of yet, they infrequently appear as cited references in their own right (Graham, 2003).

According to IFLA ISBD (ER), an electronic resource consists of materials that are computer-controlled, including materials that required the use of a peripheral (e.g. a CD-ROM player) attached to a computer- the items may or may not be used in the interactive mode. There are two types of E-resources: data (information in the form of numbers, letters, graphics, images, and sound, or a combination thereof) and programs (instructions or routines for performing certain tasks including the processing of data and programs. e.g. online services, interactive multimedia) (Bavakenthy et al., 2003).

According to Online Dictionary for Library & Information Science (ODLIS) an electronic resource is a material consisting of data and/or computer program(s) encoded for reading and manipulation by a computer, by the use of a peripheral device directly connected to the computer, such as a CD-ROM drive, or remotely via a network, such as the Internet. The libraries with their traditional holdings in print format are now being added with electronic information resources in various formats like CD-ROM and DVD-ROM databases, On-line databases, E-journals and plenty of Internet or Web resources. The content of these sources varies from bibliographic or factual to full text.

TYPES OF ELECTRONIC RESOURCES

Some of the common types of electronic resources available in the academic world are:

- Indexing and abstracting databases
- Full-text (aggregated) databases
- E-journals
- E-books
- Reference databases (directories, dictionaries, encyclopedias, etc.)
- Numeric and statistical databases

A detailed but non-exhaustive list of the different types of electronic resources is given below:

A. Text Based Document Types

Biography	Conference proceedings	Dictionary
Directory	Electronic Journal	Electronic Newspaper
Electronic Newswire	Electronic Book	Electronic Text
Encyclopaedia	Exhibition	Numerical data
Statistical data, Etc.		

B. Non-Text-Based Document Types

Animation	Architectural drawings	Architectural models
Audio file	Book illustrations	Blueprints
Computer graphics	Digital image	Maps
Multimedia	Paintings Drawings	Panoramic photographs
Panoramic views	Periodical illustrations	Sculpture Photographs
Space photographs	Sketches	Title pages
Video files, Etc.		

C. Meta Resource Types

Abstracts	Archival finding aid	Bibliography
Catalog	Index, Etc.	

GUIDELINES FOR SELECTION OF FEE-BASED ELECTRONIC RESOURCES

The electronic resource must support the curricular and research needs of the university. There should be a target audience and an expected level of use. The resource will add depth or breadth to the existing collection. Collectively, a balance should be sought among the various disciplines and intellectual levels (undergraduate, graduate, and faculty) to meet the different needs. Except for archival materials, information must be current and updated regularly. Preferably, resources with print equivalents should not lag behind their print counterpart.

The content should come from an authoritative author and/or publisher on the subject. Other indicators of quality include positive peer and professional reviews. Accuracy and completeness as compared with print format, if available. This means that the electronic resource should have all the articles, illustrations, graphs and tables as they appear in the print counterpart.

Functionality and System Reliability

The electronic resource will provide sufficient added value over the print equivalent or other formats. The interface should be user-friendly. Some common user friendliness features are introductory screens, online tutorials, context-sensitive help, and pop-ups and menus. The search and retrieval software must be powerful and flexible. Some features that should be available include command search, index and title browsing, truncation, auto-stem, thesaurus, history and alert/SDI. Preferably, the user interface should be consistent with other interfaces currently in use. The system should support multiple export options (email, printing, and downloading.)The system should provide access to other electronic resources and support resource integration via reference and full-text linking. The system capacity and network infrastructure should be technologically up-to-date and provide for optimum response time.

Access-Related Technical Considerations

Preferably, the electronic resource should be available for remote access. Stand alone CD-ROMs and dedicated work stations that require in-library use are generally discouraged.

The libraries prefer access to remote hosts via Web to other formats and methods of access, such as CD-ROM, local Web mount, etc., because it offers optimum access, faster updating, cost savings in storage, and presents fewer problems in maintenance and preservation. Acquisition in other formats is discouraged, unless there is no alternative or the cost difference between the formats is significant.

The libraries prefer IP filtering to other methods of authentication, such as login and password authentication. Unless there is no alternative or the cost difference between the methods is significant, other methods of authentication are in general discouraged.

The electronic resource should be compatible across different platforms (PC, Mac, etc.)Though local installation and maintenance are not preferred, if chosen, the electronic resource must be compatible with the existing hardware and software. Obsolete formats and platforms are not supported. The Systems Librarian and staff should be consulted in case of doubt. If the electronic resource requires any special hardware, software, audio and/or video capabilities, the Systems Librarian and staff should be consulted.

Vendor Support

The vendor of the electronic resource should be established and reliable. The electronic resource should be available for trial. Preferably, the vendor shall provide product demonstrations, if needed.

If needed, the vendor should provide initial and, preferably, ongoing product training. Customer and technical support should be timely, accurate and professional. The vendor should provide quality statistical reporting. Preferably, the reports should follow ICOLC (International Coalition of Library Consortia)'s Guidelines For Statistical Measures Of Usage Of Web-Based Information Resources and/or COUNTER (Counting Online Usage of Networked Electronic Resources)'s Code of Practice.

The vendor should be prepared to respond to the libraries' requests for customization, branding and provision of MARC records and URLs. The vendor should provide advance notifications for content and platform changes, as well as system down time.

Pricing Consideration

The vendor should offer a choice of pricing models from which the libraries may select. These models could be based on various criteria, including the number of simultaneous users and user population. Pricing models that are based on FTE should only take into account the size of the actual user community. A specialized electronic resource should not be charged based on the total user population of the university.

The cost of providing access and the cost of content should be separate. Preferably, the subscription fee for a licensed electronic resource should include permanent rights to use the information that has been paid for in the event that the electronic resource is subsequently cancelled. Alternatively, the vendor should offer either a purchase option (e.g. netLibrary PrePaid model) or a combined model with a one-off archive fee and a cost-recover annual access fee (e.g. JSTOR model).

The libraries should not be required to purchase both the print and electronic versions of a resource. The cost of the electronic resource should not exceed that of the print counterpart. Any increase in price from print to electronic format, and from CD-ROM to Web should be reflected in the increase in functionality and accessibility.

In general, the libraries support ICOLC's Statement of Current Perspective and Preferred Practices for the Selection and Purchase of Electronic Information. The libraries participate in JULAC's CDC (Joint University Librarians Advisory Committee's Collaborative Development Committee) and other consortia in order to take advantage of aggregated purchasing agreements. It actively seeks consortia purchasing opportunities and the vendor should be prepared to offer consortia pricing.

Licensing Consideration

'Authorized Users' should be defined as broadly as possible. Bonafide faculty members, students, researchers, any employees and contractors engaged by the university as well as on-site users of the university should be included as authorized users.

"Authorized Sites' should be defined as broadly as possible. Authorized users should be permitted to access the electronic resource from anywhere via the university's secure network.

The license should permit fair use of all information for non-commercial, educational, instructional, and research purposes by the libraries and authorized users. These include viewing, downloading, and printing. Other uses permitted under fair use are ILL, e-reserves and course packs. The license should reflect realistic expectations concerning the libraries' ability to monitor use and discover abuse.

In general, the vendor should employ a standard agreement that describes the rights of the libraries in easy-to-understand and explicit language.

a. Responsibilities of the Collection Development Team

The Collection Development Librarian coordinates the Collection Development Team in collection building activities. The Assistant Collection Development Librarian (Electronic Information Acquisitions) assists in the identification and negotiation of large database as well as consortia purchase with other libraries and agencies. Other identified library staff in the university library, with support from the Assistant Collection Development Librarian, are responsible for building electronic resources in their assigned areas. The Team works closely with Acquisitions Services Librarian and Systems Librarian and in consultation with the Deputies in the purchase of electronic materials.

ACQUISITION PROCESS

a. Selection Aids for Electronic Resources

In addition to the selection aids mentioned in the Collection Development strategy, a number of other sources are also consulted to identify electronic resources of potential use:

- Database listings of other university libraries
- Minutes, trial pages and reviews of other libraries' collection development committees
- Consortia's reviews and listings
- Mailing lists

b. Acquisition Procedures

Generally, electronic resources that require on-going subscriptions and/or that provide packaged or aggregated contents are processed following the Electronic Resources Collection Building Workflow (Intranet) and evaluated with reference to the Selection Guidelines using the Evaluation Checklist for Electronic Publication (Intranet). Recommendations for electronic resources should be submitted using the Electronic Resources Recommendation Online. The completed forms are routed directly to the Collection Development Department unless the requester's faculty prefers other arrangements and instructs accordingly. The form allows the Collection Development Department to gather important information regarding the resource recommended, such as method of access, expected audience, quality of content, subject coverage, and user interface. It also allows the requester to provide ranking on the resource, which is used to prioritize recommendations.

Electronic Journals

Recommendations for individual journal titles, whether electronic-only or print plus electronic, follow the same procedure as those for print-only titles. Recommendations should be submitted using the Journal Recommendation Online (University Library website). Completed forms are routed to the appropriate Faculty Library Committee Chairman to be forwarded to the Faculty Library Committee for final approval. When approved, the recommendations will be directed to the Acquisitions Services Department for processing. Recommendations for e-journal packages may be submitted directly to the Collection Development Department using Electronic Resources Recommendation Online (University Library website).

Monographic CD-ROMs, VCDs and DVDs

In general, CD-ROMs, VCDs and DVDs that are monographic in nature are not covered by the Electronic Resources Fund. Recommendations for these items should be submitted using the Book Recommendation Form.

De-Selection

This part applies to electronic resources that are in stand alone floppy diskette/CD-ROM/DVD-ROM and other media formats. These include monographic titles purchased by the faculty for general circulation, networked/standalone/dedicated CD-ROMs weeded as per the Criteria for Installing CD ROMs (Intranet), and other items transferred to the AV & Reserve collection over time.

Guidelines for De-selection

Periodic examination of materials in the collection for de-selection will be conducted. In addition to the Duplication Policy and Weeding Policy in the Collection Development Policy, the following guidelines will also apply.

- Materials non-circulated for discretionary number of years
- Materials not compatible with existing hardware and software and/or not supported by the vendors/Obsolete formats and platforms are not supported
- Outdated or inaccurate materials
- Content is duplicated in available preferred formats
- Materials damaged beyond repair

Librarians responsible for the selection of the following materials are to be consulted in case of doubt. Effort will be made to obtain a preferred format if available.

- Expensive titles
- Archival CDs, DVDs, tapes and other media formats of electronic journals, standards and dissertations.

Formats which are becoming obsolete should no longer be selected for purchase. Replacement/substitutes in a desirable format should be sought if contents are unique and deemed invaluable to research.

GUIDELINES FOR SELECTION OF FREE INTERNET RESOURCES

Free Internet resources may come in a variety of formats and document types, such as Web pages, listservs, Usenet news, FTP sites, full-text online versions of books, journals, and government documents. To supplement the breadth and depth of the libraries' collections, free Internet resources which are deemed of value to the research and teaching of the university will be identified and cataloged. While selection criteria from the general and subject policies prevail, the following specific selection guidelines should be met also. Links to these websites will be provided in the Libraries' OPAC.

Selection Guidelines Specific to Internet Resources

- Information provided or created by an authority or a reputable or reliable source on the subject.
- Website is favorably reviewed by a reputable source.
- Site is accessible freely with browser/software and compatible with existing networked environment.
- Site is stable with infrequent down times.
- Policy of periodic review and update of content, with a date of revision statement for websites. E-books, journals, and other documents should have dates of publication or posting.
- Good design with visual appeal and easy navigation of contents within the site, e.g. site index or search engine.

Exclusions

- Commercial sites which are mainly advertisement or promotion of services or products.
- Web sites or web pages of institutions, corporations, government agencies, and/or professional societies which contain largely

promotional or newsletter type materials about the activities of the organization. Institutional web sites/ pages should only be included if there is a substantial amount of full text documents useful for the university's research and learning purposes.

- Sites that require a user fee or access to the contents within requires fee.
- Portals which are merely links to hosts of other links but lack organization and /or substantial annotations, as opposed to an organized and annotated series of links which may be deemed useful as a subject bibliography.
- Other University Electronic-Resource pages.
- Websites deemed out of scope to our curriculum or level.

De-selection Guidelines

- The resource is no longer available or maintained.
- No longer current, reliable or relevant.
- Overlaps another resource which offers more comprehensive coverage or treatment of subject.

Duplication

Internet resource which duplicates an existing print resource is deemed acceptable if no fee is incurred and its inclusion provides greater access and convenience than the single point of access which a print resource provides.

The Web format is preferred generally, and print duplication is usually discouraged due to space and processing costs. The libraries will duplicate print resource with existing free Internet resource when:

- One format is unstable and retention is expected or required.
- Multiple formats meet the needs of different users.
- The print format is needed for archival purpose due to its significant historical value.

Copyright for Internet Resources

In order to protect the libraries and its users from copyright infringement in establishing hyperlinks to Internet Resources, the following policy should be observed:

- Effort will be made to identify and acknowledge the owner/creator of the Internet resource.
- Hyperlinks to the material content will not be set up in such a way

that the remote webpage or resource be brought within a frame under academic library web page link, thus implying that academic institute has created the resource.

- A disclaimer is placed on the Electronic Resources webpage, announcing who may link to our information, and to remove any of the hyperlinks made to remote webpage/resource if the copyright owner requests.

CONCLUSION

As the world of information continues its march towards the electronic format, librarians need to be savvier in handling e-collections. Librarians would never consider adding a new collection of printed books or journals without a thorough review process. Yet it appears that we often add electronic content without a rigorous process. This will have to change. Librarians need to treat e-content like printed content by developing a set of standards for the collection and management of e-resources.

REFERENCES

1. Bavakenthy, M; Veeran, M. C. K and Salih, T.K.M (2003). *Information Access Management and Exchange in the Technological Age*. New Delhi: Ess Ess Publications.
2. Graham, S.R. (2003). "Historians and electronic resources: a citation analysis", *JAHC*, Vol. 3 No. 3. pp. 18-24.
3. *Online Dictionary for Library & Information Science*. Available http://lu.com/ odlis/ search.cfm
4. Robert K. Flatley and Krista Prock, "E-Resource Collection Development: A Survey of Current Practices in Academic Libraries". Available http://www.libraryworks. com/ LW_Best Practices/BP_E-Resource_Collection_Development_ 0210.aspx
5. Sandhu, Gurdish and Sale, Anna (2005). "25 Years of Electronic Resources Collection Development at the University of Salford: Some Issues and Challenges". Available
6. http://lib.hku.hk/cd/policies/erp.html
7. http://www.lib.utk.edu/colldev/elrescd.html
8. http://*www.iusb.edu/.../collections electronic_collection_development .doc*

❑❑❑

Chapter – 3

Adoption of E-Resources in Indian Libraries for Countering Economic Challenges.

L.S.R.C.V. Ramesh and Mohd. Vali Hussain

INTRODUCTION

Digital divide is the gap in opportunities experienced by those with listed accessibility to technology especially, the Internet. This digital divide can be bridged by facility access to scholarly e-resources to the people of developing and undeveloped countries. Apart from the fact that most of the print journals are expensive and there is steep rise in the subscription price of journals and databases, financial constraint because of static/shrinking budget available to higher educational institutions have forced the libraries to cut their subscription drastically.

ELECTRONIC SUBSCRIPTION OF JOURNALS

With globalization of education and competitive research, demand for journals has increased over the years. Due to insufficient funds libraries have been forced to cut subscriptions of journals which has titled them towards the internet to cover the gap between demand and supply by way of e-journals that can be subscribed online. Most of the journals are available in electronic form. These journals are available over UGC INFONET to all the universities, thereby quality information is made accessible to the academic scholar-base speedily across the country, at an affordable price.

NEED FOR E-LEARNING

E-learning provides faster learning at reduced cost increases access to learning and clear accountability for all the learning processes.

- Learning is self directed allowing students to choose speed or slow down as necessary.
- Learning is self directed, allowing students to choose content and tools appropriate to their differing interest, needs and skills.
- Geographical barriers are eliminated, opening up broader education options.
- Overall student costs are less.
- Enhances computer and the Internet skills.
- Draws upon hundreds of years of established pedagogical principles.
- Has the attention of every major university in the world, most with their own live degree certificates and individual courses.

Z39.50 is a protocol for computer to computer information retrieval. Users can access dissimilar library catalogues from the host institution's catalogue. While using a familiar interface. Both Z39.50 client and server are needed if you want to visit others and have others visit your catalogue.

ADVANTAGES OF E-RESOURCES

Electronic resources offer a number of advantages not only to libraries but also to users, authors, editors, publishers and archivists.

- Low cost of production compared to printed document
- Saves enormous time by providing easy and instantaneous access without wasting time for processing, printing, binding and delivery.
- Eliminates printing, binding and postage cost.
- Allow interactive facility.
- Facilitate easy depiction in new media and distribution.
- Integration of different media (images, sounds, video etc)
- Saves library storage space.
- Provide hyper links to related additional resources.
- Have potential to conserve fragile/precious original material.
- Allow remote access from any where & any time
- Enable simultaneous access to large number of uses.
- Eco friendly.

CREATION OF INSTRUCTIONAL REPOSITORIES

Most of the academic, scientific and technological institutions are bringing out lot of valuable scholarly publications in the form of theses, dissertations, technical reports, study materials and papers etc. Many of their research libraries are creating digital repositories in electronic form for the use of their own user community as well as for others.

OPEN ACCESS RESOURCES

Institutional repositories are created to capture, preserve maintain and disseminate intellectual output of respective institutions. The open access movement, changes in scholarly communication to remove barriers to access, and the increasing awareness that universities and research institutions are not availing valuable digital and print materials are the driving forces for the establishment of institutional repositories.

Open access resources refer to all types of information resources freely accessible online, free of charge, and free of most copyright restrictions. The modern technology makes possible the world wide electronic distribution of the peer reviewed journal literature and completely free and unrestricted access to scholars, teachers, students and other curious minds. Removing access burners to this literature will accelerate research and enrich education.

CONCLUSION

As information becomes an indispensable form of commodity, providing information services is of paramount importance to all types of organizations. Libraries are faced with the challenge of providing letter services with shrinking budget. Fortunately, the developments in IT are creating new opportunities for libraries. For instance, libraries can now provide access to networked information sources that their libraries do not even own. They need to weigh the virtues of new approaches such as "access versus ownership".

REFERENCES

1. Mc Knight (1993). Electronic journals past present and future. ASLIB proceedings 45 (11), pp. 7-10pp.
2. Jana R (1999).Getting the most out of online learning. Info world 21 (37), p. 199.
3. Demas (1994). Collection development for the electronic library, A Concept red and organizational model. Library Hitech 12(3), pp. 71-80.
4. Singh SN (2000). Library resource sharing in network environment. ASLIC Bullet 45(2), pp. 63-71.

5. Vohara, Rajahs (2003). Collection development and management in university libraries in the connect electronic information environment. ASLIC Bulletin 48 (4), pp. 224-240.

6. Harish Chandra (2003). E-resource management with specific reference to e-reference source Interactive and Issuer: 21st Annual convention and conference, Central Library, IIT, Roorky.

❑❑❑

Chapter – 4

Library Services and Resources in Christian Mission Hospitals in Tamil Nadu with Special Reference to CMC&H, Vellore

D. Joyson Soundrarajan and Prof. B. Ramesh Babu

INTRODUCTION

The contribution of the church in the field of the health services has been well appreciated by all sections of the people as well as by government. Quite a few church personnel are fully involved in public health services, nutritional programmes and hygiene and sanitation programmes. There are mobile clinic and awareness programmes run in the rural areas. In the field of medical care the contribution of the Christianity is meritorious. The healing mission received some priority in the agenda of the missionaries and churches. Health centers run by Christians originally meant to serve the poor. Many of well equipped and well established hospitals render service in rural areas and slums others do not reach. Educational service of the Christianity has been a highly valued service to the nation.

CHRISTIAN MISSION HOSPITALS IN INDIA WITH SPECIAL REFERENCE TO TAMIL NADU

From the middle of the nineteenth century, the mission world in Britain began to change. There were many missionaries who held university degrees. They provided a wholly new context to evangelism by their emphasis first upon the importance of education and later, by being the pioneers at least in Asia and Africa, of Western scientific hospitals, organized by missionaries, ultimately developed. The full-fledged teaching hospitals were without doubt a high point of missionary achievement. American medical missionaries who were in Sri Lanka prior to the mid-nineteenth century did not belong to the artisan or mechanic class or other lower middle-class groups. John Scudder, a physician, grandfather of the founder of the Vellore College, left for the East in 1819 and worked first in Sri Lanka before moving to India. John Scudder's father has been described by one of his biographers, as a 'gentleman of the old school' and his mother it is said was a 'lady of high culture'.

The importance given to education, including female education, was a feature of this mission. In 1816 there was only one woman who could read but by 1852 an inspection of Dr. Green's dispensary register showed that there were fifty-one. The improvement, Green believed, was a result of mission education. School and college education and medical education were fields in which the missionary contribution received a mixed reception in different quarters. In South India, statistics, particularly of school and early university education at the end of the nineteenth century show that the mission contribution in the field of education was very significant. The creation of a pool of educated men and women as result of mission enterprise and doctors which facilitated the training of nurses, pharmacists and doctors in medical mission nursing schools, hospitals, and ultimately medical colleges.

Table 1 State-wise No of Christian Mission Hospitals in India

Sl. No.	State	No. of Hospitals
1	Andhra Pradesh	15
2	Assam	6
3	Bihar	6
4	Chattisgarh	8
5	Delhi	2
6	Gujarat	2
7	Jharkhand	4
8	Karnataka	13
9	Kerala	20
10	Manipur	1
11	Meghalaya	3
12	Mizoram	3

Contd...

13	Maharastra	14
14	Madhaya Pradesh	6
15	Nagaland	1
16	Orissa	6
17	Punjab	1
18	Tamilandu	42
19	Uttar Pradesh	16
20	Uttaranchal	5
21	West Bengal	4
	TOTAL	**178**

TABLE 2 List of Christian Mission Hospitals In Tamil Nadu

Sl.No	Name of the Hospital and Location
1	Christian Medical College Vellore
2	Scudder Memorial Hospital, Ranipet, Vellore
3	Besthesda Hospital, Ambur, Tamilnadu
4	Christukula Ashram Hospital, Tirupathoor
5	C.S.I. Hospital, 21, Hospital Road, Kanchipuram
6	C.S.I. Welfare Centre, Chingleput
7	C.S.I. Hospital, Via Tiruvallore, Ikkadu
8	C.S.I. Rainy Multi Speciality Hospital, Chennai
9	C.S.I. Kalyani Multi Speciality Hospital, Chennai
10	Danish Mission Hospital, Tirukoilur
11	C.S.I. Mission General Hospital, Woriur, Tiruchirappalli
12	Christian Fellowship Hospital, Oddancharam
13	Lutheran Eye Hospital, Dharapuram
14	Joseph Eye Hospital, Base Hospital, Melapudur Tiruchy
15	Joseph Eye Hospital, Ariyalur TELC Eye Clinic, Joseph Eye Hospital Branch Ariyalur
16	Joseph Eye Hospital, Perambalur TELC Eye Clinic, Joseph Eye Hospital Branch Perambalur
17	St.Luke's Eye Hospital, TELC Compound, Virudhunagar
18	Swedes Mission Hospital, Tirupattur, Karaikudi

Contd...

19	C.S.I. Immanuel Hospital, Idaiyankudi
20	T.D.T.A. St.Luke's Leprosarium, Peikulam
21	St.Barnabas Hospital, C.S.I. Tirunelveli Diocese, Nagalapuram
22	C.S.I. Bellpin Indrani, Chelladurai Mission Hospital, Palayamkottai
23	St.Luke's Hospital, Nazareth
24	Kanyakumari Medical Mission, C.S.I.Hospital, Neyyoor
25	C.S.I. Hospital, Martandam
26	C.S.I. Hospital, Kulasekaram
27	C.S.I. Hospital, Nagercoil
28	C.S.I. Hospital, Karungal
29	International Cancer Center, Neyyoor
30	C.P.M.L. Hospital, Colachel
31	St.RaPhael's Hospital, Sawyerpuram
32	Christian Mission Hospital, Madurai
33	C.S.I. Hospital, Erode
34	Christian Fellowship Community Health Center (CFCH), Ambilikkai
35	Bishop Walsh Memorial Hospital, Thadagam, Coimbatore
36	Mount Tabor Medical Mission Hospital, Mathur
37	The Salvation Army Catherine Booth Hospital, Nagercoil
38	Seventh-day Adventist Hospital, Melavastachavadi, Thanjavur
39	Moses Gnanabarnam (MG) Eye Hospital, Coimbatore
40	The Leprosy Mission Dayapuram Leprosy Centre, Manamadurai
41	The Leprosy Mission Hospital, Vadathorasalur
42	C.S.I. Jayaraj Annabackiyam, Palyamkottai

CHRISTIAN MEDICAL COLLEGE AND HOSPITAL, (VELLORE), LIBRARY: AN OVERVIEW

The Christian Medical College (CMC), Vellore, was established and is maintained by the Christian Medical College Vellore Association, a registered society, formed by over 50 different Indian Christian churches and Christian organizations. The objective of the Christian Medical College Vellore Association is "the establishment, maintenance and development of a Christian Medical College and hospitals in India, where women and men shall receive an education of the highest grade in the art and science of medicine and of nursing, or in one or other of the related professions, to equip them in the spirit of Christ for service in the relief of suffering and the promotion of health". The motto of the institution is; "NOT TO BE MINISTERED UNTO, BUT TO MINISTER".

The Christian Medical College began in 1918, when Dr.Scudder started training women for the Licentiate Diploma (LMP). Her first batch of medical students achieved a 100 percent pass in the examinations. In 1942, the medical school was raised to the status of a college and 25 students were admitted to the MBBS course. At first only men students were admitted to the college in 1947. Permanent affiliation to the University of Madras was obtained in 1950. From 1953 onwards 50 students were admitted, 25 men and 25 women and in 1964 the annual admissions were increased to 60. In 1988, the affiliation of this institution was transferred from the University of Madras to the newly established "Tamilnadu Dr.M.G.R. Medical University". In 2001, the National Assessment and Accreditation Council, an autonomous institution of the University Grants Commission awarded a five star rating to the institution.

Christian Medical College Library and its Branches

There are two main libraries, one in the College Campus known as Gault Library at Bagayam, and the other one is known as Dodd Memorial Library in Hospital Campus Vellore. There are about 120 Department Libraries in the hospital and other Campus. Among them RUHSA Department Library is located in Kavanur K.V. Kuppam Block which is specially meant for the community and rural work. The other Schell Hospital Library is located outside of the main hospital which is in the Eye Department. It covers mainly on the eye and its related diseases. Mental Health Department Library which is available in the Bagayam Campus it specializes in the mental health and related diseases. Others are Rehabilitation Institute Library and Centre for Stem Cell Research Library Anatomy Department Library, Biochemistry Department Library, Biostatistics Department Library, Community Health Department Library, Physiology Department Library, Medical Education Unit Library, Bioengineering Department Library.

Objectives of Christian Medical College & Hospital Library

- Provision of current information to users in a quick and cost effective manner
- Provision of balanced perspective on medical issues
- Provision of alternatives to formal learning in form of material support for continuing medical education

- Provision of value services, which improves information delivery
- Dissemination of health information and promotion of healthy lifestyles
- Satisfying the health information needs of the community
- Locating and assisting in the development of relevant information or materials
- Provision of effective and efficient service to the medical professional according to their need.
- Increase access health resources through improved health literacy.
- Provision of knowledge based information resources to Medical College and Hospital staff and students.
- Teaching and training on the use of various electronic resources.
- Effective and efficient Document delivery service to the users
- Develop web page with links to the finding aids.
- To provide the holding list of the journals which will enable the local and outside users to the exact titles available in the library including missing volumes and numbers.
- Extend library resources to all who require it especially for the mission hospitals.

The goal of the libraries is to provide an effective combination of print, non-print and electronic resources, and the integration of the use of these resources in support of teaching, learning and research at Christian Medical College.

Collection Development

The CMCH Library is the primary source of biomedical information resources in all formats including electronic resources central to medicine, health, and the basic life sciences as well as some materials in the allied health sciences and other relevant areas.

From 2000 onwards the library gives priority to the acquisition of electronic resources. This will result in easier use, wider access and more timely updates.

Books, journals and databases are procured continuously according to the recommendations given by the subject specialists. Books and periodicals received as gifts are also processed by library. The budget allocation for purchase of books is decided by the library committee, which consists of the CMC Director or nominee, Principal, Vice Principal (Curriculum), Medical Superintendent or nominee and few subject specialists from various departments on routine basis. The principal is the Chairman of the Committee and the Chief Librarian acts as the secretary. The budgets will considerably increase according to the need and the demand. Tables 3.8 to 3.11reveal the total number of books and journals acquired and the amount spent from 2005 to 2010.

TABLE 3 Books Acquisition - Purchase

ACQUISITION	2005 – 2006		2006 – 2007		2007 – 2008		2008 - 2009		2009 - 2010	
	P	G	P	G	P	G	P	G	P	G
DODD LIBRARY	160	40	420	28	665	25	294	12	748	23
GAULT LIBRARY	175	1	234	15	231	12	223	2	485	15
DEPARTMENTS	552	52	357	45	531	25	502	25	799	0

P = Purchase G = Gift

TABLE 4 Journal Acquisition - Purchase

ACQUISITION	2005 – 2006		2006 – 2007		2007 – 2008		2008 - 2009		2009 – 2010	
	C P	B V	C P	B V	C P	B V	C P	B V	C P	B V
DODD LIBRARY	216	564	489	25	213	521	217	545	217	20
GAULT LIBRARY	38112	39	69	38	97	38	140	38	3	
DEPARTMENTS	289	374	280	545	285	305	312	263	282	228

CP = Current Periodicals BV = Bound Volumes

TABLE 5 Journal Acquisition - Gift

ACQUISITION	2005 – 2006		2006 – 2007		2007 – 2008		2008 - 2009		2009 - 2010	
	C P	B V	C P	B V	C P	B V	C P	B V	C P	BV
DODD LIBRARY	30	37	32	29	21	28	20	71	20	18
GAULT LIBRARY	3	0	3	1	2	5	3	0	3	0
DEPARTMENTS	1	1	1	0	2	3	1	0	0	0

CP = Current Periodicals BV = Bound Volumes

TABLE 6 Budget Spent During The Year From 2005 To 2010

Particulars	2005 - 2006	2006 - 2007	2007 - 2008	2008 - 2009	2009 - 2010
Books	5,42,786	9,65,034	8,38,447	1,13,26,650	15,01,260.00
Journals	84,71,848	94,72,103	92,57,601	9,15,348	1,23,64,093.00
Binding	1,38,685	1,23,285	1,25,295	1,45,955	1,54,780.00
General Maintenance	1,66,847	1,22,700	1,42,990	2,03,923	1,53,267.95
Membership	11,500	7,500	11,526	11,525	11,525.00
Total	**93,31,666**	**1,06,90,622**	**1,03,75,859**	**1,26,03,401**	**1,41,73,400.95**

E-resources Subscription

To meet the ever increasing demands from users for remote across to information academic libraries now subscribe to electronic resources such as e-books, full text e-journals and online bibliographic databases, in addition to housing these resources in their printed formats. Each year library pays significant fees to bring these resources to their patrons. To use fee based online resources, users must be validated as belonging to an institution that has purchased a license; vendors often restrict access to resources by Internet Protocol [IP] address for the Institution network. One can access the online paid resources by the following ways:-

- Use the electronic resource at the library.
- Gain access from an office, OPD, Theatre, Ward, Residence, Connected access to the campus network.
- Access the resources from off campus via proxy server.

CMCH Library's journal subscriptions are supplemented by the numerous journals that allow free online access to their contents.

TABLE 7 E-Journals Usage Statistics From 2005 To 2010

Particulars	2005-2006	2006-2007	2007-2008	2008-2009	2009 - 2010
High-wire Hosted Journals	44548	65015	122927	73,724	68698
Science Direct Journals	10910	18575	24125	39,843	40731
OUP Journals	9047	10574	10978	14,723	16112
Blackwell Journals	7048	16965	8723		
American Medical Association Journals	19178	19278	32756	11,250	12728
Cochrane Library	425	2272	3250		
Cambridge University Journals	122	250	372	1,378	850
Ingenta Journals	1243	1159	2656	12,296	8320
LWW Journals (Ovid Platform)	5248	6206	8427	7,248	8750
Inter science Wiley Journals	985	6843	7100	4,440	20223
Springer Varley Journals	NA	NA	2,326		6503

Contd...

Informa Medical Journals	NA	NA	NA	12,450	13767
Upto Date	NA	NA	NA	14,802	32022
NEJM	NA	NA	NA	12,450	13280
Published (Full Text Accessed)	NA	NA	4,339	NA	4229

*Number of Articles accessed or downloaded during the above period.

NA-not available

The data in Table 7 exhibits the e-journals usage statistics* by the Health Science Professionals in CMC & H Libraries

Services

The following services are being provided by the library

- Online catalogue services and circulation services (borrowing, returning, renewal, reservation facility)
- Medical Multimedia collections
- Ez-proxy Server: Interoperable port
- Institutional Repository - Conference, class room lectures.
- OPAC, Books, Journals, Thesis
- Journals – Print, Electronic, Subscribed, Free
- Interlibrary Loan (Delnet, QMed)
- Photocopying Services
- Database Search Services
- Trial Services of Medical E-Resources
- Reference Services
- Purchase Recommendation
- Library Resources subscription and cataloguing services
- Instructions to authors from various publishers to write the articles.
- Compilation of published articles by Christian Medical College Staff, Vellore
- E-learning curriculum for undergraduate
- Duplicate literature weeded books.

Library Infrastructure and ICT Facilities

The libraries of CMC&H have the following infrastructure and ICT facilities:

- Fully computerized
- Over 58000 titles (Books back volumes of journals, reports)
- 1683 E-journals with archive
- Members of DELNET which library share resources with the other member
- Members of Q-med knowledge foundation for document delivery service
- Computer lab facility with branded servers with 30 Desktop in each library
- Entire campus is connected to the internet through cabled & wireless LAN
- 100.0 mbps bandwidth
- Database packages like SQL server, Java, Visual Basics
- Fully Wi-Fi secured with Firewall, Antivirus & Antispam

3.7 Library Manpower

The department of library services is equipped with 23 staff which includes professionals, semiprofessionals and non -technical staff.

- Chief Librarian 1
- Senior Librarians 4
- Librarians 6
- Library assistant 4
- Clerical 3
- Library attendants 5

3.8 Future Plans of CMC&H Library

- Library modernization project to modernize racks and interior lighting arrangement.
- Add more ICT Technology such as Internet Lab with all accessories.
- Automated library services plan to add more electronic data bases and to subscribe to E-books.
- Virtual reading hall

- Virtual library collection with archives.
- Virtual document delivery service.

CONCLUSION

Medical librarians are part of the pool of institutional capital. Their roles in project management and system lifecycles are often left unexplored and their skills remain underutilized. Librarians are a resource which some organizations evaluate for the amount of space they consume, yet their efforts go beyond physical boundaries, reach many throughout a health institution, from consumers to healthcare personnel and administrators. The study at Christian Mission Hospitals in Tamil Nadu suggest the following trends that may have implications for research institutions :

- Electronic resources are popular and extensively used. Their popularity continues to increase with time.
- E-journals and e-books title have already been related for print collections and continue to be used in their e-format. New journal titles in their online-only format, usually added to library collections in large quantity due to new acquisition strategies, also get used.
- Medical Sciences research libraries and Hospital libraries can provide new and innovative document delivery services in an effort to better accommodate to the needs of their Health Science Professions in electronic environment.

❑❑❑

Chapter – 5

Agro-informatics: Changing Trend of Using Information and Communication Technology in Agricultural Sector

Rabindra K. Mahapatra

INTRODUCTION

The 21st century has witnessed the emergence of information revolution in a dramatic way that has shaped the human lives in a new direction. Information revolution has not only made tremendous changes in the social-economic and political life of the people but also given a dramatic boost for scientific community for its right uses in their research and academic work. The society has experienced a fast change. McGarry has presented the relative rapidity of such changes in saying that progress is at glacial speed. The striking changes in the information society are also depicted by Alvin Toffler in his three books. He advocated that the chief agent of transformation of society is information and its related technologies. Moreover, it is acknowledged that information and knowledge become the principal generators of wealth in the form of educational institutions, research and development organizations, scientific establishments and information dissemination agents.

With agriculture in the present century moving rapidly away from an artisanal, labour- extensive, traditional activity towards a sophisticated, information-intensive sector of the global economy, access to information and modern communication technologies has become a necessity for the farmers of the global sphere especially in developing countries. The agriculture of the future will entail more efficient and sustainable production systems, making optimal use of land, water and other natural resources. Sustainable food production will rely more and more on agricultural information management and communication technologies.

In this context, information exchange aimed at enhancing food security will be essential to all concerned: the government, the private sector, the academic community, farmer organizations and civil society in general, (FAO,2003)

The dynamic form of ICTs application is realized in the library and information sector which has drastically changed the structure and functioning of the library and information centres over the world. The use of such technologies has made it possible to convert the traditional libraries into digital libraries whose main features are automated library management systems, on-line search and retrieval systems, development of electronic databases and the use of Internet. The agricultural libraries experience a specific importance in developing information system which has been described as '*agro-informatics*'.

The use of information technologies has become an increasingly important driver for agricultural research and education and agricultural industry. The critical role of information technologies has been realized in every aspect of agricultural knowledge generation and dissemination. U.S. farmers have been acclaimed worldwide as almost insatiable consumer for information and adopters of technology. A significant factor in the dramatic productivity increase of U.S. agriculture during the past half century has been the information on new ideas and techniques that farmers gleaned from both the public and private sector (Boehlje, 1998). The most dynamic form of technology use for agriculture is in the sphere of information generation to dissemination by the researchers, scientists, extension workers, academician and information intermediaries which are mainly acquired, processed and retrieved by the library and information centres in agricultural institutions and universities. ICT in agriculture is an emerging field focusing on the enhancement of agricultural and rural development in India. It involves application of innovative ways to use Information & Communication Technologies (ICT) in the rural domain. The advancements in ICT can be utilised for providing accurate, timely, relevant information and services to the farmers, thereby facilitating an environment for more remunerative agriculture. Given the development scenario in Indian agriculture ICT movement is still evolving.

However, all the ICT initiatives are not uniform with disparities between regions in the level and quality of telecommunications, information and the effort of individuals, public and private organizations, and differentiated nature of demand of the farmers in different areas. As a result, there have been many successes, failures, lessons learned and experience gained. While these initiatives are intended to address the needs of the farmers through ICT, their actual usage and their ability to bring significant impact on the farm productivity and socio-economic development of the intended beneficiaries is to be understood. It is relatively unknown as to whether the ultimate beneficiaries actually use the facilities provided for them meaningfully to meet their needs. The common problems in adoption of ICT in rural segments are ICT illiteracy, availability of relevant and localized contents in their own languages, easy and affordable accessibility and other issues such as awareness and willingness for adoption of new technologies among the rural people etc. One critical aspect in the usage of ICTs for farmers and their groups, as seen in some of the ICT driven initiatives is the involvement of human interface indicating that there is a human dependency in transmission of information/knowledge to farmers. Thus, there is a need to understand as to how far the ICT initiatives are able to address the farmers' need so that better solutions can be developed to address those unmet needs. In harnessing such a vast sphere of information and communication technologies uses in agriculture, a new concept called '*agro-informatics*' has emerged.

AGRO-INFORMATICS: CONCEPT AND DEFINITION

Since the use of computer and communication technologies has been widely made in different spheres of knowledge dissemination purposes, the agriculture scientists and the experts felt it worthy to use the computers in different aspects of agriculture such as, teaching, research and field works. The term agro-informatics was coined in the mid 1980's. Agro- informatics is nothing but the assimilation of computer and communication technologies in agricultural information dissemination system. According to Vanitha and Kalpana (2011) agro-informatics is an integration of computer, mathematical and statistical methods to manage and analyze the agricultural information. It is a technology–based science which is primarily used in developing computer databases and algorithms for purpose of speeding up and enhancing agricultural research. A combination of computer science, information technology, agriculture and genetic engineering to determine and analyse genetic information of plants. Agro-informatics has emerged as an important discipline in agriculture sector due to simultaneous development into the plant biotechnology and information technology and computing power.

INFORMATION SYSTEM IN AGRICULTURE

Information system in agriculture consists of components (subsystems), information related processes (generation, transformation, storage, retrieval, integration, diffusion and utilisation), system mechanisms (interfaces and networks) and system operations (control and management). In addition, the analysis of the agricultural information system in a specific farming system may provide the identification of basic components and structure of the system, the different sources of information used by different components in the system, the understanding of how successfully the system works and how to improve system performance (system management) . This approach is also useful to identify possible defaults and improve the coordination between components.

Agriculture is a knowledge intensive industry. Modern farmers need information on financial, climatic, technical and regulatory information to manage their farms. Both public and private institutions have emerged to supply farmers with information and analysis. However, inadequacies such as the inability to consistently provide accurate, timely and easily accessible information, present several challenges to farmers. One of the roles of the government is the provision of information to increase efficiency and improve the performance of the economy, but government activities are constrained by budget. Information is also provided by the private sector, and effective policy design needs to identify where investment in public information is most effective. Therefore, the agricultural research aims to understand networks of information and, in particular, who is the provider and who is the user of certain types of information. Agricultural information interacts with and influences agricultural productivity in a variety of ways. It can help inform decisions regarding land, labour, livestock, capital and management. Agricultural productivity can arguably be improved by relevant, reliable and useful information and knowledge. Hence, the creation of agricultural information (by extension services, research, education programmes and others) is now often managed by agricultural organisations that create information systems to disseminate information to farmers so that farmers can make better decisions in order to take advantage of market opportunities and manage continuous changes in their production systems. Therefore, there is a need to understand the functions and use of particular agricultural information systems in order to manage and improve them (Demiryurek *et al*, 2008)

INTELLIGENT TECHNOLOGY

The web technology has developed several natural language search engines and intelligent agents that help the users to retrieve required information. Intelligent technology is one such emerging technology that has been variously used to provide appropriate solutions to critical problems.

The intelligent technology has been widely used in agriculture, and has improved efficiency of agricultural logistics, utilization rate of resources and cultural quality of farmers in demonstration areas. All commercial crop and animal production systems are potential users for ingtelligent technology products. Many such technology systems have been developed to help farmers, extension workers and administrators to make recommendation solution. Also intelligent technology will provide powerful means for the transfer of agriculture technologies to practices.

China has used such intelligent technologies in agricultural production.

In some remote areas, China continually carried out the computer expert plan to push forward the agriculture development and increase farmers' income. In some areas with good industry bases, China has set new development orientation for the 21st century. For example, Beijing has made a blueprint to develop precision agriculture to keep pace with developed countries to establish modern agriculture demonstration areas. Some Chinese farmers have become accustomed to using computers to assist them in farming. Farmers have been using software called "Agriculture Expert System", a product of the Application and Demonstration of Intelligent Agriculture Information Tech Project under the National Hi-tech R&D Program, also called "863 Program". Since 1996, the Chinese government's 863 projects started the demonstration district of intelligent agriculture information project. It has since then increased from four to twenty provinces . China has developed agriculture technology application platforms and tools that enjoy independent intelligent property right, established more than 100 agriculture intelligent application systems, covering the areas of food, fruit, vegetable and aquatic products. The total demonstration areas have amounted to 20 million mu (1/15 of a hectare), and the extension areas reached 0.1 billion mu. The total agricultural output increased by 1.5 billion kilograms, the production cost dropped by RMB0.6 billion and accumulated economy profits amounted RMB1.5 billion.

ARTIFICIAL INTELLIGENCE IN AGRICULTURE

Artificial Intelligence (AI) is an idea raised commonly when discussing technological advancements in the future, as well as in science fiction novels and film. Artificial intelligence is the capacity of transferring to improve from mistakes to machines. John McCarthy is a scientist who worked heavily on artificial intelligence machines in the early 20th Century, and actually coined that term. He describes it as the science behind creating machines that are intelligent. The whole idea behind this branch of technology is based on the idea that intelligence, which is generally believed to only be able to be tracked and monitored in humans, is able to be simulated by a computer. This calls into question many issues about the capabilities of the mind, and the ethical drawbacks of comparing a machine to the intelligence of a human brain. The integration of this technology into popular culture has helped to bring the idea of artificial intelligence into daily conversations, and has sparked plenty of discussion and debate about what the future may hold as technology continues to advance.

Artificial intelligence is primarily addressed to the modelling and simulation methods of dynamical systems and processes in agriculture, control, operation and optimization methods, modelling issues for agro-industry, e.g. uncertainty, randomness, time variability strong external disturbances and lack of predictability, and artificial intelligence (AI) techniques for modelling, control and operation. The technological approaches of artificial intelligence are mainly concerned to the photosynthesis of crops under environmental stresses, soil and/plant atmosphere cycle, metabolism of farm animals, harvesting systems, food processing, grading, drying, storage of crops including fruits and vegetables, automation, e.g. robotics, vehicle guidance, autonomous vehicles, internal transport and packaging, distribution and marketing automation, and heating, cooling, lighting, and energy saving.

The Application of artificial intelligence in agriculture can be spread to various areas of agricultural research, field work, production and marketing, etc. The utilization of this technology has already developed models in a broad area which is often hindered by one or more factors. One frequent factor which impedes transportation is model inaccuracy. For example, when models that perform well in one region, are transported to be used in a different region, they often do not give accurate output (such as, recommendations, results, and/or indicators) in their new environment (i.e., when they are run in a new region). This is one of the major difficulties of model technology transfer. To address this difficulty, an artificial intelligence methodology is proposed. At the heart of this methodology is a genetic algorithm which is linked to the agricultural model engine (e.g., a risk assessment, provisional, or crop growth model). The general component created by this combinational methodology is called an 'Agricultural Model'.

EXPERT SYSTEM IN AGRICULTURE

Expert system is a computer programme that solves complicated problems which are rather difficult to solve through normal procedure. Expert system can be defined as a tool for information generation from knowledge. Information is either found in various forms or generated from data and/or knowledge. Text images, video, audio are forms of media on which information can be found, and the role of information technology is to invent, and devise tools to store and retrieve this information. Statistical information is a good example of information generated from data while advises generated by an expert system is a good example of information generated from knowledge. At the beginning, the concentration was mainly on textual information. Information technology used for textual information ranged from paper archiving tool to the sophisticated electronic computer software tools such as data base management systems, and hypertext tools. Images were very difficult to be included in an information system just few years ago till the scanners technology has been advanced together with the invention of the optical storage devises which have the capacity to store hundreds of mega bytes. This technology has enabled the developers to include images in their systems. Input peripherals to capture video and audio information have been commercialized and are now available in the market. Storage of audio and video would be impossible unless large storage media were invented.

The advances in data processing have led to generating efficiently information from data. Software tools and methodologies have been developed in the field of statistics and data analysis to process data and to let these data more informative to users who need them. Data base management systems have also contributed to efficient data storage, processing, and retrieval. The information is sometimes generated from knowledge and experience. When an expert in a specific area gives an advice to a less experienced person, he/she actual use his/her knowledge and experience to generate this piece of information. This is a very precious piece of information because it is generated after long time of work and experience, and interaction with other experts and practitioners.

Expert systems can be integrated with other information sources such as image bases and/or textual bases to make use of these sources. For example, images can be used for describing symptoms as it is very difficult and very confusing to describe them in words. Images can also be used for confirming the diagnosis of the cause of a certain disorder. Expert systems can also be integrated with textual data bases that may be the extension documents related to the specialty and/or commodity handled by an expert system. This textual data base can be used for explanation purposes of basic terms and operations. It can also be used to confirm the reached conclusion in some situations. The updating problem is also found in expert systems. However, the knowledge base can be maintained more efficiently than maintaining manual documents. The problem of updating the versions in the field can be eliminated in case that the expert systems are stored on a central computer and accessed through a computer network.

Expert systems technology can play a very important role in generating knowledge from information. The need of expert systems for technical information transfer in agriculture can be identified by recognizing the problems in using the traditional system for technical information transfer, and by proving that expert systems can help to overcome the problems addressed, and are feasible to be developed. The knowledge acquisition process for building an expert system facilitates the integration of knowledge and experiences of different specialties. For example, an agricultural diagnostic expert system requires the integration of specialists in nutrition, plant pathology, entomology, breeding, and production. Therefore, when a problem occurs, the system can help the user in identifying the cause of the problem in a much more efficient way than consulting a document that handles a specific problem. MANAGE has developed an expert system to diagnose pest and diseases for rice crop and suggest preventive and curative measures. Centre for Informatics Research and Advancement, Kerala has also prepared an expert system called AGREX to help the agricultural researchers to give timely and correct advice to the farmers. U.S Department of Agriculture, University of California, and Technical University of Berno, Czechoslovakia have developed expert systems in agriculture to solve difficult problems.

INTELLECTUALIZED INFORMATION TECHNIQUE

Intellectualized Information Technique (IIT) is an important subject which is developing rapidly in recent years. The use of such technique has been highly realised in agricultural sector. Using it to reconstruct and support agricultural development has become a very attentive work at present. Since the agriculture has lower content of technology and weak base of information technology in our country, advancing IIT gains immense economic and social benefits in present day situation. So the research gets government's support, recognition of science and technology department and welcome from the grass roots. A research project in China entitled "application and demonstration engineering of Chongqing IIT section" and significant project "development framework of agriculture ES" sponsored by 863 makes a series of research on platform-based IIT application in agriculture. Applying the latest fruits of information technology and artificial intelligence, hardware structure and software framework of the technique are researched on the basis of analysis and study on the development of technique inside and outside our country. The project staff have analyzed and explored some problems about the agriculture expert system (ES), agriculture database/data warehouse, GIS-based soil information system, distributed computer control technology in the greenhouse, the knowledge discovery in databases and so on. Furthermore, they have constructed intellectual agriculture information network of Chongqing which has run practically. The project analyzed the system structure of computer network and the character of required services provided by such technique, constructed internet-based computer agriculture information network (integrated with some fruit of intellectual agriculture sponsored by 863) and devised software framework structure matching it, developed the agriculture database supporting intellectual decision-making, advanced model of the agriculture data warehouse. All of these provide the platform support of the intellectualized decision-making on the field of agriculture. Again applying GIS-based technology in agriculture system, soil information system based on GIS is developed. Making use of its powerful functions of graphics and data management, users can get the data of agricultural space distribution across the clime (soil, for example) by the Network, and by virtue of the convenient multimedia interface. It can radically improve the configurations of information resource and support intellectual decision-making in the field of agriculture. They again studied the character of knowledge in the field of agriculture, bring up the use multi-media technology to express the concept of space information of many dimensions' in agriculture, developed five kinds of farm crops of cultivated expert system base on Web such as tomato, cucumber, capsicum, potato, orange and so on in the agriculture ES, and resolved intellectual decision-making concerning the breed to choose, seedtime, how to operate fertilizer, plant diseases and insect pests diagnosis etc. On the basis of synthesizing development discipline of agriculture ES, we bring up the framework of multimedia agriculture ES based on C/S mode, efficiently shorten the period of exploitation, improve the efficiency of exploitation, reduce the difficulty of exploitation in agriculture expert system, and refer non-computer person to use.

AGRO-INFORMATICS IN INDIA

The Department of Agriculture and Cooperation, Government of India have taken steps to establish Agricultural Information System Network (AGRINET) in collaboration with National Informatics Centre during Ninth Five Year Plan. The proposal recommended that the state-of the-art information technology infrastructure requirement to establish AGRISNET as the Intranet over NICNET and development of databases and information systems for decision support for evaluation, monitoring and policy formulations and improvement of human resource development, managing multimedia based training and demonstration of transfer technology and to strengthen farm research education using broadcast VSATs. In addition to this there is a need for creation of special interest group for problem solving situations, developing different programes schemes. The most important activity of the system is to develop on-line for Internet and Intranet access through AGRISNET nodes. AGRISNET is designed to be established at headquarter at Krishi Bhawan at New Delhi, attached offices, regional offices, subordinate offices, regional units public sector undertakings, autonomous undertakings, state agriculture departments, district agriculture offices and block agriculture offices. The basis of the technology is network-centric using data warehousing technique, expert system, GIS technology, remote sensing technology and web technology which will be available in AGRISNET nodes.

CONCLUSION

The impact of information and communication technology has changed the spectrum of the information use in digital formats. Agriculture is the most viable used area in which the use of information technology has been realised. The scientists, researchers, faculty and academicians, bureaucrats, farmers and information intermediaries have adopted new information technologies in disseminating agricultural information. Such a wide uses of ICTs in agricultural sector has given birth to the concept of agro-informatics. The advent of Internet has made agricultural sector more dynamic in dissemination of electronic information to a variety of users in a global village. The shift of information resources in agricultural science from print to soft copy has transformed the uses pattern. The utilization of intelligent technology has improved efficiency of agricultural logistics, utilization rate of resources and cultural quality of farmers. Intelligent technology has made tremendous impact upon the commercial crop and animal production systems. Similar type technological systems have been developed to help farmers, extension workers and administrators to improve the quality of work and products. The use of artificial intelligence is basically addressed to the modelling and simulation methods in agriculture, control, operation and optimization methods, modelling issues for agro-industry.The agricultural research, field work, production and marketing, etc. are the most used areas by application of artificial intelligence. The expert systems in agriculture have been utilized by recognizing critical problems which are difficult to solve by the beneficiaries. While diagnosing a problem agricultural expert system requires the integration of specialists in nutrition, plant pathology, entomology, breeding, and production. Considering the emergence of such technologies, the concept of agro-informatics has got a good momentum in India. The Government of India has introduced a number of computer based schemes for development of agriculture. The emergence of computer based network called AGRISNET, IT enabled information systems, consortia based information sharing through CeRA are some of the recent developments in India. However, the process of ICT application in agriculture is growing rapidly and is a welcome gesture for the farming community.

REFERENCES

1. Rafea, Ahmed. Expert System Applications: Agriculture
2. Demiryurek, K., *et al* (2008). Agricultural information systems and communication networks: the case of dairy farmers in Samsun province of Turkey. *Information Research*, **13**(2), p. 343. (Available at *http://InformationR.net/ir/13-2/paper343.html)*
3. McQueen, R; Garner, S; Manning, C and Witten, I. (1995). Applying machine learning to agricultural data. *Computers and Electronics in Agriculture* 12(4): pp. 275-293.
4. Vanitha, G and Kalpana, M (2011). Agro-Informatics New Delhi, New Indian Publishing Agency.
5. Report of Prime Minister's Task Force on India as Knowledge Superpower'.
6. Planning Commission, Government of India, New Delhi.
7. Jones, G.E. (1997). The history, development and the future of agricultural extension. ***In*** B.E. Swanson, R.P. Bentz and A.J. Sofranko (1997) Improving agricultural extension – a reference manual. Rome: FAO.
8. McConnell, S (2001). Connecting with the unconnected: Proposing an evaluation of the impacts of the Internet on unconnected rural stakeholders. Mc Connell International. http://mcconnelinternational.com/evalnation.html
9. Meera, S. N (2002). A Critical analysis of information technology in agricultural development: Impact and implications. Unpublished PhD thesis, IARI, New Delhi.

10. Richardson, D (1996). The Internet and rural development: recommendations for strategy and activity – final report. Rome: Sustainable Development Department of the Food and Agriculture Organization of the United Nations.http://www.fao.org/sd-dimensions.

11. Swaminathan, M.S (1993). Information technology: Reaching the unreached. Chennai: Macmillan India.

12. Zijp, W. (1994) Improving the transfer and use of agricultural information – a guide to Information Technology. Washington DC: World Bank.

❑❑❑

Chapter – 6

Electronic Resources Management: Opportunities & Challenges in Digital Era

K. Veeranjaneyulu, N. P. Ravi Kumar and T. Sreenivasa Rao

INTRODUCTION

Providing access to the nascent information is the main motto of the library. Electronic resources management (ERM) is the latest phenomenon in the field of Library and Information Science. In a nutshell it is responsible for the evaluation, selection, pricing, securing, maintenance and provision of electronic resources to the users. As electronic resource collections continue to expand, allied workflows and processes encompass growth in complexity. Advances in printing technology and information communication technology (ICT) have resulted in transforming the publishing industry into e-publishing. It has resulted in considerable impact on the library collection building process in terms of print collection, electronic and online resources.

Now a days many reputed publishers have started e-publishing and many of them are now issuing their publications in electronic version besides conventional printing. The libraries are upgrading their collection in terms of documentary resources and electronic resources and infrastructure to sustain in the fast moving knowledge society.

"Libraries have struggled to manage the burgeoning number of electronic resources..." (Tull, Crum, Davis, & Strader, 2005, p. 103).

"Several factors have rendered the job of librarians who deal with electronic resources extremely challenging…" (Sadeh & Ellingson, 2005, p. 208)

NATIONAL KNOWLEDGE COMMISSION'S REPORT ON LIBRARY

Library is a gateway to knowledge. A great responsibility rests on the present day Librarians in making India a Knowledge Hub. National Knowledge Commission emphasized the main areas to be focused are:

- Access
- Concepts
- Creation
- Applications
- Services

The libraries attached to all the institutions and organizations haverecognized the importance of library and its services. The implicit concept behind the NKC report on libraries is that to access the world of knowledge and make use of it to create more knowledge. Information which enables in terms resulted in the development of a vibrant knowledge-based society.

E-RESOURCES

World Wide Web (WWW) facilitates the delivery of electronic content to the libraries and the desktops of its users. Libraries began acquiring the new online resources with few ideas of where this revolution would be leading. Procedures were developed to fit the small scale of available materials at the time, and then hastily underwent revisions. Online journals were at first merely adjuncts to their print counterparts.

Electronic resources consists of data (information representing numbers, text, graphics, images, maps, moving images, music, sounds, etc.), programs (instructions etc., that process the data for use), or combinations of data and programs. E-resource is an individual electronic journal such as Nature, as is an electronic book or an abstracting and indexing database such as MEDLINE. An e-resource can also be a package of e-journals such as CeRA (Consortium for e-Resources in Agriculture), EBSCO, J-Gate etc.

CHARACTERISTICS OF E-RESOURCES

- Timely and Instant access to nascent information
- any time any where access (24 x 7)
- saves lot of time in terms of publishing, dissemination, usage.

- Portability
- Occupies less physical storage space and resources
- Unlimited simultaneous use
- Downloading, saving, reading, forwarding and many more.
- It can be edited as per the user requirement
- Allows federated search facility.
- Real time simulations can be possible
- More interactive
- No theft, pilferage, mutilation etc.
- Up-datedness

NEED FOR E-RESOURCES

The driving force of present day society is information. The information seekers mainly depend on the information sources which provide instant access to current information for various applications. With the rapid advancements the user expectations are changing in the same proportion. The field of publishing aims to publish the information in the format as desired by the end-user. Reputed publishers located around the globe have switched over from conventional printing to electronic publishing. In electronic publishing the delivery of information is instant and authentic. Users can browse the resources from any where any time i.e., 24 X 7 access. Unlike the traditional library workflow of ordering and paying for print resources, cataloging those items, and processing them for the shelves, in e-library a workflow different library units know their roles and responsibilities. Most libraries consolidate all things electronic such as A-Z lists, federated search engines, e-journals, abstract-and-indexing databases, statistical databases etc.

Maintaining the balanced collection to fulfill user demands i.e."Best Reading for the Largest Number at the Least Cost" is a great challenge before the library and information officers, more so in academic institutions who are confronted with many problems. Not only they have to bank on book trade for supplying the information on new arrivals, they also have to manage with meager funds to meet the information needs of large community of students, researchers and the faculty. If regular flow of funds is ensured by the management, library may think of subscribing to online databases. Membership of Consortia may also help in meeting the demands of user community.

LIFE CYCLE OF AN E-RESOURCE

The lives of e-resources are as complicated and challenging as those of human beings. E-resources are born, and at times they also die or reincarnate under a different name or in a different shape; they form families, and the families may unite with other families, quarrel, or split up; treaties between families are signed and can be later discarded; and so on.

ELECTRONIC RESOURCES MANAGEMENT

Responsibility for handling electronic resources was at first the province of the interested or the co-opted. However, this does not fit well within the traditional workflow such resource selection, ordering, and payment which may be easily managed within the traditional ILS workflow, but the similarity ends there. Once an order is placed, there is no mechanism in an ILS to notify a library of non-receipt or the availability of a resource to the library user.

E-Resource management is the rapid growth of electronic resources. Because of this growth libraries are experiencing issues related to time management, staffing, and the time-honored task of deliberating the set-up of logical workflow systems for such resources and allow an electronic resources librarian to handle most, if not all, responsibilities from pre-order activities to access set-up. When all these activities are left in the care of one or two people in a library, many of them are unsure what to do.

The development of ERM became necessary in the early 2000s as it became clear that traditional library catalogs and integrated library systems were not designed to handle metadata for resources as mutable as many online products are. Electronic resource management (ERM) is the practices and software systems used by libraries to keep track of important information about electronic information resources, especially internet-based resources such as electronic journals, databases, and electronic books.

ADVANTAGES OF ELECTRONIC RESOURCE MANAGEMENT

- Supporting acquisition and management of licensed e-resources
- May be integrated into other library system modules or may be a stand-alone system
- May have a public interface, either separate or integrated into the OPAC
- Providing descriptions of resources at the package (database) level and relate package contents (e.g. e-journals) to the package record
- Encoding and perhaps publicly displaying licensed rights such as e-reserves, course packs, and interlibrary loan
- Tracking electronic resources from point of order through licensing and final access
- Providing information about the data providers, consortia arrangements, access platform

- Providing contact information for all content providers
- Logging problems with resources and providers
- Providing customizable e-mail alerting systems (e.g. notices to managers when actions are expected or required)
- Linking license documents to resource records
- Systematic usage reporting and tracking.
- Generating and maintaining alphabetic and subject lists of journals and/or databases.
- License term negotiation, tracking, and communication processes.
- Multiple staff and department involvement in selection & support of e-resources, i.e. communication and workflows.
- Problem tracking and trouble shooting activities including escalation/ triage support.

REVIEW AND DE-SELECTION

Electronic resources could be removed from the collection at any time at the discretion of the Library and information officer. The following are some reasons an e-resource may be un-subscribed/cancelled.

- usage statistics are too low to justify cost
- the quality of the content is too poor to justify cost, or the content is covered by another resource
- a better comparable option becomes available
- a vendor fails to honor the terms of the license, or the price of the subscription or maintenance becomes too high.
- lack of up-datedness
- restrictions on perpetual access
- limitations on archives

CONCLUSION

Electronic resources planning, policy development, workflow and the documentation (publisher's price strategy, licensing, perpetual access etc) are very crucial aspects of electronic resources management. An important attribute for keeping the privacy of the library and information services and controlling the access to resources, devices and services organized in virtual communities. However, the success of electronic resource service and management depends on its usage. To create awareness among the users is a crucial factor and is mandatory to ensure authentic usage.

REFERENCES

1. Bergman, B. J. (2005). Looking at electronic resources librarians. Is there gender equity within this emerging specialty? New Library World, 106 (1210/1211), 116-127.
2. Chang, S. (2003). The DLF electronic resource management initiative. OCLC Systems & Services, 19(2), 45-47.
3. Smith, Carol (2006). Electronic Resource Management Systems. The Impact of DLF ERMI standards a review of recent literature.
4. Sadeh, T. and Ellingsen, M. (2005). Electronic resource management systems: the need and the realization. New Library World, 106(5), 208-218.
5. Alan, R. (2005). Electronic resource management: transition from in-house to in-house/vendor approach. *The Serials Librarian, 47*(4), 17-25.
6. http://en.wikipedia.org
7. Parker, Kimberly (2008).Tools for Mature Management of Electronic Resources Lifecycles in Libraries.
8. Jewell, T.D., et al (2004). Electronic Resource Management: Report of the DLF Electronic Resource Management Initiative. Washington, D.C.: Digital Library Federation.
9. Vashishth, C P (2011). Building Library Collection In E-Environment : Challenges & Opportunities. *Library Herald.* Vol 49 No 1
10. NKC: Libraries Gateways to Knowledge, p. 1.

❑❑❑

Chapter – 7

Electronic Publishing: Impact of Information Communication Technology on Research Knowledge Resource Centres

Rajpal Walke and N K Wadhwa

INTRODUCTION

Knowledge Resource Centres play a very important role in this fast changing e-environment of publishing. Their role includes identification and selection of information, its organization and management, storage, retrieval and dissemination to right users at the right time at right place at right price and in right format. The dawn of information revolution is considered to be one of the marvels of 21st century. It is well known that paper and printing were originated in China in the 2nd and 5th century of Christian era, respectively.(1) There is a " wordless heaven book", " published in oral or paper less form among the Chinese. The word less book is actually an adaptation and extension of"the song of baked dough by Pie-wen Lu" (2) of the 14th century. The "elite" in every generation have access to the timelessly flexibly text of the heaven-book to interpret the contents and to predict, accordingly, the great events of the world, particularly when it is in chaos. The world refers to, of course, the "middle kingdom," which is China in Chinese. Although the work is only a legend, the wordless heaven-book can be considered as the pioneer prototype of modern electronic publishing and as the earliest idea of the recently developed hypertext.

Another classic concept of e-publishing can be traced in *Gullivers Travels* by Jonathan Swift first published in 1726. The work has a passage describing a writing machine developed by the Lagadonians in the Grand Academy of Lagado. The Lagadonian writing machine used the method of a fixed syntactic structure and the filling in of that structure with contents by a random procedure (3).

Recently, Edwin B Brownrigg and Clifford A Lynch of the Division of Knowledge Resource Centre automation University of California, Berkely, declared that " electronic publishing was established... in East Pittsburg in 1919-1920 with Frank Conards music broadcasts at radio station KDKA....(4)

The information technology has changed the way the information is stored and disseminated and has threatened the traditional approaches to the Knowledge Resource Centre and its services. The digital revolution has taken on the world of publishing also. Now paperless publishing or electronic publishing is gaining more prominence. In the changing scenario, libraries and librarians will have to play a crucial role in handling conventional and electronic resources. Thus the era of electronic publishing has begun affecting Knowledge Resource Centre and information professionals. The ultimate goal of electronic publishing is to provide fast and easy access to the information contained in the objective publications with simple, powerful search and retrieval capabilities. Thus, e-publishing can be used effectively in the context of Dr. S.R. Ranganathan's fourth law "Save the Time of User" for many purposes. The U.G.C Infonet E-Journal Consortium is a unique ICT programme for facilitating free electronic access to scholarly research databases and journals to 100 universities and is the largest research network in the world.

ELECTRONIC PUBLISHING

Electronic publishing, involves the digital publication of electronic articles and e-books. It also includes the development of digital catalogs and libraries. There are many non-network electronic publications such as encyclopedias and reference and technical publications relied on by most users. Today however, network distribution is also being strongly associated with electronic publishing. Electronic publishing does not generate a hard copy, unlike desktop publishing.

The emergence of the internet, particularly the World Wide Web, as a new medium of information storage and delivery represents a revolution which will have a lasting impact on the publishing and information delivery system in the 21st century. An increasing number of publishers are using the internet as global way to offer their publications to the international community of scientists and technologists. It is basically a form of publishing in which books, journals and magazines are being produced and stored electronically rather than in print. These publications have all qualities of the normal publishing like the use of colours, graphics and images and they are much convenient also. Electronic

Publishing = Electronic Technology + Computer Technology + Communication Technology + Publishing

DEFINITION

Definition of Electronic publishing on the web: Electronic publishing or ePublishing includes the digital publication of e-books and electronic articles, and the development of digital libraries and catalogues....en.wikipedia.org/wiki/E-publishing (5)

Kist (1989) defined electronic publishing as "the application by publishers of a computer aided process, by which they find, capture, shape, store and update information content in order to disseminate it to a chosen audience" Grolier Electronic Publishing, 1995 defines electronic publishing as:

The term E-publishing refers more precisely to the storage and retrieval of information through electronic communications media. It can employ a variety of formats and technologies, some already in widespread use by businesses and general consumers and others still being developed. E-publishing technology can be classified into two general categories:

l) information is stored in a centralized computer source and delivered to the users by a telecommunication systems including online database services and videotext, represents the most active area in E publishing today, and, 2) the data is digitally stored on a disk or other physically deliverable medium.

TYPES OF E PUBLISHING MODELS

1) **Electronic Books**: (E-Books) is quiet popular document to meet the research needs of user community. Publishing a book electronically is to achieve quick publishing and dissemination of information. A book may not have contemporary value that a journal has but it certainly an archival and reference value. A number of encyclopedias do come out on CD-ROM. It is felt that the Internet is not a satisfactory platform for publishing full text of documents but CD-ROM is appropriate medium for publishing books. Book length e-text is also available on Floppy disc and CD-ROM, although distribution by floppy disc is decreasing due to the convenience and growing popularity of CD. Most e-Texts published on CD-ROM are public domain works including encyclopedias. Using the E-publishing language on Internet like SGML presented and published attractively with multimedia effect especially for documents like Yearbooks, Encyclopedias.

2) **Electronic Periodicals:** E-Periodicals are accessible to all users regardless of geographic location. Anyone with proper computer software and browser services can access online journals. This accessibility leads to a more diverse audience throughout the world

as well as a readership that may include not only researchers, but students and lay people. This new media is a vehicle of scientific communication and purely a product of scientific research. This category includes electronic journals, newsletters, magazines, and discussion lists. Perhaps no other area in E-publishing has received more study than the area of E-journals. As they apply to scholarly research, are very useful source of information for Research Knowledge Resource Centre System.

3) **Electronic Database:** With the emergence of computers and communication technologies the strength of research information system in the development of modern database has taken new shape. The holding of the research Knowledge Resource Centre database consisting of books, periodicals, reports and theses which can be converted to electronic form that allows access for public use through digital networks. The online electronic Knowledge Resource Centre card catalog (OPAC) shows how it enables the user to search the document with various access points like author, title, subjects etc. Various electronic database publishers today account for publishing information both bibliographic and full text on CD-ROMs as well as making them available for online retrieval. The prominent online publishers include DIALOG, BRS, and EBSCO host etc. An excellent example of electronically published databases in the ERIC (Educational Resource Information Centre) which is the largest educational database in the world that adds more than 800,000 records per year. ERIC is available in CD-ROM format as well as on the net free of charge.

4) **Electronic Publishing on CD-ROM:** CD-ROM has provided new dimension for information storage and retrieval. Publishing information mainly abstracting sources are quiet common in CD-ROM. Although much of the work on e-journals has concentrated on distribution via the Internet, there has been some work on CD-ROM as well. The advantages of CD-Rom are:

   a) More material can be included, both in terms of quantity (650+megabytes) and type (multi-media resources). b) Full text searching is relatively easy to include.

5) **Print-on-Demand (POD):** Print-on-Demand is a new method for printing books. It is a mix of electronic and print publishing. The book is held by the publisher in electronic form and is printed out in the hard copy form only on order. This method helps free publishers from the process of doing a traditional print run of several thousand books at a time. The technology involves complex laser printing systems and electronically formatted text that the printers can read. The technology is currently very expensive and the New York Times

recently reported that Lightning Source, Inc., a leading provider of e book fulfillment, charges publishers over $4.00 per book, which is a higher cost per unit than that of small print run. Prices should come down as more publishers and retailers purchase the technology. POD is very hot right now; in a sense, it is a good intermediary step between the regular method of printing paper books and electronic books. However, in the long run, POD could decline in popularity when consumers become comfortable with electronic reading software and e book reading devices.

6) **Digital Content:** Digital content generally refers to the electronic delivery of fiction that is shorter than book-length, nonfiction, and other written works of shorter length. Publishers of digital content deliver shorter sized works to the consumer via download to handheld and other wireless devices. Technology used for delivering digital content includes Adobe PDF, XML, HDML, WAP (Wireless Application Protocol). The security of the data being delivered is the major concern of publishers who want to ensure they can deliver digital content without the risk of someone copying the work and selling or giving away the works.

7) **Electronic Ink:** Electronic Ink is a developing technology that could have a huge impact on the media and publishing industries. Electronic Ink could be used to create a newspaper or book that updates itself. In addition, this content could be programmed to change at any time. For example, you could have a billboard that rotates different ads, or you could receive a coupon in the mail that is frequently updated with the latest offer. For media companies, the possibilities are almost endless. Someday your electronic newspaper will simply update itself every day. E- Ink Corporation and Xerox are two companies currently developing this technology.

8) **Email Publishing:** Email publishing is designed specifically for delivering regular content-based email messages. Email publishing, or newsletter publishing, is a popular choice among readers who enjoy the ease of receiving news items, articles and short newsletters in their email box. The ease of delivery and production of email newsletters has led to the development of a massive number of available email newsletters, mailing lists and discussion lists on a large variety of topics. Newsletters are also widely used by media companies to complement their web and print offerings. Many authors and writers publish their own newsletters in order to attract new readers and to inform their fans about new books and book signings.

9) **Web Publishing:** Web publishing is not a novel practice any longer, but it continues to change and develop with the introduction of new

programming languages. HTML is still the most widely used web programming language, but XML is also making headway. XML is valuable because it allows publishers to create content and data that is portable to other devices.

BENEFITS OF ELECTRONIC PUBLISHING

Thousands of manuscripts get rejected every day by traditional publishers. This is the reason behind "e-publishing" becoming a popular and profitable alternative. You have a better chance of getting published with the help of electronic publishing. The costs involved in traditional publishing methods are comparatively high and the publishers are very selective. Electronic publishing has removed much of the cost and risk involved in print publishing. Due to this, a larger number of authors are now able to get their works published.

Since the cost of electronic publishing is significantly lower, an author can expect a higher income from the sale of an e-book. If an author decides to pay for the creation of his e-book up front and distribute the work on his own, he gets to keep all the profit. He can negotiate with the e-publisher about the royalty. E-publishers grant more freedom to the authors for discussion about the contract.

Different aspects such as the duration of contract, royalties, electronic publishing and print rights, advertising, design input and marketing and distribution are negotiated to benefit both parties. E-Publishers even encourage the authors to get involved in the creation of their e-book and ensure that the final product meets their expectations. Articles and e-books can be published and offered for sale within a few months, unlike conventional publishing, where it can take up to two years for the manuscript to get printed and reach the bookstore.

The magic of multimedia can be included in electronic publishing. Multimedia elements such as graphics, animation, audio, short video clips, music or expandable photos elevate the quality of electronic publication and illustrate the textual content more effectively. These elements also enhance the reading experience. The publication can be packaged and distributed in more than one format.

Electronic publishing is increasingly popular in works of fiction as well as with scientific articles. Electronic publishers are able to provide quick gratification for late-night readers, books that customers might not be able to find in standard book retailers (erotica is especially popular in e-Book format), and books by new authors that would be unlikely to be profitable for traditional publishers. The biggest advantages of e-publishing are the cost saving in printing and paper as well as better data storage and maintenance. It is most ideally suited for publications like journals, research reports and newsletters. It is also suited for all information that is dynamic or constantly changing. E-publishing finds great use and acceptance in researches, in the online publishing of educational books or tutorials. With an increase in distance learning programs, the need for quality educational material is on the rise. These e-books and study material need to recreate an active learning atmosphere as can be found in a class full of students and a teacher.

CONCLUSION

Electronic reserves projects and systems have been a tremendous success for many libraries and have provided development opportunities for librarians, staff and users.

With documents getting published electronically and the Internet resources growing at the rate of 20 percent a month, the selection of documents is going to be a difficult job. The 21st Century librarian will basically become a resource sharing librarian, whose resources will have no boundaries, local, national or international. The services, the librarian can offer to the users, will compel them to create new methods of classifying and cataloguing internal resources, developing such type of search engine, which specialize in certain subject areas only and interlink each bit of information which has relevance to anything else in the universe of knowledge. In this changing scenario, the librarian is going to be a highly skilled professional whose total commitment would be as a navigator to global intellectual resources as facilitators, instructors, gatekeepers of knowledge interpreters, evaluators, consultants, researchers, information managers, promoters.

REFERENCES

1. McMurtrie, D.C. (1943). The book: the story of printing and bookmaking; Oxford University Press, pp. 61 & 86
2. Wsift, J. Gullivers Travels; Heilman RB, Random House, New York, 1969, pp209
3. Brownrigg, E B and Lynch, C A (1985). Electrons, electronic publishing and electronic display. Information Technology Knowledge Resource Centre 4, pp. 201
4. www.wikipedia.org/wiki/E-publishing

❑❑❑

Chapter – 8

Bibliometric Analysis of the Nursing Literature: A Study at Sri Venkateswara Institute of Medical Sciences University, Tirupati

V. Nireekshan Babu, M. R. Murali Prasad and A .Omkar Murthy

INTRODUCTION

During the last three decades, libraries have shown a considerable degree of momentum in the collection building and readership programme activities involving considerable expenditure of funds. This rapid development of libraries as a consequence, generated several evaluative studies on the usefulness of libraries to society. Until recently evaluations were subjective, based purely on opinions expressed by an individual or group. However, developments in the field of mathematics, statistics, operations research, management science, economics and system analysis have led to a minimization of this subjectivity. In particular, the systems analysis approach has led to the identification and application of appropriate quantitative measuring techniques for evaluating the effectiveness and efficiency of the information services offered by the librarians. This has generated a new field in library and information science viz; 'Bibliometrics'.

Bibliometric analysis which has now become a well established part of information research and quantitative approach to the description of documents and examination of services is gaining ground both in research and practice. Librarians are facing the problems arising out of ever increasing cost of different types of reading materials and decreasing budgets of libraries.

Bibliometric studies are helpful in solving the problems of librarians. Pritichard[1] defines Bibliometrics as "application of mathematical and statistical methods to books and other media of communication".

According to Fairthorne[2] Bibliometrics in "the quantitative treatment of the properties of recorded discourse and behavior pertaining to it".

REVIEW OF LITERATURE

Sangam and Biradar[3] analysed 7,576 citations appended to 145 Master of Science (M.Sc.) dissertations in surgery accepted by the Gulbarga University, during the period of 1982 to 1989.

Vimala[4] studied the pattern of the use of information by researchers in Biological Sciences by analyzing the citations appended to 200 doctoral theses in Biological Sciences, submitted to Sri Venkateswara University, Tirupati.

Aruna Prasad Reddy[5] studied the citations appended to 186 doctoral dissertations in Chemistry accepted by Sri Venkateswara University, Tirupati.

Omkar Murthy[6] studied the citations appended to 135 doctoral dissertation in Geography submitted to Osmania University, Hyderabad, Andhra University, Visakhapatnam, Sri Venkateswara University, Tirupati and Sri Krishnadevaraya University, Ananthapur.

Nisha[7] studied the citations appended to 159 doctoral dissertations in Psychology accepted by Sri Venkateswara University, Tirupati.

OBJECTIVES OF THE PRESENT STUDY

1. To know the authorship patterns in the field of Nursing ;
2. To know the bibliographic forms of Nursing;
3. To know the rank list of journals in the field of Nursing
4. To know the extent of availability of citations in Sri Venkateswara Institute of Medical Sciences (SVIMS) University Library.

DATA AND METHODOLOGY

The citations in M. Sc. Nursing dissertations are given as a footnote at the end of the each of chapter. All the citations mentioned in dissertations were noted down on slips of size11.5 x 7.5 Cm. The information which is provided in each citation is taken as it is on the slips. The present study is mainly intended to describe the characteristic features of Nursing based on the analysis of citations collected in the Nursing dissertations and to know the extent of the availability of citations in Sri Venkateswara Institute of Medical Sciences University Library. The sources of data for the present study are the 7757 citations which have been cited in 77 M.Sc. Nursing dissertations submitted to Sri Venkateswara Institute of Medical Sciences University, Tirupati during the years 2005-2010.

ANALYSIS AND DISCUSSION

It is evident from Table 1 that journals (56.20%) and books (38.48%) are the major source of information for the M.Sc. Nursing students. The remaining (5.31%) of total citations are distributed in other bibliographic forms. It can be concluded from the Table that the Post graduate students in Nursing are using journals mostly for their research work.

Table 1: Distribution of cited literature in different bibliographic forms in Nursing

Sl.No.	Bibliographic Forms	No. of Citations	%
1.	Journals	4135	56.20
2.	Books	2831	38.48
3.	Seminars/Conference/Proceedings	118	1.60
4.	Govt. Publications	105	1.43
5.	These/Dissertations	93	1.26
6.	Reports	75	1.02
	Total	**7357**	**100**

The distribution of citations of books and journal articles according to the number of authors in nursing literature is shown in the following Figure.

It can be seen from above figure that most of the citations (32.79%) are contributed by two authors, three authors (22.01%) and the remaining (45.20%) are contributed by single author and more than three authors. From this, it can be concluded that majority of the authors in nursing are conducting research and publishing books and articles in collaboration.

Fig. 1 Distribution of citations in books and journals according to Number of authors

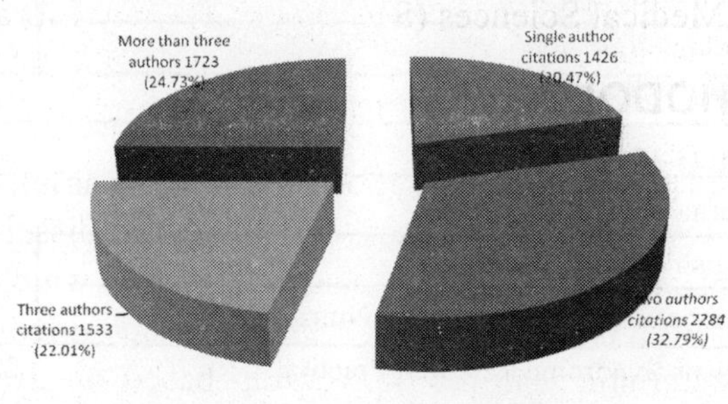

Table 2: The rank list of cited journals

Sl. No.	Rank	Name of the Journal	Citations	
		No.	%	
1	1	Indian Journal of Preventive Medicine	182	4.40
2	2	Nursing Research	172	4.16
3	3	Indian Journal of Maternal & Child Health	159	3.85
4	4	Indian Journal of Pediatrics	152	3.68
5	5	Nursing Outlook	150	3.63
6	6	Indian Journal of Psychiatry	149	3.60
7	7	Indian Journal of Community Medicine	124	3.00
8	8	Indian Journal of community Medicine	119	2.88
9	9	Indian Journal of Clinical Obstetrics and Gynecology	117	2.83
10	10	Journal of Occupational Environmental medicine	109	2.64
11	11	Indian Journal of Nursing	100	2.42
12	12	British Journal of Gynecology	96	2.32
13	13	American Heart Journal	85	2.06
14	14	Journal of Pediatrics	82	1.98
15	15	Circulation	75	1.81
16	15	Pediatrics Today	75	1.81
17	16	Nursing Clinics of North America	74	1.79
18	17	Health for Millions	69	1.67
19	18	Indian Journal of Radiology Image	64	1.55
20	19	Journal of Bone and Mineral Research	60	1.45
21	20	Indian Journal of Communicable Diseases	59	1.43
22	21	Journal of Cancer Education	56	1.35
23	22	Orthopedic Nursing	52	1.26
24	23	Journal of Clinical Obstetrics and Gynecology	50	1.21
25	24	Hypertension	46	1.11
26	25	Kidney International	44	1.06
27	26	Saudi Medical Journal	41	0.99
28	27	American Journal of Psychiatry	39	0.94
29	28	Journal of Neurology	36	0.87
30	29	Urology Research	35	0.85
31	30	JAPI	30	0.73
32	30	Journal of Endourology	30	0.73
33	31	Journal of Midwifery	29	0.70
34	32	British Medical Journal	27	0.65
35	32	American Journal of Clinical Nutrition	27	0.65
36	33	Downs Syndrome Research Practice	25	0.60

Contd...

37	33	Journal of Surgical Oncology	25	0.60
38	34	Obstrics and Gynecology Today	24	0.58
39	34	The Australian Journal of Obstetrics and Gynecology	24	0.58
40	35	Indian Journal of Nephrology	22	0.53
41	35	American Journal of Human Biology	22	0.53
42	36	Canadian Journal of Nursing	21	0.51
43	37	American Journal of Physical Medicine and Rehabilitation	19	0.46
44	38	Lancet	17	0.41
45	39	British Journal of Obstetrics and Gynecology	16	0.39
46	39	Journal of Virology	16	0.39
47	40	Nursing Times	15	0.36
48	41	American Journal of Epidemiology	14	0.34
49	41	Journal of Infectious Diseases	14	0.34
50	42	American Journal of Dietic Association	12	0.29
51	43	Health care for Women	11	0.27
52	43	Indian Heart Journal	11	0.27
53	43	Journal of Indian Medical Association	11	0.27
54		11 Journals each 10 citations	110	2.66
55		9 Journals each 9 Citations	81	1.96
56		7 Journals each 8 Citations	56	1.35
57		14 Journals each 7 Citations	98	2.37
58		17 Journals each 6 Citations	102	2.47
59		22 Journals each 5 Citations	110	2.66
60		21 Journals each 4 Citations	84	2.03
61		45 Journals each 3 Citations	135	3.26
62		58 Journals each 2 Citations	116	2.80
63		108 Journals each 1 Citations	108	2.61
64		Unknown	02	0.05
		Total	**4135**	**100**

It can be observed from Table 2 that the Journal literature used by the M.Sc. Nursing students is scattered in 367 different periodicals. However most of the citations are found in Indian Journal of Preventive Medicine (4.40%), Nursing Research (4.16%) and Indian Journal of Maternal and Child Health (3.85%). Indian Journal of Preventive Medicine gets the first rank for being cited more number of times. 'Nursing Research' and Indian Journal of Maternal and Child Health get second and third rank respectively. It is also evident that 50% of citations are contributed by 10 periodicals and 75% citations are contributed 34 periodicals. That means less number of periodicals are contributing more number of citations.

Table 3: Country-wise distribution of cited journals

Sl.No.	Name of the Country	No. of Journals	%
1	India	147	40.05
2	U.S.A.	127	34.61
3	U.K.	37	10.08
4.	Europe	14	3.82
5.	New Zealand	09	2.45
6.	Africa	06	1.63
7.	Russia	05	1.36
8.	Pakistan	03	0.82
9.	Others (17)	17	4.63
10.	Unidentified	02	0.54
	Total	**367**	**100**

The name of the country of the citied journals was found out from the Ulrich's International Periodicals Directory. As revealed by many previous studies, it is a well known fact that U.S.A. and U.K. are the main producers of journals. It is apparent from the above Table that India ranks first by producing 40.05% of cited journals followed by U.S.A. (34.61%) and U.K. (10.08%). These three countries produce nearly 95% of cited journals. The remaining 5 per cent of journals are from 22 other countries. It is evident from it that Indian journals are mostly cited compared to the journals from other countries.

Table 4: Distribution of journal citations according to number of years they are old

Age of Old in years	Citations	
	Number	%
0-5	28	0.68
6-10	40	0.97
11-15	57	1.38
16-20	52	1.26
21-25	75	1.81
26-30	52	1.26
31-35	186	4.49
36-40	193	4.67
41-45	102	2.47
46-50	126	3.05
51-55	191	4.62
56-60	294	7.11
61-65	302	7.30

Contd...

66-70	361	8.73
71-75	319	7.71
76-80	270	6.53
81-85	287	6.94
86-90	260	6.29
91-95	309	7.47
96-100	263	6.36
101-105	368	8.89
Total	**4135**	**100**

It can be noticed from Table 4 that most of journal citations (86.70%) used by researchers are 0-35 years old. It is evident from that (13.30%) of citations used by them are 36-115 years of old. From this it can be concluded that researchers are depending upon journal articles which are of from 0-35 years old.

Table - 5: Availability of citations in SVIMS University Library

Bibliographic forms	Total No. of Citations	No. of Availability of Citations	%
Journals	4135	2509	60.68
Books	2831	969	34.23
Seminars/Conference/Proceedings	118	46	38.98
Govt. Publications	105	11	10.48
These/Dissertations	93	29	31.18
Reports	75	18	24.00
Total	**7357**	**3582**	**48.68**

It is also evident from Table 5 that most of the cited references (48.684%) are available in SVIMS University Library. The students might have read the other references which are not available in the University library by visiting other libraries, by getting the reading materials on interlibrary loan, browsing the internet or by borrowing materials from their faculty members or friends. Finally it can be said that SVIMS University Library is meeting of the requirements M. Sc. Nursing students.

SUMMARY

The present investigation is mainly to describe the characteristic features of literature used by the M.Sc. Nursing students of SVIMS university.

- The analysis of authorship pattern of journal articles reveals that the publications with single authors are more in number in English.
- The rank list of cited journals based on the analysis of citations reveals that the cited journal literature is scattered in 367 periodicals. The

periodical Indian Journal of Preventive Medicine gets first rank for being cited more number of times.

- The chronological scattering of journal citations indicates that most of the citations (86.70%) used by the researchers in English are from 0-35 years old.

CONCLUSION

This type of studies will help in collection building of the libraries as well as to assess the user needs, utilization of the literature available in the library to meet the information requirements of the readers.

REFERENCES

1. Pritchard, Alan (1969). Statistical Bibliography or Bibliometrics?. *Journal of Documentation* 25, pp. 348-349.
2. Fairthorne, Robert A (1987). Empirical Hyperbolic distribution. *Encyclopedia of Library and Information Science* 42, p.153.
3. Sangam, S L and Biradar, B S. (1990). Patterns of information use by Indian Surgical Scientists. *Annals of Library Science and Documentation* 37, pp.133-142.
4. Vimala, V (1997). Bibliometric Study of citations in Ph.D. theses in Biological Sciences. Tirupati: Sri Venkateswara University. Ph.D thesis.(Unpublished).
5. Arun Prasad Reddy, C. (1999). Bibliometric Study of citations in Ph.D. theses in Chemistry accepted by Sri Venkateswara University, Tirupati: 1964-1997. Visakhapatnam: Andhra University. Ph. D. thesis (Unpublished).
6. Omkar Murthy, A. (2006). Bibliometric Study of citations in Ph.D. theses in Geography. Tirupati: Sri Venkateswara University.Ph.D. thesis. (Unpublished).
7. Zaffarunnisha, Y (2009). Citations analysis of psychology Ph.D. theses. Tirupati: Sri Venkateswara University. Ph. D. thesis. (Unpublished).
8. Aravinda, P.(1986). Citation analysis in the Annual Review of Anthropology for the years 1980 to 1982. Tirupati: Sri Venkateswara University, M.L.I.Sc. Dissertation. (Unpublished).
9. Pangannaya, N. B and Kumaraswamy, S (1981). Leisure, Subject, Scatter, Journal dispersion and other characteristics: A Citation analysis. *ALIS Bulletin* 5, pp. 7-24.
10. Srinivasulu, T. (1993). Citation pattern in M.Sc. (Ag) theses of Andhra Pradesh Agricultural University in Agronomy. Tirupati: Sri Venkateswara University. M.L.I.Sc. dissertation. (Unpublished).

Chapter – 9

User Education in the Age of Information Technology

M. Suresh Babu and D. Chandran

USER EDUCATION

User Education can be defined as a program to guide and to instruct the potential users either individually or collectively. User education is an action taken by the Library staff to train / educate their users so as to make full use of the existing knowledge to develop their community.

ALA Glossary defines user education as it encompasses all types of activities designed to teach users about library services, facilities and organizations library resources and search strategy.

User education can be defined in the context of electronic sources of Information as educating the users how to operate computer and searching Information on Net using various search strategies and to educate them how to use electronic sources of information and various databases.

Users of the library must be convinced that continuing learning is worthwhile and that the process of education does not end with examination. They must have confidence to be learners and to stand of their own, to possess autonomy to select and to direct their own future study experience. User education has been defined by Mews as "instruction given to readers to help them to make best use of library". User education was not solely to stimulate library use as this but one of the sources of Information. According to Nancy, Fjalbarnt and Lan Malley " User Education is concerned with the whole

Information and communication process and one part if this involves the total interaction of the users the library. This should be a continuous process starting with schools and public libraries and with possibility of extension to academic and specialized libraries. According to Jacques Tacathan, Director of UNESCO general Information Program "User Education is to include any effort or program which will guide and instruct existing and potential user in the recognition and information service and their assessment.

OBJECTIVES OF USER EDUCATION

In every institution there is a need to train the student/staff members for regular and rational use of vast information resources available in their library. User education is an essential part of general education. The ability and skill for using a library which are provided in the academic institution, serve one's needs beyond the formal education.

Due to scientific and technological revolution, a new alarming situation regarding Information has been reated in the world by the rapid increase in the flow of information due to information explosion, wide dispersal of information, greater research on complex and inter disciplinary topics and the number of users.

The specific objectives of user education are to create awareness and understanding of the basic relevant library and information sources and service, to bridge the gap between the potential user and education, to enhance users ability to select appropriate information sources and systems for their specific information needs

It is necessary that user education must be given to the users in their initial academic careers, because as the academic level increase their demand for information will increase accordingly.

Association of College and Research Libraries, USA refers to user education as "information literacy". They further stated "information literacy is a set of abilities requiring individuals to recognize when information is needed and has the ability to locate, evaluate and use effectively the needed information.

Information literacy forms the basis for life long learning. It is common to all disciplines, to all learning requirements and to all levels of education. It enables the user to master the content and their investigation becomes more self – directed and assumes grater control over their own learning. Information literate individual is able to determine the extent of information needed; assess the needed information effectively and efficiently; evaluate information and its sources critically; incorporate selected information into one's knowledge base; use information effectively and accomplish a specific purpose; understand the economic, legal and social issues surrounding the use of information and access and use information ethically and legally.

The education of the user is an important aspect of the library and information centers. If the user is unable to retrieve the information he needs, no matter how splendid a library or efficient its service, the ultimate purpose of all reference service will not be achieved. The most urgent need therefore is to ensure that awareness is created about the tremendous out –pour of new information, desire to read and assimilate and the ability to find one's way about the expanse of recorded information becomes a part of every individual.

USER EDUCATION IN THE AGE OF INFORMATION TECHNOLOGY

All procedures of the library and information centers already contain artificially of the procedures a good librarian/ information officer must guide/ educate/train his users to access required information effectively and efficiently. In the present day of information technology the library functions are automated. The automation is multifaceted in that it also encompasses the functions of acquisition, cataloguing and circulation. Today it is expected that the library management system will incorporate OPAC's, CD–ROM, and networks, desktop publishing, office automation, virtual reality, multimedia, hypermedia, hypertext, web pages, websites etc.

In this changing scenario the functions of the user education rather became more complex because of this new technology, and the user education will be in two steps. Firstly the library staff themselves have to be trained and familiarized with the technology. Secondly, the library staff prepare simple and easy instructions to train their user to acquire the desired information.

User education or information literacy is a survival skill in the information age, because information literate people know how to find, evaluate and use information effectively for making decision. User education/ information literacy given by the library to the individual is related to information technology skills, but has broader implications for the indivual, the educational systems, and for the society. Information technology skills enable an individual to use computers, software applications, databases and other technologies to achieve a wide variety of academic work related and personal goals. Information literate individuals also develop some technological skills.

According to Freeman,Raoul J., the training for users includes instruction regarding the overall operation of the new system, detailed delineation of how particular subsystems operate, guidance on the operation of computer hardware , and hands on practice in the actual operation of the system. He emphasizes on developing easy – to - understand user manuals that provide information relative to various other matters i.e. operation of terminals and printers, functioning of and entering information into screen displays, retrieveing information from databases, formats of reports provided by the new system etc. Meadow, Charles T. says that the intelligent user will rationally choose between system power and simplicity. The uninformed will not recognize that a choice is being made, and may opt for simplicity instead of the complexity that might be needed to solve certain problems.

Tschudi, C.M says that training online searcher in not an easy task for several reasons. First of all, new searcher comes from a wide variety of backgrounds with very diverse levels of skills. We also have vastly different learning rates as well as different career goals and interest.

For the successful implementation and operation of scientific and technical information systems in the future, a new training system for information specialists should be established

USER EDUCATION AND NETWORK LITERACY

There are three main elements that are different from traditional bibliography instructions for providing instruction to user education on network literacy. Firstly, librarians should organize and design an efficient teaching environment including facilities and select a suitable teaching method to provide instructional programs on network literacy to users. Networked information must be based on a networked environment. To set up physical equipment or facilities for network training would involve collaboration with computer/network specialists, and also it should be based on the existing library network system. Secondly, librarians need to determine what course contents should be provided in the instruction. The contents for network literacy instruction varies based on the purpose, target group and subjects of networked information.

Thirdly, combine library information literacy training programs with other educational programs such as teacher's course offerings in academic and school, library, public education programs in public library, and in special library and computer/network specialists workshops on computer/networks literacy. The cooperation between librarians and users, between librarians and other educators will be important. Network/computer specialists can provide instruction for computer literacy and network technology. Librarians focus on instructions on network literacy programs in specific subject fields as needed in their courses. The teacher can also consult with librarians to update their sources for networked information needed.

COMPUTER AIDED INSTRUCTION

Computer aided instruction/computer assisted instruction (CAI) is probably the most imaginative of the new application of the computer in education. In essence, CAI tries to use the computer as an all knowing teaching "Brain" in such a way that the student can interact directly with it without the immediate mediation of a human factor. However, human effort is required in massive amounts in preparing the system and the specific instruction material to be stored in the computer.

The academic institutes have accepted programmed instruction or computer aided instruction. This is now being used by several libraries and information centers quite effectively and efficiently. Most of the CAI programs are pre-packaged, thus learning times for librarians providing user education are forced to concentrate on the essentials/CAI programs take care of library instruction program or user education program automatically. It has one more substantial advantage that every librarian has not been adequately trained to provide library instruction, so it takes the charge of search a specific reading material or information. Computer assisted learning would have considerable educational potential on instruction and training for off-line and entire searching of information. A specific method is needed for rationalization of instruction in terms of sequencing presentation and feedback as to progress. Computer assisted instruction can be used to present the subject matter in logical searches and articulated hierarchy of task. The user can receive instruction in a number of cognitive modes, whilst at the same time training in the use of tool-modems and terminals and experiencing the interaction of an offline and online system.

As a training of instructional device the computer acts as a link between the instruction programs and the student. The instruction program can be either linear or branched. Formerly the student is given one unit of instruction and then is tested. In the latter the student is routed to appropriate parts of the instruction program based on the responses made of the computer more fully than the simpler linear mode. CAI is an interface between the user and the real online/offline system, by translating commands in one language into commands appropriate for other system; to provide practice on a real online/offline system using a subject of a database or several databases; by providing diagonistic messages and responding to the help command during online/offline searching. These features, which have been originally built into online/offline system to improve system performance, are of considerable instructional value to searchers.

USER EDUCATION FOR VARIOUS NEW INFORMATION TECHNIQUES

In this information technology age various techniques have been launched such as OPAC, Video, Internet, CD-ROM technology etc. Use of Internet has already made tremendous impact on the research activities of the teachers, research scholars, social scientists and users of e-libraries. Various purposes for which users are attracted towards Internet are:

1. Keeping them up to date
2. Publication of research papers
3. Electronic journals
4. E-mail facility
5. Surfing etc.

USER EDUCATION PROGRAM FOR INTERNET

To educate in the information technology environment, a detailed users education program is required .Finding information from net is difficult due to on-indexed information on net .It takes a lot of time and even a very few results are relevant to users after a searching of several hours .The user educating program in such a condition needs :

- a particular user must have clear understanding of how to prepare a search.
- how to identify the main concept in the related topic
- use to search tools
- knowledge of search enginees etc
- knowledge of web sites
- knowledge of e-mail
- knowledge of content direct services
- knowledge of different search tips
- knowledge of patent information services
- knowledge of e-journals
- knowledge of newspapers and magazines
- downloading

USER EDUCATION FOR CD –ROMs

Users are to be instructed about various CD-ROM databases available in the library and how, when and where to use them. Users must be trained for the services offered by INFLIBNET. Users must be trained for the techniques for subscribing information materials on net. They can be informed with the help of some brochures, leaflets or pamphlets etc.

Various tools and techniques to educate users in the information age.

- Searching databases
- Classes on information literacy
- Use of keyboard of computer
- Web tutorials
- Instructions on how to use key search engines effectively including Yahoo,Google, Excite etc
- Computer assisted Learning packages for the new students
- OPAC for searching

- Guides for citing e-information
- Use of video
- Educational programs for Internet services
- Interactive tutorials for evaluating tutorials for evaluating the quality of information.

CONCLUSION

User education in the age of changing information environment has opened new ways of teaching and learning use of the library –collection. With the arrival of computer, internet, multimedia and other sophisticated technologies, it has become essential to educate the user so that they can feel the information environment friendly. Their hesitation, lack of understanding towards the various tools of information in the library can be minimized and finally removed. User education plays a very important role in exploiting the resources of any library and making it most useful in the service arena.

❑❑❑

Chapter – 10

The Diffusion of Library and Information Science in the Modern Age in Andhra Pradesh

R. Pommal Rao and M. Muniya Naik

INTRODUCTION

Libraries have become Library and Information Centers (LIC) and Knowledge Resource Centers (KRC). Many LICs and KRCs have stepped forward towards establishing Digital Libraries and Digital Repositories. These wings require the professionals with adequate qualifications and should have good command over the latest technologies. The trained candidates prior to their recruitment may immediately take up a project with a challenge. The professionals who are in service may enhance their skills through sponsorships to long term / short term programs.

In the present era, LIS is treated as multi-disciplinary subject and has integration with all newly emerging subjects. The other side, the LIS departments in the Universities have to respond properly (towards requirement) in incorporating suitable latest topics in their curricula and implement it very strictly. The research activity in LIS field in the country has to grow suitably along with the developed countries. In Andhra Pradesh, similar response is needed from the Government in providing and releasing funds to the state universities to start LIS departments. The preference has to be given by the State Government to LIS research in public libraries in proportionate with

Science, Humanities and Social Science libraries. In future, it is expected that the LIS research should lead.

LIS EDUCATION

The primary aim of LIS education is to provide the professional training to intellectuals in the areas of information capturing, refining preparation, retrieval and display formats, etc. The goal of such programs is to achieve wisdom in promoting better utilization of information. As said in the above paragraphs, the modern LICS and KRCs require qualified and trained professionals for strengthening systematical functioning.

At present, the Library and Information Science courses are being offered by many Indian institutions at various levels such as Certificate, Diploma, Bachelor Degree - BLISC, Post Graduate Degree - MLISC, or Integrated Course MLISC (2 years), M.Phil., Ph.D., etc. Among these, except the Certificate and Diploma Courses, all other courses are being offered in various Universities in the country. Among 531+ universities in India (42 Central, 275 State, 130 Deemed and 85 Private Universities), many Universities could not establish LIS departments because of concentrating on burning topics in their catchment areas. Total 118+ Universities are offering these courses countrywide.

The first library school in Andhra Pradesh was "Andhra Desa Library Association" located in Vijayawada (now Andhra Pradesh Library Association). It started conducting library training courses during 1920s. The certificate course and diploma courses were started during 1935 by Andhra University, Waltair. Later the diploma course was changed and upgraded to Bachelor degree program during 1960s. Gradually this program has started by other Universities in the state.

In Andhra Pradesh, there are four central universities, 30 state universities, and seven deemed universities. Among these 40+, only ten Universities are teaching library science courses. There is acute necessity to establish LIS departments in all other universities in the state.

LIS RESEARCH

Many Government and Private Universities are offering M. Phil. and Ph.D. research courses to the Post Graduates i.e. MLIS / MLISC qualified students through regular stream. These two courses were also available through distance education mode prior to 2009. The MHRD has discontinued these distance courses mentioning the necessity of protecting suitable academic values in the research programs. Dr.B.R. Ambedkar Open University, Hyderabad is only institution which is offering M.Phil. and Ph.D. courses via distance mode.

However, many universities are offering off-campus research courses with a condition i.e. an attendance of 3-6 months is compulsory and to stay on the campus.

It has been noticed that the working librarians who are waiting for senior pay scales and selection grades, are very much disappointed towards the above decision of the UGC. In general, the employees at an age of 50 / 50+ also do not prefer either regular courses or off-campus programs. They may much depend on distance mode of learning.

The below mentioned table shows the List of Universities which are offering Library Science Courses (including M. Phil. and Ph. D.) in Andhra Pradesh State.

Sl. No.	University	Location	Type	Established
1.	Andhra University	Visakhapatnam	State	1926
2.	Dr.B.R. Ambedkar Open University	Hyderabad	State	1982
3.	Dr. B.R. Ambedkar University, Srikakulam	Etcherla	State	1988
4.	Dravidian University	Kuppam	State	1997
5.	Kakatiya University	Warangal	State	1976
6.	Osmania University	Hyderabad	State	1918
7.	Sri Krishna Devaraya University	Anantapur	State	1981
8.	Sri Padmavathi Mahila Viswavidyalayam	Tirupati	State	1983
9.	Sri Venkateshwara University	Tirupati	State	1954
10.	University of Hyderabad*	Hyderabad	Central	1974

* offers only PGDLAN Course coordinated by The Indira Gandhi Memorial Library.

LIS TRAINING

The available training resources and tools in the field of Library and Information Science can be grouped as following.

- Long Term Programs
- Short Term Programs
- On Site Training
- Off Site Training

Long Term Programs: The programs which are designed to admit the candidates for a period of one month to a maximum of one year training may be consider as long term programs.

- Internships
- Associateships
- Post Graduate Diploma in Library Automation and,
- The regular and continuously attending training programs are examples of long term.

The advantage is, a candidate may thoroughly learn practical knowledge and may enhance the power of management of each task in a library whenever returned to native library. The disadvantage is, stay away from his/her native library and could not cope up with the changes occurred in the native library.

Short Term Programs: The programs which are designed to provide training and awareness towards latest advancements in the field of LIS are grouped here such as:-

- Seminars (1,2,2-3 days)
- Conferences (1,2,2-3 days)
- Workshops (1 week / 2 weeks)
- Refresher Courses (3 weeks)
- Basic and Advance Training Courses (1 week)
- Dr. S.R. Ranganathan Birth Centenary Celebrations (Particular on the 12th August every year)
- Round Table Meetings (1/2 a day / 1 day), etc.

Very few research organizations in LIS are admitting candidates for Internships and Associateships outside the state. No doubt, a candidate who qualifies the internship / Associateship course will be familiar with latest advancements in LIS field and has practical knowledge than the learners of other courses. These candidates are easily qualifying the recruitment tests as well as facing interviews, group discussions and getting jobs early. The PGDLAN program of one year duration is being offered by very few Universities which can be counted on finger tips.

It is clear that the short term programs are much impressive and became popular than the long term training programs.

The training provided by a vendor of Hardware or Software at the work place itself is called as onsite training. The training programs whichever conducted by external universities, institutions and organizations are called offsite training programs. Many women employees prefer onsite training and men prefer onsite and offsite training simultaneously.

CONCLUSION

The UGC has contributed their efforts well to develop LIS departments in Indian Universities as well as the state universities. The UGC has constituted several committees especially Curriculum Development Committees to restructure the LIS syllabus with IT and multimedia courses since the year 1992. A comprehensive State Government's Policy has to be formulated and norms are to be framed towards the changed LIS scenario in the state. For this the guidelines, instructions and recommendations may be downloaded from the reports of National Committees and a suitable policy may be prepared. Certainly this may enhance the power of 'Information Literacy' and encourage young students and research scholars in the state.

REFERENCES

1. Toney, Bernard (1967). Indian Library Science training. Journal of Education for Librarianship 8, pp.115-123.

2. Nishavathi, E (2007). Research trends in LIS : A subjective analysis of doctoral theses published in India. Proceedings of NACLIN -2007, pp. 559-568.

3. www.vidyanidhi.org.in

❑❑❑

Chapter – 11

User Education in Agricultural Libraries in Digitized Environment

Monisha Mishra and Rabindra K. Mahapatra

INTRODUCTION

The emergence of Information and Communication Technology (ICT) has made the libraries more powerful in the collection development, processing and retrieval of information. The advent of internet has not only made it possible to connect the libraries over the world, but also to search a huge repository of databases. The technology has developed to online system to connect commercialize vendors as well as learned societies with the databases to seek and obtain the needed information. The use of computer and digital technologies in teaching and learning has been evolved not just through the increase of distance learning or virtual courses but through the use of cyber education as an adjunct to the traditional classroom. This increased the trend of access to technology in Library and Information Centers and has given the opportunity to use those resources and improve the skill. In order to acquaint themselves with the new technological environment, the users are required to be more conversant with those skills.

Libraries & Information Centers play an important role in supporting the teaching, learning, research and extension programme of universities. These are made possible by building and developing good collection of selected documents both in print as well as digital form and by supporting it with various services for their dissemination. There is such an exponential growth of information in today's era that students, faculties, research scholars often lack the scope of getting proper education or instruction to use those resources to the optimum possible limit. To overcome this difficulty and to maximize the use of such resources proper library instruction must be imparted to the user community which is otherwise known as *Library User Education.*

DEFINITION

ALA Glossary of Library & Information Science defines "User Education as the term which encompasses all types of activities designed to teach users about library activities, services, facilities, resources, organization and different search strategies. It also includes instruction in the use of one or more reference sources as apart of the reference transactions, library use, presentation and bibliographic instruction." Tactlian, Director of UNESCO General information program mentioned that "User education is to include any effort or program which will guide and instruct existing and potential users in the recognition and formulation of their information needs in the effective and efficient use of information services and their assessment." Fleming (1990) defines "user education" as various programs of instruction , education and exploration provided by libraries to users to enable them to make more effective, efficient and independent use of information sources and services to which these libraries provide access.

NEED

The "inner incentives" which drive librarians to serve users are no different from those which inspire teachers. Librarians are as concerned about the new users as are the classroom teachers for the new students. These concerns come normally in three phases. First, there is the feeling of responsibility to the profession. If this is taken seriously, every effort will be made to help the user towards his learning objectives. Second, there is a strong desire to assist in the growth and maturity of users as intellectuals and as citizens. Third, there is the fulfillment and satisfaction that come from successfully promoting and engaging in the learning process. To satisfy all these needs the term of "Library User Education" was coined.

The main objectives of User Education are : -

- To make aware about the resources and facilities available inside the Library
- To develop users knowledge and skills to retrieve information required.
- To enhance user abilities to select appropriate information
- To bridge the gap between potential users and the resources

USER EDUCATION IN A DIGITIZED ENVIRONMENT: WHY?

Information and Communication Technologies (ICTs) are the clusters or interrelated systems of technological innovations in the field of microelectronics, computing electronic communications including broadcasting and the Internet (Preston, 2003).These technologies are immensely revolutionary and have influenced the creation, distribution, dissemination, sharing and repackaging of information (Britz, 2006). ICTs have facilitated the following–more people can be reached simultaneously and may be exposed to more information in an interactive way; information can be customized, integrated, altered, copied and distributed or even destroyed at absolutely no cost; knowledge can be shared in real time without time and space barriers. Due to rapid strides in ICTs there has been paradigm shift from acquiring, cataloging, circulating physical collections to synthesizing, specializing and mobilizing web based services (Murray, 2007).

The advent of Internet, advancement of ICT facilities, 24x7 accessibility of information resources have made the Libraries and Information Centers (LICs) not only to change in outlook but also in functions, services, methods and collection development, processing and dissemination of information. With so much of information being added to the web, it becomes imperative to sieve internet information resources before disseminating to the end user. Libraries and information centers need to draw upon their expertise to identify, select, evaluate and sift internet resources so as to provide their clientele access to only quality resources. Now-a-days information explosion, diversified user needs, multidisciplinary research, duplicity of resources, escalation in cost of foreign journals, and financial crunch have made libraries to opt for resource sharing. Various factors like emergence of digital collection , electronic sources of information, library automation and networking etc. have posed a challenge before the library professionals to equip themselves with the latest technologies as well as make the users compatible with the web environment to use the resources independently and get the maximum possible benefit out of those collection.

The use of IT in libraries enhances users' satisfaction and provides numerous advantages to the users. Some of the advantages are (Henderson, 1992).

- Provide speedy and easy access to information
- Provide remote access to users
- Provides round and close access to users
- Provide information flexibility to be used by any individual according to his or her requirements
- Provides increased flexibility
- Facilitates the reformatting and combining of data from different sources

RELEVANCE OF USER EDUCATION IN AN AGRICULTURAL LIBRARY

Agricultural research is a continuous process and requires updated inflow of concord knowledge which is generally managed through libraries in research institutions. Agricultural University libraries also support teaching, learning and research work. The inflow of knowledge can be met through different types of sources such as Books, Journals, Research reviews, Electronic media etc.To render those services though different resources, the State Agricultural University libraries are offering one credit hour practical course to the Post graduate as well as PhD 1st year 1st semester students. As those libraries are going hi-tech with the use of information and communication technology the relevance of these courses has become important. To use the digital resources like different databases, online journals and search engines, Institutional Repositories, Web OPACS, the users need to for educated. As such the course on "Library and Information Services" not only acquaint the users with various sources of information but also help them to be less dependent on the library staff and use the library resources independently and thus save the valuable time of themselves.

Objective of the Course

The basic objective of the course curriculum is to acquaint the users with the principles of library use and library ethics and to teach them to help themselves to retrieve the required literature desired by them at the time of their use.

1. To train the users about the concept of university library and its resources
2. To make them aware about the different services offered by the university libraries
3. To acquaint the users about using library catalogue both manual and OPAC in the automated environment.
4. To provide knowledge about CD-ROM databases, Consortium ,Online Journals, Search engines etc
5. To train them to compile bibliographies, writing scientific reports, theses/ dissertations, etc
6. Bibliographical control such as indexing and abstracting services, Current Awareness Service (CAS) and Selective Dissemination of Information(SDI)
7. To help the users in literature search and problems associated with scientific literature etc. over the internet

8. To impart knowledge about various institutional repository and subject gateways

There are number of methods by which the "User Education" can be imparted such as lectures, Seminar/Workshops, Tutorials/ demonstrations, Visual Instructions, Print media, Computer aided instruction etc. In the digital era there are specific web related instructions to make the users savvy with the digital environment.

DIGITAL RESOURCES

The rapid growth of ICT has changed the functioning of the libraries. Database information system, Web OPAC has replaced the traditional libraries. The presence of ICT inside the Library can be seen on the following areas.

- Open Source Journals
- Web OPAC
- CDROM Databases
- Consortium of E-Resources
- Digital Repository
- e-Granth (NARS)

Open Source Journals

There are several open access journals available on the internet which the agricultural users can access in the time of their need. A few such resources are mentioned below.

- Indian Journal of Agricultural Science
- Indian Journal of Animal Science
- Karnataka Journal of Agriculture Sciences
- Current Science
- NISCAIR Research Journals
- Indian Academy of Sciences – Journals
- The Madras Agricultural Journal
- Journal of Tropical Agriculture
- Krishi Munnade
- Journal of SAT Agricultural Research (ICRISAT)
- Vet Scan
- Proceeding of the Royal Society a Mathematical, Physical & Engineering Sciences

- Proceeding of The Royal Society B Biological Sciences
- Proceedings of the Indian National Science Academy
- Directory of Open Access Journals – Agriculture & Food Sciences

Web OPAC

The development of ICT has influenced the implementation of OPAC available through internet. By searching and browsing online library catalogue, the end users can directly order or transmit request directly to the Web OPAC available at different University Libraries.

CD-ROM Databases

Due to the complexities and high cost of online information searching, readers find it easier to use CD-ROM which offers unlimited access to databases at a fixed cost, interactive searching in comparison to hard copy or microfiche. In addition, it provides the potential to browse, though it is a single-user system. CD-ROM may not replace online services or hard copies completely, but it does offer an alternative option to searchers.

CDROM databases provide mainly abstracting and indexing services. Those are the most cost effective tools for information storage and retrieval. Information can be stored in different formats such as text, audio, video etc. Searches can be made through author, subject, Journal Title, Publisher etc. Boolean operators like AND, OR, NOT can be used to refine searches. Those CDROM databases not only minimize subscription cost but also facilitate quick and speedy search. Some of the important CDROM databases of Agriculture are AGRIS, AGRICOLA, VET CD, CAB abstracts etc.

AGRICULTURE DATABASES

AGRIS

AGRIS is the International Information System for the Agricultural Sciences and Technology. Together with CARIS, (Current Agricultural Research Information System), AGRIS is maintained, promoted and disseminated all over the world by means of a network of scientific documentation centers.

In 1975 the AGRIS network began publishing a bibliographic database which now holds more than 3 million records. This CD contains a subset of the AGRIS database; the complete AGRIS database can be found on the Internet at http://www.fao.org/agris. The latest version of the multilingual agricultural thesaurus, AGROVOC, is now accessible on the Internet at http://www.fao.org/agrovoc; in addition, details on 30 000 agricultural research projects and their current status as reported by the CARIS participating centre can be consulted at http://www.fao.org/agris, and are available on CD-ROM.

AGRICOLA (Agricultural On-Line Access)

It is a database created and maintained by the United States Department of Agriculture(USDA). The database serves as the catalog and index for the collections of the United States National Agricultural Library, but it also provides public access to information on agriculture and allied fields.

AGRICOLA indexes a wide variety of publications covering agriculture and its allied fields, including animal and veterinary sciences, entomology, plant sciences, forestry, aquaculture and fisheries, farming and farming systems, agricultural economics, extension and education, food and human nutrition, and earth and environmental sciences.

CAB ABSTRACTS

Covering the literature from 1910 to 1972, CAB Abstracts Archive makes over 1,860,000 records on every aspect of agricultural science, veterinary medicine, nutrition and natural resources, available electronically for the very first time.

The Archive contains seminal research that will help today's researchers:

- Build on earlier scientific work
- Learn from past mistakes
- Learn from past techniques
- Assess long-term trends and changes
- Access valuable research about rare and infrequent events
- Find 'missing' pieces of research
- Gain insights about the past

Much of the research covered in the archive such as climate change / biodiversity / pest control / pollution / animal diseases (such as TB and avian flu) / food production / managing natural resources / plant and animal breeding is still relevant today.

WEB OF SCIENCE: Largest Science Database. Covers agriculture, food and natural resources.

ANR-INDEX: Agriculture and Natural Resource Index and Archive (1975-)

GEOREF: Available through Geoscience World (1985-). It deals mainly with soil scienceand natural resources.

NETLIBRARY: Agriculture, Food and Natural resources.

AANRO: Australian Agriculture for Natural Resources Online.

ABS: Australian Bureau of Statistics

EVA : Deals with Environmental Abstracts

WISE : Water Information System for the Environment

CONSORTIUM BASED E-RESOURCES

An Agricultural Library is a special library which primarily renders service to the policy makers, specialists, scientists, teachers, students, researchers, and farmers in agriculture and allied subjects. To maximize discipline-wise coverage, to supply economics of pricing models given by publishers for using additional advantages like unlimited access, unlimited downloads, easy accessibility, any where at any time accessibility, full-text downloads, etc., made the authorities of ICAR to think about formation of e-Consortium under the Project of National Agriculture Innovation Project (NAIP) in the name of CeRA.

6.4.1. Consortium for e-Resources in Agriculture (CERA)

CeRA was launched successfully on 30 April 2008 at its headquarters at Indian Agricultural Research Institute (IARI), New Delhi. The purpose of CeRA is:

- To develop the existing R & D information resource base of ICAR institutes/ State Agricultural Universities (SAU) etc,
- To create an e-access culture among scientists/teachers in ICAR institutes/SAU.
- To develop a Science Citation Index (SCI) facility at IARI for evaluation of scientific publications.
- To access the impact of CeRA on the level of research publications measured through Science Citation Index (SCI)

The project envisages to digitize all PhD theses numbering over 10,000 submitted (since year 2000) to the SAUs and Deemed universities of ICAR. The entire work has been outsourced to a common agency so that all the theses would be digitized following uniform and standard protocol.

Digital Repository (KrishiPrabha)

Through this project all agricultural research scholars can get the benefit to access the digital e-theses repository free of cost. KrishiPrabha is a full-text electronic database of Indian Agricultural Doctoral Dissertations submitted by research scholars to the State/Deemed Agricultural Universities during the period from 1.1.2000. This database, listing about 7500 Doctoral Dissertations with a full text of about 6000 Dissertations has been created by Nehru Library, Ch. Charan Singh Haryana Agricultural University, Hisar with financial support from Indian Council of Agricultural Research, New Delhi under its National Agricultural Innovation Project having the following objectives:

- To develop, organize and sustain knowledge base of Indian Agricultural Dissertations in digital form and make it accessible on-line.
- To develop a standard format for submission of e-theses to the SAUs/ DUs.
- To upgrade skills of human resources of SAUs/DUs.
- To publish a journal in electronic form/ hard copy form from the Database.

e-Granth

The aim of this project is strengthening of digital library and information management under National Agricultural Research Scheme (e-GRANTH) .The lead is being taken up by Indian Agricultural Research Institute (IARI), New Delhi with the following objectives:

- To create Online Public Access Catalog (OPAC) under "Indian Agricultural Research Group Catalogue" of all 12 library resources with Online Computer Library Center (OCLC) partnership
- To digitize important institutional repositories (limited to IARI, IVRI, Izatnagar, Bareilly, ANGRAU, Hyderabad and UAS, Bangalore) including rare books and old journals and make them open access under NARS
- To strengthen capacity building for library and information management system (open to all libraries of NARS)

CONCLUSION

Agricultural research, the backbone of agricultural growth in the country, demands timely dissemination of knowledge being generated and updated across the globe from time to time. It is therefore important for librarians and documentalists to examine the effectiveness of their services and products vis-a-vis the user and to create mechanisms by which they can receive regular feedback. As Drucker (1976) implies in a talk on the public service institution, a library does not exist merely to collect books or even to practice librarianship but to provide information to people. It follows that understanding people deserves as much thought and effort as collecting and organizing information. Only by understanding how users obtain and use information can one see how the library or information service fits into the process of information transfer. It focuses on the complex interconnection, interdependence, and intercommunication between users and information professionals. and consists of three sections. The first point is to identify the profile of users of agricultural information; who they are, some features they share, and problems they face. The second point is to study the trends in agriculture and information delivery.

Lastly implications of these characteristics should be examined and necessary suggestions and recommendations be made based on them.

REFERENCES

1. Singh, Neena (2002). LIS User education Courses in Agriculture Universities: An Analysis into objectives and reality. *Annals of Library and Information Studies* 49 (2), pp. 37-44.
2. Mundhe, B T (2008). Use of Library for effective instruction. *Indian Journal of Agriculture Library and Information Services* 24.
3. Kumar, Surendra and Kumar, S (2008). Free e-Journals in Agriculture. *SRELS Journal of Information Management* 45 (3), pp. 295-304.
4. Perumalsamy, K (2006). Role of Agricultural University Libraries in enhancing the National networks for the Collection and dissemination of Agricultural information. *IASLIC Bulletin*.51(4), pp. 221-227.
5. Padmaja, M and Kumbhar, Mallinath (2008). ICT's for Dissemination of Development information: An Analysis of Selected Cases. *Indian Journal of Agriculture Library and Information Services* 24.
6. French, Beverlee A (1990). User Needs and Library Services in Agricultural Sciences. *Library Trends* 38 (3), pp. 415-41.
7. Raju, Nemani Govinda (2010). Use and User Awareness of E-Resources in Andhra University Library : A Study. *PEARL- A Journal of Library and Information Science* 4 (3), pp. 183-188.
8. *http://www.naip.icar.org.in/project.htm* (Accessed on 28.6.2011)
9. *http://202.141.47.8:8080/HAU/thesis.html* (Accessed on 28.6.2011)
10. *http://www.naip.icar.org.in/downloads/Summary/C1_IARI_Egranth.pdf* (Accessed on 28.06.2011)
11. Satyanarayana, M (2009). Library user education in the digital era: A study of academic Libraries. *All India IASLIC Conference*-2009, KIIT Deemed University , Bhubaneswar, pp. 425- 432.
12. Mishra, Monisha and Mahapatra, R K (2010). Capacity Building and Library User Education ***in*** *Capacity Building and restructuring of Library and Information Centres*. Ess Ess Publications, New Delhi.

❑❑❑

Chapter - 12

Awareness of Information Literacy and Computer Literacy Awareness among Teachers: A Case Study

D. Konappa, K. Kumar, M. Tholkappian and D. Chandran

INTRODUCTION

Research and teaching increasingly rely on global networks for the creation, storage, evaluate, and disseminate the knowledge. The 21st century has brought enormous change in higher education throughout the world as a result of new information and technological developments. We are outfitting our schools, libraries, and homes with electronic technologies, but are we preparing our students and teachers for the onslaught of information that is provided by these technologies? What happens when the student can get more information from the Internet than previously conveyed by a teacher or a textbook? What should a student do when faced with so many informational possibilities? Which of the information is credible and which is not?

The teacher's role must evolve from the giver of knowledge into being more of a coach or guide. Teachers, librarians, administrators, and the community must collaborate to develop ways to involve the student not only in using classroom materials but also in using resources from the broader community and the mass media.

Teachers must be prepared to teach student to become critical thinkers, intellectually curious observers, creators, and users of information. In this context university libraries need to be dynamic, take a leading role in assessing the information literacy and computer literacy competence of the teachers and plan for conducting such programmes to improve the situation. One such attempt has been made by the Authors and the result is reported here.

INFORMATION LITERACY AND COMPUTER LITERACY DEFINITION

Information Literacy: American Library Association's (1998), Presidential Committee on Information Literacy, Final Report states, "To be information literate, a person must be able to recognize when information is needed and have the ability to locate, evaluate, and use effectively the needed information".

Computer Literacy: Computer literacy is defined as the knowledge and ability to use computers and technology efficiently. Computer literacy can also refer to the comfort level someone has with using computer programs and other applications that are associated with computers. Another valuable component of computer literacy knows how computers work and operate. Having basic computer skills is a significant asset.

NEED FOR INFORMATION LITERACY AND COMPUTER LITERACY IN HIGHER EDUCATION

Solution to the data smog

Now we are living in information age wherein the information resources are proliferating and individuals are faced with diverse and abundant information resources in their studies, in their workplace and in their lives. Information is available through libraries, mass media, manufactures and service providers, and the internet. It refers to the idea that too much information can create a barrier in our lives called the "data smog". Information literacy is the solution to Data Smog. It allows us to cope by giving the skills to know when we need information and where to locate it effectively and efficiently. It includes the technological skills needed to use the modern library as a gateway to information. It enables us to analyze and evaluate the information we find, thus giving us confidence in using that information to make a decision or create a product.

Supporting the users to achieve a range of skills & self directed learning

In the field of education in general and higher education in particular, there has been a shift toward building teacher-center learning environment, which enable them to understand and appropriateness of a variety of information sources, access them efficiently, evaluate the information and use them effectively. Information literacy extends learning beyond formal classroom settings and supports individuals in self directed learning in all areas of life.

ESTABLISHMENT OF ASC IN S V UNIVERSITY, TIRUPATI

In pursuance of the National Policy on Education 1986 and its Programme of Action, UGC at the first instance established 48 Academic Staff Colleges all over the country. The UGC-Academic Staff College at SV University was established in August, 1988. The centre is 100% funded by UGC. The objective of ASC is to enhance motivation of teachers, to develop professional competency, inculcate values among the teachers and encourage creative work. The College has a separate Computer Centre, Library and Audio-Visual facilities. The Academic Staff College has so far conducted various training programmes for College/ University teachers, principals and officers. The EDUSAT facility will be developed soon at the centre.

Objectives of the study

1. To examine the teacher's ability to use computers.
2. To know the teacher's ability to use the Internet.
3. To know the teacher's ability to specify electronic information sources to solve specific information problems to fulfill the student's information need.
4. To know the need of teachers about the information literacy and computer literacy programmes in making them self-learners and life-long learners.

Limitations

The study is limited to the participant teachers of *of 68th Orientation course, held from 23-May to 11-June, 2011.*

Methodology

The survey method was adopted for the present study and a questionnaire was used as a data collection tool. Majority of the questions were objective type designed keeping the objective of the study in view. The questionnaire was distributed to all the participant teachers. In total 83 (coming from 22 different faculties also LISc Professionals) teachers were included. The questionnaires were distributed among the sample population and were asked to fill-up the same by allowing sufficient time. Assistance to clear the doubts, if any with regard to the question was extended by the investigator (library professionals).

TEACHERS CAPABILITY TO USE COMPUTER

In order to use the information available in electronic form the teachers are expected to be computer literate which includes skill to operate computes, knowledge of hardware, software, and storage devices. The questions were realized to examine the computer literacy of the teachers and the data is given in Table 1.

Table 1: Teachers ability to use Computer

Teachers have ability to Use of Computer	Teachers does not have ability to Use of Compmuter	Teachers not Respondents
59 (71.08)	19 (22.89)	5 (6.02)

(Figures in parentheses indicate percentage)

Table 1 reveals that 71.08% of the teachers know how to operate computers. 22.89% of the teachers do not know computer operation, and 6.02% of the teachers have not responded to the question.

In order to know the familiarly of some popular aspects of the IT environment few questions were raised and the data is presented in Table 2.

Table 2: Teacher's Knowledge of Computer

S.No	Computer Related Questions	No. of Teachers Possess Knowledge	No. of Teachers does not Possess Knowledge
1	"Bit" means Binary Digit	47 (79.66)	12 (20.34)
2	Expanded form of "CD-ROM"	48 (81.36)	11 (18.64)
3	Expanded form of RAM	51 (86.44)	8 (13.56)
4	Expanded form of CPU	52 (88.14)	7 (11.86)
5	"C" refers to Programming Language	46 (77.97)	13 (22.03)
6	Hardware of Computer	44 (74.58)	15 (25.42)
7	Software of Computer	42 (71.19)	17 (28.81)

(Figures in parentheses indicate percentage) **N=59**

Table 2 reveals that among the teachers who indicated that they know how to operate computer are unaware of the software(28.81%), hardware (25.42%), 'C' as a programming language (22.03%), and 'Bit' meaning (20.34%). And 18.64% of the respondents do not know the full form of CD-ROM, 13.56% of RAM and 11.86% of CPU.

TEACHERS ABILITY TO USE INTERNET

The Internet, the network of networks has been considered as a powerful source of information. The teachers should know how to use the Internet for various purposes including for finding the latest information needed for their studies, for communication with teachers and friends, for finding information regarding higher education, job opportunities etc. However, the use of, Internet presupposes the use of computer. Hence, in order to know the teachers competence in using internet, a question was asked to those teachers who have said that they are competent to use the computer and the responses are tabulated and presented in Table 3.

Table 3: Teacher's Capability to Use the Internet

Teachers have ability to Use of Internet	Teachers does not have ability to Use of Internet	Total
41 (69.49)	18 (30.51)	59 (100)

(Figures in parentheses indicate percentage)

The data presented in Table no. 3 clearly indicates the fact that the majority (67.5%) of the respondents possess the competence to use the Internet and (32.5%) of them have indicated that they are not competent to use the Internet. In order to cross-check thc ability of the respondents who have indicated that they are competent to sue the Internet, few more questions were asked and the responses are presented in Table 4.

Table 4: Teacher's knowledge of the Internet

S.No	Internet Related Questions	No. of Teachers possess Knowledge	No. of Teachers does not Possess Knowledge
1	Description of the Internet	18 (43.90)	23 (56.10)
2	E-Mail	32 (78.05)	9 (21.95)
3	Expanded form of WWW	19 (46.34)	22 (53.66)
4	Search Engine	23 (56.10)	18 (43.90)

(Figures in parentheses indicate percentage) **N=41**

A glance at the data present in Table 4 reveals that among the 41 respondents, who have indicated they are competent to use the Internet, 56.10% of them do not know the applications of the Internet. And 21.95% of them think that E-mail means a system of sending letters through courier service.

The majority (53.66%) of this category of respondents do not know the expanded form of WWW and 43.90% of them do not know that the search engines help users locate the websites containing useful information and references to such information. This actually shows the ignorance of even those respondents who have said they are competent to use the Internet.

TEACHER'S CAPABILITY TO IDENTIFY DIFFERENT E-RESOURCES OF INFORMATION

There is variety of information sources available in the market. It may be available in traditional or in electronic form. The teachers are expected to be aware of wide range of information sources and use the appropriate ones to solve specific information problems. In the present study a series of specific information problems were given with several alternative answers. The teachers were asked to tick the best sources of information to find specific information among different sources in order to determine their ability to use the appropriate source of information to solve specific information problem. The data is presented in table 5.

Table 5: Teacher's Capability to Identify Specific E-Resources of information

S.No	Information Sources	No. of Teachers able to Specify Specific Resources	No. of Teachers does not able to Specify Specific Resources
1	Dictionaries	17 (41.46)	24 (58.54)
2	Encyclopedia	20 (48.78)	21 (51.22)
3	Bibliographies	12 (29.27)	29 (70.73)
4	Journals	28 (68.29)	13 (31.71)
5	Directories	23 (56.10)	18 (43.90)

(Figures in parentheses indicate percentage) N=41

The data presented in Table 5 reveals that the majority of the respondents could specify specific resources for the information problems related to Journals (68.29%), Directories (56.10%). On the contrary, it is highly disturbing to note that large number of the respondents could not specify specific resources for the information problems related to Bibliographies (70.73), Dictionaries (58.54%). and Encyclopedias (51.22%)

IMPORTANCE OF INFORMATION LITERACY AND COMPUTER LITERACY PROGRAMMES FOR TEACHERS

In order to elicit the teacher's opinion about the need of information literacy and computer literacy programmes in the Orientation course in the University Library, the teachers were asked to indicate the degree of importance of such a programme and the results are given in Table 6.

Table 6: Teacher's Opinion about the Need of Information Literacy and Computer Literacy Programmes

S.No	Degree of Importance	No. of Responded	%
1	Most Important	64	77.11
2	Important	11	13.25
3	Somewhat important	0	0.00
4	Not Important	3	3.61
5	No Response	5	6.02
	Total	83	100.00

Analysis of data in Table 6 reveals that the majority 77.11% of the teachers feel that information literacy and computer literacy programmes are 'Most important', 13.25% of them opine that such programmes are 'important', and only 3.61% think that it is 'not important' for them. And 6.02% of the teachers have not responded to the question.

FINDINGS

The findings of the present study have been summarized hereunder.

- Majority of the respondents (22.89%) do not know how to operate computer.
- Majority of those who have indicated that they know how to operate computer indeed do not know the basic concepts like hardware, software, programming languages, storage devise etc.
- Among those who indicated that they have ability to use the computers, 30.51% of them do not have capability to use the Internet.
- Nearly half of the total respondents, who indicated that they know the use of Internet, do not know the description of the Internet. Also more than half Internet users do not know about expanded form of WWW.
- The majority of the respondents are not aware of the Electronic information sources like Directories, Encyclopedias, Dictionaries, and Bibliographies etc. Many of them opine that information literacy and computer literacy programmes in the Library are 'most important' and they are enthusiastic to undergo such programmes to become self-learners and life-long learners.

SUGGESTIONS

In the present study the authors find that the information literacy and computer literacy rate of the majority of the teachers are very low. In 21st century we have need to improve our knowledge with the awareness of computer information literacy. In order to improve the situation and make the teachers and students sustainable in the growing higher education system the following suggestions are put forth.

1. The UGC and the University has to take the steps to impart information and computer literacy programmes among teachers and students engaged in higher education. College and university librarians have to take a leading role in teaching the teachers and students with basic skills of information literacy and computer literacy are organizing different orientation courses.
2. The UGC and the University has to provide sufficient funds to colleges to arrange such type of orientation programmes.

CONCLUSION

We are living in information age and ICT are the basic tools used in higher education for more effective learning. ICT have become necessities in order to stay abreast in the current globalized knowledge-based economy. It is often perceived that ICT literacy automatically equates to information literacy. In information age teachers have responsibility to give effective, accurate, evaluated, reliable and skillful education to the students. Teachers must be prepared to "teach students to become critical thinkers, intellectually curious observers, creators and users of information because today's education system is totally changed from teacher centered learning to the student centered learning. But due to barriers of information, teachers have created disturbance in their information understanding, evaluating and presenting, thereby they do not have the capability to present their knowledge effectively. Especially in "arts" field teacher faces the problems of computer literacy and information literacy.

UGC and Universities play an important role to impart information and computer literacy programmes. If UGC undertaken imparting such types of programmes in teacher's orientation courses with the help of libraries, then teachers will be more literate about e-resources and their accessibility and able to present it effectively. The survey results support this aspect.

REFERENCES

1. Wisconsin Educational Media Association (1993). Information Literacy: A Position Paper on Information Problem Solving, WI. ED 376817.
2. Lenox, Mary F and Walker, Michael L (1993). Information Literacy in the Educational Process. The Educational Forum, Vol. 57 (Spring).
3. American Library Association Presendial Committee on Information Literacy - 1989. Final Report. Washington, DC. URL: www.ala.org/acrl/nili/ilit1st.html
4. Ramakrishna Gowda K.C and Walmiki R.H (2004). Assessment of Information Literacy and Computer Literacy among Post Graduate students: A case study of Kuvempu university library users. SRELS Journal of Information Management, Vol.41, No.4; p.367-382.
5. http://www.svuniversity.in/centres/index.html
6. Gilton, Donna L (1994). A World of Difference: Preparing for Information Literacy Instruction for Diverse Groups. Multicultural Review, Vol. 3 (3).

Chapter – 13

Total Quality Management Approaches in Agricultural Libraries in India: An Introspection

D R Meher and Rabindra K. Mahapatra

INTRODUCTION

Library and information centers are primarily service institutions which are expected to provide information to the entire satisfaction of user groups. However, in recent times, it is observed that there is conglomeration of several services in a pin-pointed manner in which the libraries are facing problem of confusion. Therefore, leading library and information centers have started adopting emerging management principles and practices in their functions and operations. Among all these new traits of management the concept of quality management appears to have a dynamic impact upon the improvement of organizational objective and functions. Since agriculture libraries are vibrant information organizations their quality of services needs to be improved in the modern technological era. The application of Total Quality Management (TQM) is one of the vital aspects of the management techniques that appears to be very much applicable and can bring about a great transformation in quality of library services. The present paper makes an analytic discussion on the applicability of TQM in Agriculture Libraries in India.

TOTAL QUALITY MANAGEMENT (TQM) : DEFINITION AND CONCEPTS

Definition

The following definitions give a very closer idea of Total Quality Management.

TQM is a system of continuous improvement employing participative management and centered on the needs of customers (Jurow & Barnard, 1993).

According to Zaira and Jurow (1991) TQM is the combination of socio-economic and technical process towards doing the right things (externally), everything right (internally) first time and all the time, with economic viability considered at each stage of each process.

Thakur defines the TQM as a concept which makes quality, the responsibility of all people within an organization. All the persons involved are expected to contribute to the overall improvement of quality. TQM is the preferred method to increase the user satisfaction. It reduces the defects of the organization and increases the productivity" (Pramanik, 2010).

When an organization needs to involve its employees for improving their performances, undertaking problem solving strategies, improving the quality of work by statistical methods, the concept of TQM emerges. TQM is now being practiced in business as well as in government, the military, and the education and in nonprofit organizations including service organizations. TQM is a management technique that is designed to improve the effectiveness, efficiency, flexibility and competitiveness in business organization. It is a management philosophy used by enterprises that seek to improve product and service quality and increase customer's satisfaction by restructuring traditional management practices (Sravan, 1997).

What is Quality ?

According to Juran quality is fitness for use. But on the other hand Crosby defined quality as conformance to requirements. Japanese Industrial Standards Committee has defined that quality is a system of means to economically produce goods or services which satisfy customers' requirements. Leffler says that quality refers to the amounts of the un-priced attributes contained in each unit of the priced attribute. International Organization for Standardization (ISO) defines quality as "the totality of features and characteristics of a product and service that bear on its ability to satisfy given needs". All of us whether we touch on issues of quality, excellence, compliance, or performance at work, or whether we encounter these concepts as customers—know quality when we see it. Defining quality is one thing; enhancing it for our organizations is another (Richman)

STATE OF AGRICULTURE LIBRARIES IN INDIA

Although ICAR institutes are doing tremendous professional work in dissemination of agricultural information they are not being privileged to enjoy the status equivalent to other research institutes under CSIR and ICMR organizations in India. A survey by IARI library staff in 1991 reveals that ICAR libraries are still in a poor state with poor collections and inadequate manpower. The budget allocations to libraries is on average, remain below the mark of one per cent (Kumar, 2008). Due to the present trend of economic globlization the agricultural development is imminent and second "green revolution" is the future requirement of the society. In this critical situation the role of libraries in dissemination of information for agricultural development is vital. Although ICAR has given adequate attention in strengthening and rejuvinating the agricultural libraries system in India by giving adequate funding for modernization, the libraries are still in a poor state for some reason and the other.

NEED FOR TQM IN AGRICULTURAL LIBRARIES

Scientists and researchers in agriculture sector normally use the library to seek information for improvement of crop production, protection and improvement as well as variety creation. The agriculture libraries are replete with various types of knowledge in agriculture research, extension and education, which invokes the most interdisciplinary subjects such as biology, medicine, chemistry, various crops with their scientific and economic implication, veterinary and animal husbandry, biotechnology, environment science, various branches of engineering, climatology, agribusiness marketing and so on. In view of such multidisciplinary subjects, agriculture libraries are to provide useful platform for building agricultural knowledge base for different types of user community. These libraries are to empower agriculture scientists, academicians, technocrats and farmers to manage vast amount of information for optimizing agriculture research, extension and education.

Agricultural knowledge generated in the research institutions are to be improved and utilized and it is imperative on the part of agriculture libraries to change its operational strategies and adopt a viable management. TQM is such a management technique which appears to be the most applicable in agricultural sector.. With TQM, where continuous improvement is core principle, agriculture libraries can improve their information mechanization system so that their very establishments for catering to the information needs of the communities relating to agricultural education, research and extension can be actualized.

TOTAL QUALITY MANAGEMENT IN AGRICULTURAL LIBRARIES

Quality management is a technique which is applied to bring about changes in the organizational structure for an optimum result-oriented objective. Quality can be achieved by either providing good products or good services. While the library is a service institution, it is required to provide service to the entire satisfaction of the user community. When developing a library system some keys issues are given importance. Organizational, financial and strategic issues are such management functions which are required to be covered at designing stage. According to Brophy, the 'quality trilogy of Joseph Juran' is to be considered first while applying quality management techniques to any organization. Such trilogy is quality planning, quality control and quality improvement.

QUALITY PLANNING

While undertaking a perfect quality planning, the librarian has to develop a strategy of setting goal. It is an established fact that the goal of the library is to satisfy the users and in order to achieve this objective, it is required to

- Identify proper customers (user community) and their needs.
- Set the quality goals
- Design or develop quality plan for achievement of the set goals
- Identify and allocate or acquire the resources required for implementation of the quality plan
- Ensure every action taken is right action

QUALITY CONTROL

Quality control is basically required to evaluate the action taken and measure those indicators for further determination of goals. It necessitates:

- Development of meaning quality measures (choosing an unit of measure)
- Evaluation of action taken
- Measure actual performance
- Interpretation of the difference of actual versus standard planned
- Action on the deference

QUALITY IMPROVEMENT

In this stage of quality improvement, to reduce wastage of resources and to ensure greater customer/ user satisfaction it is needed

- Proof of the need for improvement
- Diagnosis to find the causes
- Provision of remedies

RESOURCE MOBILIZATION IN AGRICULTURE LIBRARIES

In India there are 48 ICAR Institutes (5 National Institutes), 12 Project Directorate, 5 National Bureaux and 48 Agricultural Universities under ICAR and all the institutes have a library. In addition to this there are more than 75 all India Co-ordinated Research Projects undergoing under ICAR. The librarians who are actually the managers of those libraries have practically little to say for library planning because most of the libraries are headed by Professor-in-Charge who seldom find time to get into the problems of libraries to be functional one as they are busy in their study, teaching and research works in their respective fields. In some libraries the librarians are not even members of the library committee. In fact the librarian should be the key person in planning, controlling and coordinating so that he can bring about any changes in the library.

In case of finance, the budgetary provision of agriculture libraries are very poor. Few libraries have standing budget. ICAR is doing a good job by giving developmental grants to the libraries for procurement of reading materials and infrastructure development. But in the absence of a regular budget, for example, in case of journals a library could not subscribe for one year and after availing budget in the subsequent year it would not be possible on its part to get the journals of previous year. Because of this the library will be unable to provide its users the journals of the gap period and its journal database will be an incomplete one forever.

In mobilization of information resources librarian has to standardize the information acquisition, processing, organization, dissemination etc. Policies are to be made for each sphere having a slant towards user satisfaction.

CONCLUSION

Agriculture libraries must work in a digital and modern environment to provide user satisfaction. Adequate of information services must be provided so that information is reached from the policy maker level to the farmer level. In order to make wide publicity the library and information centers must create service brochures and information kits to make the users aware of the information available and the service provided by the respective libraries. The librarians must take up user surveys to identify information needs and information seeking behavior of users as well as requirements of the present library system so as to redefine future actions. To keep the libraries more useful a specific time of working hour may be provided in order to facilitate the user target group. All library managements are to maintain good relationship with their authority or higher department and funding agencies for favourable inflow of fund and for availing incentive for development of the organization. The library staff-both seniors and juniors must have thorough orientation about the new product and services required for the libraries. It is has also to develop and popularize library outreach programmes by which remote users can be benefited.

Quality is a buzz word now a days . Every organization needs quality in their products, functions and services. Library is also a service institution which is striving for improving of the quality of its functions and services. Total Quality Management (TQM) is the emerging management technique which appears to be more applicable for library and information centers for effective improvement of its functions and services. Agriculture libraries in India are not in a very good state in relation to its financial, manpower and organizational set up. In this situation it is high time to implement TQM techniques in those libraries which is sure to make a viable improvement in library services.

REFERENCES

1. Jurow, S and Barnard, S. B (1993). *Integrating total quality management in a library setting.* New York: Howorh Press.
2. Kumar, P. S (2008). *Agriculture librarianship*. Delhi : B R Publishing Corporation.
3. Richman http://www.qualitydigest.com/inside/quality-insider-column/defining-quality.html
4. Pramanik, A (2010). Total quality of management in college library. *IASLIC Bllitin*, pp. 103-108.

❑❑❑

Chapter – 14

Usage Pattern of Electronic Resources by Physics and Chemistry Research Scholars in Periyar University, Salem

N. Subramanian

INTRODUCTION

Information has now become one of the basic needs of human being in addition to air, water, food and shelter. There is no human activity in the world without information. It is a basic raw material for right decision making from the governmental level to the personal level. It is an indispensable tool for teachers and research scholars.

Now-a-days, ICT advancements and developments have changed the libraries from mere store house of printed materials into gateways to knowledge of the world of information. The collection of modern library is not restricted to print media only but libraries are adding e-resources to their existing collections. Users need not come to library to meet their information needs. They may use online catalogue, web based database, online e-journals etc remote from library. In view of the above, information need and seeking pattern of users particularly research scholars are likely to change. Based on this, an attempt has been made to study on use pattern of electronic resources by Physics and Chemistry research scholars.

OBJECTIVES

The study has been designed with the following objectives.

- To find out the information needs of the Physics and Chemistry research scholars of Periyar University
- To examine the awareness of the e-resources among the sample research scholars
- To know the places of access of e-resources by the scholars
- To find out the frequently used e-resources by the research scholars under study.

METHODOLOGY

Questionnaire method was applied to this study. Questionnaires were administered in person by the investigator to 150 physics and chemistry research scholars . A total of 130 questionnaires were received back.

SCOPE AND LIMITATIONS

The scope of the present study is confined to only physics and chemistry research scholars. The sample respondents are doing their research either full time or part time mode. They are working or doing in various categories of colleges such as Government colleges, Aided colleges and Self financing colleges.

ANALYSIS AND INTERPRETATION OF THE DATA

1. Distribution of Questionnaires

Table 1

Sl.No	Type of Colleges	No. of Colleges	No. of Questionnaires Distributed	No. Questionnaires of Received	% of Respondents
1	Govt. Colleges	9	36	30	20%
2	Aided Colleges	4	50	42	28%
3	Self-Financing Colleges	12	64	58	38.7%
	Total	**25**	**150**	**130**	**86.7%**

Table 1 shows that the 150 questionnaires were distributed to the physics and chemistry research scholars in Government colleges, Aided colleges and Self-Financing Colleges. Out of which 130 questionnaires were received and the response rate is 86.7%. The majority (38.7%) of the respondents are from Self-Financing Colleges followed by the respondents are from Aided colleges (28%).

2. Age group and Subjects of the respondents

Table.2

Sl.No	Types of College	Depart-ment	Between 25 and 30 years	Between 31 and 35 years	Between 36 and 40 years	Above 40 years	Total
1	Govt.	Physics	96.9%	64.6%	10.8%	-	1612.3%
		Chemistry	75.4%	53.9%	21.5%	-	1410.8%
2	Aided	Physics	86.2%	96.9%	21.5%	-	1914.6%
		Chemistry	118.5%	96.9%	32.3%	-	2317.7%
3	Self-Finance	Physics	1612.3%	107.7%	21.5%	-	2821.5%
		Chemistry	1410.8%	1310%	32.3%	-	3023.1%
	Total		6550%	5240%	1310%	-	130100%

Table 2 indicates that the 50% of the respondents are in the age group between 25-30 year followed by 40% of the respondents in the age group between 31-35 years. It is interesting note that no Physics and Chemistry research scholars are in the age group above 40 years. Out of 130 respondents, 51.6% of respondents are from Chemistry subjects and 48.4% of the respondents are from Physics subjects.

3. Gender-wise and Qualifications of the Respondents

Table.3

Sl.No	Types of College	Subjects	Male	Female	Total	PG	M.Phil	Total
1	Govt.	Physics	12 9.2%	4 3.1%	16 12.3%	5 3.8%	11 8.5%	61 2.3%
		Chemistry	8 6.2%	6 4.6%	14 10.8%	6 4.6%	8 6.2%	41 0.8%
2	Aided	Physics	13 10.0%	6 4.6%	19 14.6%	8 6.2%	11 8.5%	91 4.6%
		Chemistry	15 11.5%	8 6.2%	23 17.7%	9 6.9%	14 10.8%	31 7.7%
3	Self-Financing	Physics	19 14.6%	9 6.9%	28 21.5%	12 9.3%	61 2.3%	82 1.5%
		Chemistry	20 15.4%	10 7.7%	30 23%	9 6.9%	21 16.2%	30 23%
		Total	87 66.9%	43 33.1%	130 100%	49 37.7%	81 62.3%	130 100%

Table.3 shows that while 66.9% of the respondents are male and 33.1% are female. Majority of the respondents (62.3%) are M.Phil Degree holders , whereas 37.7% are PG Degree holders. It clearly infers that the physics and chemistry research scholars are interested to do their research degree after having M.Phil degree.

4. Mode of Research of Respondent

Table 4

Sl. No	Type of College	Respondents				Total	
		Physics		Chemistry			
		Full Time	Part Time	Full Time	Part Time	Full Time	Part Time
1	Govt.	53.8%	118.5%	43.1%	107.7%	96.9%	2116.2%
2	Aided	64.6%	1310%	53.8%	1813.8%	118.5%	3123.8%
3	Self-Finance	96.9%	1914.6%	96.9%	2116.2%	1813.8%	4030.8%
	Total	2015.4%	4333.1%	1813.8%	4937.7%	3829.2%	9270.8%

Table 4 shows that the majority of the respondents (70.8 %) of physic research scholars are doing their research on part time basis.i.e.33.1% of respondents in Physics and 37.7% of respondents in Chemistry. Only 29.2 % of the respondents are doing research on full time basis.

5. Having Personal PC and Experience of Internet Usage

Table 5

Sl. No	Types of College	Department	Own Computer Available			No. of years using Computers			
			Yes	No	Total	1-3 yrs	3-5 yrs	5 yrs and above	Total
1	Govt.	Physics	5 3.8%	11 8.5%	16 12.3%	5 3.8%	8 6.2%	3 2.3%	16 12.3%
		Chemistry	9 6.9%	5 3.8%	14 10.7%	2 1.5%	8 6.1%	4 3.1%	14 10.8%
2	Aided	Physics	8 6.2%	11 8.5%	19 14.7%	7 5.4%	8 6.2%	4 3.1%	19 14.7%
		Chemistry	11 8.5%	12 9.2%	23 17.7%	6 4.6%	9 6.9%	8 6.2%	23 17.8%
3	Self-Finance	Physics	11 8.5%	17 13.1%	28 21.6%	8 6.2%	11 8.5%	9 6.9%	28 21.6%
		Chemistry	18 13.8%	12 9.2%	30 23.1%	12 9.2%	10 7.7%	8 6.2%	30 23.1%
Total			62 47.7%	68 52.3%	130 100%	40 30.8%	54 41.5%	36 27.6%	130 100%

Table 5 indicates that 47.7 % of the respondents are having personal computers or laptop. On the other hand 52.3% of the respondents are not having either personal Computers or laptop. The research scholars are not only using the Institutional Computer facilities, but also using their personal computers and laptops. Moreover, 41.5% of the respondents are using computers frequently between 3 and 5 years followed by 30.8% of the respondents are using computers between 1 and 3 years. From the above analysis it is inferred that the research scholars are using computers / laptops for their research.

6. Place of Internet Access

Table 6 indicates that majority of the respondents (54.6%) are using Internet access at the Departmental Library, followed by (29.2%) of the respondents are using at University Library and 16.2 % of the respondents are using Internet at their home for their research.

Table 6

Sl. No	Types of Colleges	Department	Home	Departmental Library	University Library	Total
1	Govt.	Physics	21.5%	96.9%	53.8%	612.3%
		Chemistry	32.3%	75.4%	43.1%	410.8%
2	Aided	Physics	32.3%	107.7%	64.6%	914.6%
		Chemistry	32.3%	118.5%	96.9%	317.7%
3	Self-Finance	Physics	53.8%	1612.3%	75.4%	821.5%
		Chemistry	53.8%	1813.8%	75.4%	023.1%
		Total	2116.2%	7154.6%	3829.2%	130100%

7. Frequency of using Internet & Method of Internet Learning

Table 7

Sl. No	Type of Colleges	Dept	Frequency of using Internet Access					Methods of Learning Internet skills			
			Rarely	Occassionly	Twice in a week	Daily	Total	Trial & Error	Guidance from Colleague friends	Orientation courses	Total
1	Govt.	Phy	1 0.8%	1 0.8%	6 4.6%	8 6.2%	16 12.3%	4 3.1%	8 6.2%	4 3.1%	16 12.3%
		Chem	2 1.5%	3 2.3%	4 3.1%	5 3.8%	14 10.8%	2 1.5%	6 4.6%	6 4.6%	14 10.8%
2	Aided	Phy	1 0.8%	3 2.3%	7 5.4%	8 6.2%	19 14.6%	4 3.1%	10 7.7%	5 3.8%	19 14.6%
		Chem	-	2 1.5%	8 6.2%	13 10%	23 17.7%	3 2.3%	13 10%	7 5.4%	23 17.7%
3	Self. Finance	Phys	3 2.3%	3 2.3%	9 6.9%	13 10%	28 21.5%	5 3.8%	16 12.3%	7 5.4%	28 21.5%
		Chem	2 1.5%	2 1.5%	6 4.6%	20 15.4%	30 23.1%	4 3.1%	18 13.8%	8 6.2%	30 23.1%
	Total		9 6.9%	14 10.8%	40 30.8%	67 51.5%	130 100%	22 16.9%	71 54.6%	37 28.5%	130 100%

Table 7 shows that a majority (51.5%) of the respondents are using Internet daily for their research work followed by 30.8% and 10.8% of the respondents are using twice a week and occasionally, respectively. Only a meager percentage of (6.9%) the respondents are using Internet rarely.

Majority of (54.6%) the respondents are learning to use Internet through guidance from colleagues and friends ,followed by 28.5% of the respondents learning through attending Orientation courses. Only 16.9% of the respondents are learning self study by trial and error methods

8. Methods of Identification of Electronic Information Sources

Table 8

Methods of Identification of E-Resources	Govt.	Aided	Self-Finance	Total
Personal Communication	6(20.0%)	7(16.7%)	11(19.0%)	24(18.5%)
Attended Seminars	7(23.3%)	11(26.2%)	22(37.3%)	40(30.8%)
Citation in E-resources	9(30.0%)	12(28.6%)	18(31.0%)	39(30.0%)
Bibliographical Citation	5(16.7%)	10(23.8%)	15(25.9%)	30(23.1%)
Search Engines	10(33.3%)	10(23.8%)	17(29.3%)	37(28.5%)
Browse Regularly	10(33.3%)	10(23.8%)	25(43.1%)	45(34.6%)
Subscribe Mailing List	1(3.3%)	1(2.4%)	3(5.2%)	4(3.1%)

Table 8 indicates how physics and chemistry research scholars are identifying the e-resources for their research. This analysis shows that 34.6% of the respondents are using Internet Browse regularly. A good number of respondents (30.8%) are attending Conferences and seminars, Citation in E-Resources (30.0%), 28.5% of the respondents are getting information through search engines and 23.1% respondents are using Bibliographical Citations. 18.5% of the scholars are using personal communications for identifying E-resources. A meager percentage (3.1%) of respondents are subscribing mailing list for finding their e-resources.

9. Time Spent in using Internet

Table 9

Type of Colleges	Time spent / per week					
	30 minutes	1 hrs	1 to 2 hrs	2 to 5 hrs	More than 5 hrs	Total
Govt.	4 (13.3%)	10 (33.3%)	14 (46.7%)	1 (3.3%)	1 (3.3%)	30 (23.1%)
Aided	4 (9.5%)	12 (28.6%)	17 (40.5%)	6 (14.3%)	3 (7.1%)	42 (32.3%)
Self-Finance	5 (8.6%)	16 (27.6%)	25 (43.1%)	8 (13.8%)	4 (6.9%)	58 (44.6%)
Total	13 (10.0%)	38 (29.2%)	56 (43.1%)	15 (11.5%)	8 (6.2%)	130 (100%)

Table 9 shows the average time spent per week for using electronic resources by the respondents. The majorities (43.1%) of the respondents are spending 1 to 2 hours on an average for using Internet, followed by 29.2% of the respondents spend one hour per week for assessing e-resources. Only 6.2% of the respondents are spending more than 5 hours per week for their research purpose.

10. Users Satisfaction

Table 10

Types of College	Users Satisfaction with e-resources			
	Fully	Partially	Least	Total
Govt.	17 (56.7%)	9 (30%)	4 (13.3%)	30 (23.1%)
Aided	24 (57.1%)	14 (33.3%)	4(9.5%)	42(32.3%)
Self-Finance	34(58.6%)	18(31.0)	8(13.8%)	58(44.6%)
Total	75(57.7%)	41(31.5%)	14(10.8%)	130 (100%)

Table 10 shows that 57.7% of the respondents are fully satisfied with the available recourses followed by 31.5% of the respondents who are partially satisfied. Only 10.8% of the respondents are least satisfied.

11. Internet services and Resources

Table 11

Sl. No	Internet Services and Resources	Govt.College		Aided College		Self-Finance College		Total	Rank
		Phy	Chem	Phys	Chem	Phy	Chem		
1	E-mail	13 10.0%	18 13.8%	12 9.2%	12 9.2%	20 15.4%	22 16.9%	97 74.6%	1
2	News Group	1 0.8%	1 0.8%	-	2 1.5%	1 0.8%	3 2.3%	8 6.2%	8
3	Catalogues/ Databases	3 2.3%	6 4.6%	5 3.8%	7 5.4%	4 3.1%	6 4.6%	31 23.8%	5
4	Documentary Delivery Services	1 0.8%	2 1.5%	2 1.5%	3 2.3%	4 3.1%	6 4.6%	31 23.8%	5
5	Electronic Journals	5 3.8%	9 6.9%	7 5.4%	8 6.2%	6 4.6%	13 10.0%	48 36.9%	3
6	Electronic Books	8 6.2%	6 4.6%	6 4.6%	9 6.9%	13 10.0%	8 6.2%	50 38.5%	2
7	DVD/CD Rom Databases	4 3.1%	4 3.1%	6 4.6%	6 4.6%	10 7.7%	8 6.2%	38 29.2%	4
8	FAQ	4 3.1%	5 3.8%	3 2.3%	4 3.1%	6 4.6%	8 6.2%	30 23.1%	6
9	Chat	2 1.5%	-	3 2.3%	1 0.8%	3 2.3%	3 2.3%	12 9.2%	7

Table 11 shows that 74.6% of the Physics and Chemistry research scholars are using e-mail through internet services. It is in the first position.38.5% of the research scholars are using and searching of E-books followed by 36.9% of the scholars are using Electronic journals and it has second and third position. 29.2% of the scholars are using DVD/CD –ROM databases followed by 23.8% of the scholars are using Catalogues / databases and Documentary Delivery Services. It is placed in the fourth and fifth position respectively. Meager percentages (6.2%) of the scholars are using News group services.

12. Users Approach to search

Table 12

Sl.No	Type of Colleges	Department	Users Approach to search Information				
			By Author	By Subject	By Keyword	By Title	By Classified
1	Govt.	Physics	8 6.2%	14 10.8%	9 6.9%	13 10.0%	2 1.5%
		Chemistry	9 6.9%	18 13.8%	14 10.8%	18 13.8%	4 3.0%
2	Aided	Physics	6 4.6%	17 13.1%	13 10.0%	15 11.5%	3 2.3%
		Chemistry	15 11.5%	21 16.2%	15 11.5%	13 10.0%	1 0.8%
3	Self-Finance	Physics	13 10.0%	21 16.2%	16 12.3%	14 10.8%	3 2.3%
		Chemistry	8 6.2%	17 13.1%	19 14.6%	20 15.4%	1 0.8%
		Total	59 45.4%	108 83.1%	86 66.2%	93 71.5%	14 10.8%
		Rank	4	1	3	2	5

Table 12 shows that majority of the physics and chemistry research scholars (83.1%) are using subject-wise approach of searching information and it is in the first position followed by the title wise approach (71.5%). 66.2% of the scholars are using keyword approaches followed by 45.4% of users are using author-wise approaches and it has third and fourth positions respectively. Only meager (10.8%) percentage of the scholars search information through classified approach and it has last position among them.

13. Problems faced by Respondents

Table 13

Sl .No	Variables	Govt. College		Aided College		Self-finance College		Total	Rank
		Phy.	Chem	Phy	Chem	Phy	Chem		
1	Difficulty of find relevant information	4 3.1%	7 5.4%	6 4.6%	9 6.9%	8 6.2%	9 6.9%	43 33.1%	4
2	Overload of information	3 2.3%	5 3.8%	12 9.2%	6 4.6%	17 13.1%	10 7.6%	53 40.8%	3
3	Electricity failure	11 8.5%	16 12.3%	9 6.9%	13 10.0%	7 5.4%	9 6.9%	65 50.0%	2
4	Lack of time	4 3.1%	6 4.6%	6 4.6%	9 6.9%	8 6.2%	10 7.6%	43 33.1%	4
5	Low speed of access	18 13.8%	9 6.9%	15 11.5%	13 10.0%	7 5.4%	8 6.2%	70 53.8%	1

Table 13 shows that the respondents are facing various problems while accessing information. The majority (53.8%) of the respondents are facing low speed to access information and ranked first position among the problems followed by the 50.0% of the problems are in electricity failure.40.8% research scholars are facing the problem of overload of information in the internet and ranked third position, followed by 33.1% of the respondents are facing problem with the difficulty of find relevant information and lack of time to get required information and ranked fourth place among the problems.

14. Frequency of use of Electronic Journals of INFLIBNET Consortium

Table 14 shows that the physics and chemistry research scholars are frequently using (49.2%) the Springer Link journals through INFLIBNET Consortium followed by the American Institute of Physics journals (40.0%) and ranked first and second respectively. 38.5% of the scholars are using Nature and the American Chemical Society journals and ranked third position. Elsevier reviews (36.2%) and Cambridge University Press journals (32.3%) are ranked in fourth and fifth position. 30.8% of the scholars are using American Physical Society journals and the Royal Society of Chemistry journals and ranked in sixth position. 28.5% of the scholars are using Oxford Press journals followed by 22.3% of the scholars are using Science Online journals and ranked seventh and eighth position respectively. 18.5% of the scholars are using Annual Reviews, 17.7% of the Institute of Physics journals are using and ranked nineth and tenth position. Only 9.2% of the scholars are using Kluwer online journals and ranked last position. It inferred that all the electronic journals are not available at all institutions and the available journals are used by the scholars.

Table 14

Sl. .No	Name of the Electronic Journals	Research scholars			
		Physics	Chemistry	Total	Rank
1	American chemical society	86.2%	4232.3%	5038.5%	3
2	American institute of physics	3829.2%	1410.8%	5240.0%	2
3	Cambridge university press	129.2%	3023.1%	4232.3%	5
4	Nature	2216.9%	2821.6%	5038.5%	3
5	American physical society	3526.9%	53.8%	4030.8%	6
6	Oxford press	1813.8%	1914.6%	3728.5%	7
7	Royal society of chemistry	75.4%	2821.6%	4030.8%	6
8	Springer link	2519.2%	3930.0%	6449.2%	1
9	Science online	118.5%	1813.8%	2922.3%	8
10	Elsevier reviews	2519.2%	2216.9%	4736.2%	4
11	Annual reviews	107.7%	1410.8%	2418.5%	9
12	Kluwer online	43.1%	86.2%	129.2%	11
13	Institute of physics	1914.6%	43.1%	2317.7%	10

CONCLUSION

The study reveals that majority of the (44.6%) physics and chemistry research scholars are working in self-financing colleges affiliated to the Periyar University and the electronic resources have changed the search and use pattern of research scholars of physics and chemistry. They are widely using Internet and facing lot of difficulties while accessing information. The first and foremost problems faced by the scholars are low speed of Internet connectivity. Majority of the research scholars of physics and chemistry of Periyar University area are using subject-wise search information followed by the title-wise searching information. Almost all the research scholars are using e-mail service through internet for getting information and communication to others. Most of the research scholars are using electronic journals available in INFLIBNET consortium. It is clear that the high impact factor journals are not used more by the scholars due to their non availability in all institutions. So, the research scholars are using only available electronic journals in the institutions.

REFERENCES

1. Ibrahim, A E (2004). Use and User perception of electronic resources in the United Arab Emirates University. Libri 54, pp. 18-24
2. Kumbar, M; Kumar, N.G and Parveen, J K (2005). Use of Electronic resources by research scholars in CFTRI, Mysore. ILA Bulletin. 41 (3), pp.16-20.
3. Asemi , A. (2005. Information searching habits of internet users: a case study on the medical Sciences University of Isfahan, Iran. http://www.webology.ir/ 2005/v2n1/a10.html.
4. Franklin, B and Plum, T (2004). Library usage patterns in the electronic information environment. Information Research 9 (4). http://InformationR.net/ir/9-4/paper187.html
5. Subramanian, N (2002). Information needs and information seeking behavior of faculty of engineering institutions in Tamil Nadu. Thesis submitted in partial fulfillment of the Ph.D. Degree. University of Madras, Chennai (Unpublished).

❑❑❑

Chapter – 15

Use of Digital Information Resources: A Librarians Perspective

C. Krishna Reddy and M. Anjaiah

INTRODUCTION

Digital libraries are a set of electronic resources and associated technical capabilities for creating, searching, and using Information; they are an extension and enhancement of information storage and retrieval systems that manipulate digital data in any medium. The content of digital libraries includes data and metadata. Digital libraries are constructed, Collected, and organized by a community of users and their functional capabilities support the information needs and uses of that community.

A digital library is a library in which collections are stored in digital formats and accessible by computers. The digital content may be stored locally, or accessed remotely via computer networks. A digital library is a type of information retrieval system. Man is a communicator of information, not simply a user of tools. The history of civilization is the history of improved means of communication. Man always desires to improve the means of communicating. Documents are the artifacts of recorded knowledge that is information. Documents are meant for communication knowledge to larger audiences. Libraries have stored and served the documents to the users.

Thus, libraries have performed as one of the links between generators of information and its users. The developments of libraries from print paper based libraries to digital libraries seem an illustration of man's never-ending desire to improve his means of communication. In the digital world highway, there is stress on three factors (a) Awareness of information: it provides breadth of vision (b) awareness of technology: gives the power to make the visions manifest, and (c) awareness of needs facilitates the insight to use professional skills and talents to greater effect.

MEANING

The term '**Digital Library**' has a variety of potential meanings, ranging from a digitized collection of material that one might find in a traditional library through to the collection of all digital information along with the services that make that information useful to all possible users. As there are many definitions of a "digital library," terms such as "electronic library" and "virtual library" are often used synonymously. A digital library is nothing but a large database for the people who are working on hypertext environment. It is an environment, which supports the full life cycle of creation, storage, preservation, dissemination and use of data, information and knowledge.

THE DIGITAL LIBRARY CONCEPT

Digital Libraries (DL) are becoming an integral part of digital learning environments. At the same time, the notion of "digital library" is subject to a broad range of definitions. Different audiences associated with a digital library have different Interpretations; they evaluate a digital library differently and use different terminologies. On one end of the range, DLs are considered to be related to physical libraries performing similar functions, thus creating a hybrid library (combining traditional and electronic resources). On the other end, DLs are considered to be knowledge repositories, and services, organized as complex information systems. For example, global information repository projects are devoted to the accumulation of digital forms of information related to the Earth, universe, art, environment, or humans.

THE DIGITAL LIBRARY CONCEPT

A Common Term with Many Interpretations:

Information services than has been possible in the past, by offering the following advantages: faster delivery, a wider audience, greater availability, more timely information, more comprehensive". The Technical Committee on Digital Libraries of the IEEE (Institute of Electrical and Electronics Engineers) Computer Society (IEEE-CS) uses the more general term "(digital) collective memory" to emphasize the convergence of libraries, museums, archives, and collections of all kinds including those of private citizens. Collective memory development faces challenges in several areas, including storage, classification, and indexing; user interfaces; information retrieval; content delivery; presentation, administration; and preservation. Diversity of understanding of what digital libraries are leads to a wide range of possible visions for DL frameworks and methodologies of use: from the conventional library metaphor to knowledge-based systems.

DEFINITIONS OF THE DIGITAL LIBRARY

Digital libraries are a set of electronic resources and associated technical capabilities for creating, searching, and using information; they are an extension and enhancement of information storage and retrieval systems that manipulate digital data in any medium. The content of digital libraries includes data and metadata. Digital libraries are constructed, collected, and organized by (and for) a community of users and their functional capabilities support the information needs and uses of that community. — ***COVB99***

The Digital Library Federation (USA) agreed in 1999 on the following working definition of a digital library representing a definition of the practicing community. In this definition the emphasis is on an organizational or institutional setting for the collection of digital works and aspects related to its functioning in the larger context of service.

Digital libraries are organizations that provide the resources, including the specialized staff, to select, structure, offer intellectual access to, interpret, distribute, preserve the integrity of, and ensure the persistence over time of collections of digital works so that they are readily and economically available for use by a defined community or set of Communities. — ***DLFS99.***

The United Nations Task Force on Digital Libraries gives the following definition of digital libraries: "Digital libraries are organized collections of information resources in digital or electronic format along with the services designed to help users identify and use those collections. Digital libraries promise to provide more effective".

ESSENTIALS OF DIGITIZATION

The Digital Library, simply stated is an organized collection of digitized objects along with methods of access and retrieval and selection, organization and maintenance of collections. The collection in digitized form and methods to organize, retrieve, maintain and provide access to these digitized collections are thus central to the notion of a digitized library. As regards the need, conventionally, the digital libraries are said to have three principal advantages over the conventional ones: (i) they are easier to access remotely, (ii) they offer more powerful searching and browsing facilities, (iii) they serve as a foundation for new value added services. In a context where the collections are rare and unique the digitization also serves a preservation tool.

ISSUES IN DIGITIZATION

It is important to see that when the digitization project proposes, the following basic issues are to be considered.

- Digitization and its need
- Document selection
- Copy'right and legal formalities
- Application Technology
- Library Policy
- Manpower
- Monitoring
- Utilization

DIGITIZATION POLICY

- **Digitization** is a technology of future and needs to be taken advantage of for improving access to library collections, offer more powerful searching and browsing facilities, to serve as a foundation for new value added services and enhancing preservation of the collections.
- In the **ensuing phase**, the digitization would be confined to the material (1) which is unique, rare and of artistic and heritage value (2) the readers for which are wide-spread geographically and temporally, and (3) the retrieval of information is cumbersome and copies of such material cannot be supplied to the users quickly and easily. The manuscripts and rare books in the collections of library are thus the natural candidates for digitization.
- Considering that the **digital technology** would continue to evolve and there are inherent uncertainties associated with use of any particular technique or software, the libraries with a very large collection of material would take up pilot projects involving up to little part of their respective collections. Organizations with relatively small collections can digitize the entire material subject to the availability of funds.
- Necessary and appropriate **safeguards** would be put in place to ensure the security and safety of original documents. These include that the original documents would not be taken out of institution, insistence on equipment to minimize their prolonged exposures to heat, security of material if provided on web in form of watermarks, etc.
- **Each organization** shall put in place clearly defined objectively verifiable benchmarks, standards, scope of work that they intend to take up.

- Since the **software** for providing full text facilities for Indian scripts and languages are presently in the evolution stage, the scope of digitization initiative would not include provision of full text accessibility. However, the necessary content metadata derived from approved international standards for bibliographic classification standards would be developed and provided to support advanced search and retrieval and to make the digitized material widely available.

THE DIGITAL LIBRARY

For most of the users of the Electronic Information System, a ***digital library*** is simply a collection of information stored in electronic format. However, some of the information scientists and experts of information technology defined digital library **as follows:**

- Digital libraries are libraries in which the controlled collections are in digital form and access to the information in the collection is based almost entirely on digital technology.
- A digital library is understood to have the information stored predominantly in electronic or digital medium. It is expected to provide access to the digital information collection.
- Digital libraries are electronic libraries in which a large number of geographically distributed users can access the contents of large and diverse repositories of electronic objects. Electronic objects include networked text, images, maps, sounds, videos, catalogues and scientific, business and governments' datasets.
- Controlled collections of Information Bearing Objects that are in digital form and that may be organized, accessed, evaluated and used by means of heterogeneous and extensible set of distributed services that are supported by digital technology.
- Clifford Lynch, a well known expert on Internet and Web technologies, has defined a digital library as a "system providing a community of users with coherent access to a large, organized repository of information and knowledge. The digital library is not just one entity, but multiple sources seamlessly integrated.

NEED FOR DIGITAL LIBRARIES

In 1990 **Alvin Toffler** estimated in his book, *'Power Shift'* that in one year the United States runs our 1.3 trillion documents. By now the number of documents may have risen to four trillion. According to another estimate, there are close to 50,000 periodicals in science and technology. This information explosion not confined to any particular subject and is also taking place in social sciences and humanities and in every country. With libraries facing manpower and monetary constraints, it is impossible to acquire every publisher's document under one roof and thus evolved the concept of resource sharing and networking. Since information can be digitized, the participant libraries are coming together to convert their holding to electronic form and then putting them on the network. The technology for electronic transfer of information is developing rapidly electronic publishing; electronic storage, processing and delivery of information including text and images are all feasible and operational.

Further, presently most of the information is produced on paper. The legibility of documents, which are produced, is poor, and the transmission of the same to other users is difficult. Moreover, it requires a large amount of storage space. Hence digital library seems a suitable solution at the moment.

CHARACTERISTICS OF DIGITAL LIBRARIES

A digital library is popularly viewed as an electronic throughout replacing conventional archival and print media by electronic version with the inclusive sense of greater information exchange and value added professional elevations. This received three major areas of differences, viz: storage in digital form, direct communication to obtain material and accessibility, and copying from a master version.

The gradual facelift of overall libraries from the past, there appears some tangible impacts recognizing the predictions of Lancaster's paperless society to reality. The transformation effects that digital technology brings into information system are as follows:

DIGITAL INFORMATION RESOURCES

The resources of a digital library are those, which the computer can store, organized, transmit and display without any intervening conversion process. It includes both print and electronic or digital material. The digital material may be of multimedia types or any other i.e. only digital audio, video, full text information, photograph, drawing, digitized sound, e-book, v-book, electronic tax, map, image, 3D representation etc. The collection may also include structured /unstructured text, scanned images, graphic audios, video recording etc. There are basically ***two*** types of Digital E-resources which are mentioned below:

On Line Resources

- Local Database of Traditional Books In Machine-Readable Form.
- E-Book, V-Book, Electronic Tax, Map, Image, Sound, Video, and Multimedia Etc.
- E-Journal
- LAN, MAN, WAN for web browsing, e- mail etc.

Off Line Resources

- C.D-ROM, Jukebox etc.
- Audio Visual Aid etc.

From above the digital resources, some of the very important were discussed below:

1. **CD-ROM Database** (Compact Dick read Only Memory): The CD-ROM technology has given ample opportunities for information professionals to introduce more information services to end-users. Optical Storage is making a major impact on the multimedia market as a result of the benefits that it offers in terms of capacity, lifespan and cost. The different types of optical media reviewed include analog video disk, compact disk and the use of writeable storage media such as write only, read many and magnetic optic disks. All forms of optical storage disk provide higher storage capacity, random access to data, a guaranteed lifespan of between 30 and 40 years, resolvability and portability.

   CD-ROM is an economic medium for the duplication and distribution of information to users. Users will be able to access information that is stored in multimedia databases on optical disk. Already an increasing number of companies are using CD-ROM as a distribution medium for software. Some also use it for distributing information. The majority of publishers of books and journals, online vendors and various learned societies are bringing out new titles in CD format with powerful, user-friendly retrieval software. Electronic information resources in CD format include abstracting and indexing services, encyclopedias, dictionaries, directories, yearbooks, back volumes, patents, standards and many other reference works.

2. **DVD-ROM Database:** The advent of DVD- Digital Video Disk or Digital Versatile Disc, with its 17 GB of high data storage capacity, has made it possible to include more multimedia elements like video and to integrate many reference sources on a single disc. "The other features like higher quality of sound and video, higher rate of data transfer, data security, etc. are making DVD a more viable option than CD-ROM. But, at present due to some problems like a lack of standards among the manufacturers of DVDs and drives, and for extra hardware on PCs and their higher prices are making the growth of DVD 99, Webster's International DVD Encyclopedia-2000, Grolier Multimedia Encyclopedia, Eyewitness World Atlas DVD-ROM Deluxe Edition, the Complete National Geographic on DVD-ROM, etc.

3. **FIDONET: Fidonet** is just one form of electronic communication that provides a means to bridge time and distance, to facilitate interpersonal communications. The simplest is a bulletin board system. In its basic form the idea of the system can post a message in a public area. Any other member of the system can browse through the bulletin board reading items of interest. Electronic Mails, Conference mails, and file transfer when these services are integrated with an interactive electronic bulletin board system, such as remote access, they can be accessed by people using only a modem and ordinary phone lines.

4. **INTERNET:** The Internet is a cooperative computer network of networks that links libraries, schools, governments, corporations, individuals and others to each other and to cast information resources. The internet protocol links many independent networks together so that they appear as a single network to the user. The internet currently consists of about 28,000 registered networks, about 2 million host computers and an estimated 15 million users. About 149 countries have connections to some sort of an international computer network; of theses about 63 countries have direct connections to the Internet. Internet can be used to send and receive electronic messages, to contact and search other computers – Telnet-to copy files. The Internet is an open network. Any one or any group is welcome to use it as long as that person or group has a terminal or a computer with the correct software and the ability to pay the costs. Since most users of Internet are affiliated with institutions, the computers they use are attached to LAN which is in turn connected by a router to a regional or wide area network.

   Gopher, Archie, Veronica, Jughead, WAIS and the WWW are the tools supported by Internet that help users to find and retrieve information. The information available on the net is increasing rapidly and the task of providing relevant information to patrons is gaining paramount importance in all types of libraries. Most of the reputed publishers, learned and commercial societies are hosting their products on the net and also many libraries are sharing their internal and external information resources by means of Web pages and Web-OPACs. The powerful search engines over the net are aiding the information location quite efficiently.

   The **Internet services** like e-mail, Bulletin boards, Newsgroups. Discussion lists, etc. are gaining importance in libraries and are becoming indispensable resources for the users. Owing to the impact of Internet, there is a swift migration from offline to online, as the Web is becoming a popular user interface for providing access to remote and frequently updated resources.

5. **ONLINE:** Online makes information available in different formats. It is a means of constant access to databases around the world from any location using an inexpensive telecom link and a PC terminal. The online databases services like Dialog and STN are now moving towards being web centric. The usage of online databases against their CD-ROM counterparts has to be evaluated and decided on the basis of cost-effectiveness and timeliness. A few online information services are KR Science Base and STN. The KR Science Base includes information sources like BIOSIS, CA Search, Elsevier Science Publishers, Reuters, NTIS, etc. The STN international provides a complete collection of in-depth databases in science and technology.

6. **ELIRON: Eliron"** is one of the first electronic library developments in the UK. It has given the user aspects of the electronic library a high priority in the research programme. In fact, from the outset it is clear that a user friendly interface as one of the important selection criteria, on which the electronic library system could be based. The basic objective of Eliron is to set up a large image database of complete books, journals and course materials which can be directly accessed by students and teaching staff via windows based IBM and Macintosh PCs. ELIRONELS employs current Graphical User Interface technology, the basic feature of which is WIMP, i.e. Window, Icon, Mouse and pull-down menu.

7. **E-Journals:** With the emergence of Internet Electronic Journals or E-journals are gaining more importance. Most of the publishers provide a full text of journals and other publications through Internet. The most frequently used format is Hyper Text Markup Language (HTML), Extensible Markup Language (XML) and Adobe Acrobat and its associated Portable Document Format (PDF). These Journals are also called ***networked E-Journals.***

   In USA most of the universities have launched a project to provide access to E-journals, as a partner in the project, to assist in the design of the use interface, help resolve licensing issues with publishers and to determine the best access options. Electronic Journals have now been recognized as a major link in scholarly communication. The timely publication, ease in delivery, incorporation of multimedia contents, hyper linking and search facility, etc. are some of the features which have attracted interest of both libraries and the scholarly community. However, along with these advantages it has created a number of challenges, out of which archiving is still an unsettled issue.

8. **E-Books:** Electronic Books **or** e-Books are electronic forms of printed books. E-Books are texts that have been "published" in a digital format that needs specialized reading devices or computers for using or

reading. During this decade, their growth and popularity has gone up drastically particularly in the filed of Education. Recent **UK Survey** results shows that there will be high growth in e-Books over the next year. It was also found that three-quarters of academic libraries and half of public libraries in the UK intend to increase their collections of e-Books over the next year, in spite of the current fiscal climate.

9. **Catalogue Databases**: Telnet access to the Online Public Access Catalogues server is a very simple solution over a TCP/IP network. A user telnets to the OPAC server opening a VT 100 terminal window logs in using a guest account, which usually starts the OPAC, access programs. It is however desirable that the users access the OPAC using within the Web browser interface. He should be able to access the OPAC and similar catalogues using HTML based query forms, obtained by selecting an appropriate link in the library home page. After the user fills the query form and submits it, the Web server initiates a search program that carries out a search on the catalogue database and returns the results in HTML form to the users and browsers screen via the web server. Most of the present day library automation packages have extended their functionality to support web access. Many web complaints in the public domain text indexing and search packages are also available which can be used for bibliographic and full text data.

USES OF DIGITAL RESOURCES

- Access to information is instant.
- Effective searching can be possible to retrieve a particular information
- Digital information obtains full networking capability
- Information that is digitized can become available to anyone anywhere in the world at minimal cost and its source does not get exhausted with unlimited use.
- Presentation of information through the digital resources can be done within a reasonable time with speed and ease.
- Multiple access to electronic resources is possible
- Downloading of the required information is very easy.
- It develops a distributed learning environment by which all the users can be benefited at a time.
- Remote access to information is also possible
- Large volumes of data can be stored in the digital resources and made accessible to the users.

- Information transfer can be provided with speed and accuracy.
- Addition of information to the collection of digital resources is faster.
- Cataloguing, editing, referring, indexing, etc can be done with ease and speed.

ROLE OF LIBRARIAN IN THE DIGITAL ENVIRONMENT

Though the digital environment is built as a system, which can be used by its ultimate end user directly from their desktop pc, the role of librarian cannot be overlooked. In digital environment also the librarian and information scientist will be needed for packaging and repackaging of information, for electronic publishing, for reference purpose, to advise the user about the strategy to identify relevant electronic sources etc. thus the librarian will be more or less a hypertext engineer. In the new environment it will be very difficult for the librarian to decide what should be organized? How to give citation? How to organize the collection? Etc because the new environment will be really challenging one for the librarian to decide who are author who are publisher and who are user? . In the new environment any one who has access to the network of digital libraries can be a publisher by merely posting messages to an online discussion group or by other means. A virtual environment is really open for all. In some cases, librarians have the opportunity to digitize unique material in their libraries' collections, which can then be made accessible to users of the World Wide Web at large. Some US libraries have done this with local history collections.

ADVANTAGES OF DIGITAL LIBRARIES

The advantages of digital libraries as a means of easily and rapidly accessing books, archives and images of various types are now widely recognized by commercial interests and public bodies alike.

- **No Physical Boundary:** The user of a digital library need not to go to the library physically; people from all over the world can gain access to the same information, as long as an Internet connection is available.
- **Round the Clock Availability:** A major advantage of digital libraries is that people can gain access **24/7** to the information.
- **Multiple Accesses:** The same resources can be used simultaneously by a number of institutions and patrons. This may not be the case for copyrighted material: a library may have a license for "lending out" only one copy at a time; this is achieved with a system of digital rights management where a resource can become inaccessible after expiration of the lending period or after the lender chooses to make it inaccessible (equivalent to returning the resource).
- **Information Retrieval:** The user is able to use any search term (word,

phrase, title, name, and subject) to search the entire collection. Digital libraries can provide very user-friendly interfaces, giving clickable access to its resources.

- **Preservation and Conservation:** Digitization is not a long-term preservation solution for physical collections, but does succeed in providing access copies for materials that would otherwise fall to degradation from repeated use. Digitized collections and born-digital objects pose many preservation and conservation concerns that analog materials do not. Please see the following "Problems" section of this page for examples.
- **Space:** Whereas traditional libraries are limited by storage space, digital libraries have the potential to store much more information; simply because digital information requires very little physical space to contain them and media storage technologies are more affordable than ever before.
- **Added Value:** Certain characteristics of objects, primarily the quality of images, may be improved. Digitization can enhance legibility and remove visible flaws such as stains and discoloration.

From the above **advantages** of digital libraries, we may conclude/ summaries as follows in brief.

- It is quick, accurate, and easy to locate by using searching and browsing mechanisms.
- Binding, preservation and shelf maintenance do not exist.
- Language techniques are exploited in fields such as cataloguing, indexing and abstracting.
- Digital conversion increases accessibility to users.
- Easily and rapidly accessing books, archives and images of various types
- The user of a digital library need not to go to the library physically; readers from all over the world can gain access to the same information, as long as an internet connection is available.
- The readers can gain access to the information at any time (round the clock)
- Digital libraries have the potential to store much more information, simply because digital information requires very little physical space to contain it. (Traditional libraries are limited by storage space)
- Low cost maintenance comparing with traditional libraries (on staff, book maintenance, establishment, etc.).

DISADVANTAGES OF THE DIGITAL LIBRARY

The computer viruses, lack of standardization for digitized information, quick degrading properties of digitized material, different display standard of digital product and its associated problem, health hazard nature of the radiation from monitor etc. makes digital libraries at times handicap.

1. **Copyright**: - Digitization violates the copy right law as the thought content of one author can be freely transfer by other without his acknowledgement. So One difficulty to overcome for digital libraries is the way to distribute information. How does a digital library distribute information at will while protecting the copyright of the author?
2. **Speed of access**: - As more and more computer are connected to the Internet its speed of access reasonably decreasing. If new technology will not evolve to solve the problem then in near future Internet will be full of error messages.
3. **Initial cost is high**: - The infrastructure cost of digital library i.e. the cost of hardware, software; leasing communication circuit is generally very high.
4. **Band width**: - Digital library will need high band for transfer of multimedia resources but the band width is decreasing day by day due to its over utilization.
5. **Efficiency**: - With the much larger volume of digital information, finding the right material for a specific task becomes increasingly difficult.
6. **Environment**: - Digital libraries cannot reproduce the environment of a traditional library. Many people also find reading printed material to be easier than reading material on a computer screen.
7. **Preservation**: - Due to technological developments, a digital library can rapidly become out-of-date and its data may become inaccessible.

CONCLUSION AND SUGESSTIONS

Digital libraries are not going to replace the physical existence of document completely but no doubt to meet the present demand, to satisfy the non local user digitization must be introduced so that at least libraries becomes of hybrid nature. The initial cost of digitization is high but experiment shows that once digitization is introduced then the cost to manage this collection will be cheaper than that of any traditional library. Day by day the cost of digitization is decreasing, the online publication is increasing, and the needs of user are shifting towards a different environment. So, it's needless to say that within no time, all the traditional libraries will go to be digitized.

Finally, there is urgent need to conducting the IT trainingprogrammes to LIS professionals to upgrade their professional's skills, Knowledge for providing the ICT services to users' community in the speediest digital environment Era. For this, The Central and State Governments and funding agencies like, UGC, CSIR, ICAR, ICMR, NASSDOC and DST should be provide **Budgetary Provisions** to the libraries for digitization and introducing the newly services like digital library services and reference services which are more important in the present electronic environment arena.

REFERENCES

1. Anjaiah.M. (2011). Web Resources for Distance Learners: Need of the Hour, Paper Presented at 16th IDEA Annual Conference, Organised by the School of Distance Learning & Continuing Education (SDLCE), Collaboration with Indian Distance Education Association (IDEA), Kakatiya University, Warangal, 26-27 March2011.
2. Ansari, Mehtab Alam. (2003). Digital Libraries: Needs, Technology and Benefit, *ILA Bulletin*, 38(3), pp.22-26.
3. Banerjee, Swapna and Chakrabarty, Biplab (1999). Digital libraries: Some Issues and Perspective, *ILA Bulletin* 34(3-4), October 1998 to March 1999, pp. 60-63.
4. Benahrat,A.(2004).International Summer of School of Digital Library, BBF,Vol.49,No.2.pp.110111.
5. Cyric, Jiji, Deshmukh, G.R. and Rajalakshmi (2002). Digitization of Libraries: In Modern Era, *ILA Bulletin,* 38(3) pp.68-73.
6. Dhaka, R.P.S. and Arora, Kamlesh (1995). Electronic libraries: A Myth or a Reality, Annals of Library Science and Documentation.42 (4). pp.152-59.
7. Khan, Shakeel Ahmad, Khayat, Roshan and Yunus, Mohad (2003), Digital Libraries: The Present Scenario, *ILA Bulletin,* 39(2), pp.3-7.
8. Koteswara Rao, M (2003). Digital Libraries: Challenges, Opportunities and Implications, paper presented at SIS-2004 Conference 22-23 January 2004, Madras.
9. Kumar, Bhuvan and Reddy, V.Sreeniuas (2003). Digital Library Use: A Case Study of NIT Library, Warangal, *ILA Bulletin* 39(2), pp.40-45.
10. LISWiki. (2010). Digital Library and Its Different Aspect, *Digital library,*(12).pp.12-21
11. Ravichandra Rao I.K. and Suma P. (1996). Digital Libraries, Challenge and Issues, Digitized Information, paper presented at the SIS-96, 18-

20 January 1996, Bangalore, T.B.Rajasekhar, I.K. Ravi Chandra Rao and N.V. Satyanarayana (Eds).pp.185-95.

12. http://en.wikipedia.org/wiki/Digital_library. Retrieved on 20.7.2011.
13. http://scholar.lib.vt.edu/DLI2/defineDL.html
14. http://www.clir.org/pubs/issues/issues04.html#dlf
15. http://www.dlib.org/metrics/public/papers/dig-lib-scope.html
16. http://www.firstmonday.org/issues/issue6_6/lynch/#l2
17. http://www.kmentor.com/socio-tech-info/archives/000694.html
18. http://www.www9.org/final-posters/poster17.html

❑❑❑

Chapter - 16

Institutional Repository (IR): Need and Future Trends in Indian Libraries

Sunil Kumar Satpathy

1. INTRODUCTION

With the rapid development of Information Communication Technology (ICT), many new services have been introduced in libraries to satisfy the need of users in a better way. Institutional Repository is a type of information service which involves collection, organization, preservation and dissemination of digital scholarly materials such as theses, dissertations, technical reports, journal articles and teaching materials. It is created and maintained by an individual library/ organization or a group of libraries/organizations with an aim to preserve the institutional knowledge .Thus basically it is an online locus for collecting, preserving and disseminating the intellectual output of an academic or research institution in digital form, created and maintained by the institution itself.

"Clifford Lynch defines " a university based Institutional Repositories as a set of services that a university offers to the members of its community for the management and dissemination of digital materials created by the institution and its community members. It is most essentially an organizational commitment to the stewardship of these digital materials, including long-term preservation where appropriate, as well as organization and access or distribution" [1]

Similarly Mark defines IR as "An institutional repository (IR) is defined to be a web-based database (repository) of scholarly material which is institutionally defined (as opposed to a subject-based repository); cumulative and perpetual (a collection of record); open and interoperable (e.g. using OAI-compliant software); and thus collects, stores and disseminates (is part of the process of scholarly communication). In addition, most would include long-term preservation of digital materials as a key function of IRs"[2].

The main objectives of an institutional repository are to provide access to institutional research output and other institutional digital assets, including unpublished or grey literature .It also facilitates its organization, preservation and dissemination.

The basic contents of IR are preprints, post prints, author post prints, publisher PDFs, technical reports, working papers, theses and dissertations, books and chapters of books, research databases, conference proceedings, text audio-video recordings, teaching materials, digital research, materials, unpublished work, datasets, research papers, working papers etc.

2. NEED FOR INSTITUTIONAL REPOSITORY

Keeping pace with the development of education, the number of research and publications in all fields of knowledge has increased tremendously. Contrary to this ,the institutional library have not enough space to store and preserve these materials for future use since all most all libraries are running with space problems. Further, the rapid development and impact of ICT in all walks of life have changed the library users' preference more towards e-resources than print resources. Accordingly ,there is every need to create Institutional repositories which preserve the institutional knowledge in digital format which solve the space problems and also effective use of these preserved knowledge.

Charles W. Bailey[3] has identified four factors to justify the need for building an institutional repository. These are:

a) To increase the visibility and citation impact of the institution's scholarly materials.

b) To provide unified access to the institution's scholarly materials.

c) To provide open access to the institution's scholarly materials.

d) To preserve the institution's scholarly materials".

Similarly, Barton and Waters[4] have identified various ways of using IR by university and research libraries around the world, which are as follows:

- Scholarly communication,
- Storing learning materials and courseware,
- Electronic publishing,
- Managing collections of research documents,

- Preserving digital materials for the long term,
- Adding to the university's prestige by showcasing its academic research,
- Institutional leadership role for the Library,
- Knowledge management,
- Research assessment,
- Encouraging open access to scholarly research,
- Housing digitized collections,

3. ESSENCE OF INSTITUTIONAL REPOSITORY

The creation of an Institutional Repository mainly depends upon the culture of the organization and the collaboration and trust among the staff members. In a competitive environment where cooperation and trust are not nurtured, building a repository will be a tough task. Institutional Repository advocates for an early decision on the purpose and scope of the repository and effective communication among users community. A repository may be limited to archiving of research outputs of faculty members and students or may include the intellectuals output and administrative documents for the whole institutions. Besides, Library and Information Science professionals and administrators responsible for operating and maintaining repositories need to ensure that all legal requirements are met properly. These may include appropriated software and content licenses.

4. SOFTWARE FOR CREATION OF INSTITUTIONAL REPOSIOTORY

Software is the key element in the construction of an institutional repository. Basically, there are two types of software available in the market i.e. Commercial/ subscribed software and open/ open source software. Open source software is software which is created by generous programmers and released into the public domain for public use. The underlying programming code is available to the users so that they may read or make changes and build new versions of the software incorporating their changes for software. Usually these software are distributed under an Open-Source License – General Public License (GPL). Such a license requires that the source code should be distributed along with the software, and that the source code is freely modifiable with least restrictions.

The most commonly available open source software for building Institutional Repository is listed below.

4.1. CDsWare:

CERN Document Server Software (CDsWare), developed by CERN

Document Server is compatible to electronic preprint server, online library catalogue or a document system on the web. It is compatible with the Open Archives Initiatives Metadata Harvesting Protocol (OAI-PMH) and uses MARC-21 as its underlying bibliographic standard.(http://cdsware.cern.ch)[5]

4.2. DSpace:

DSpace was developed as a joint research project of the MIT libraries and Hewlett- Packard (HP). It was developed in response to expressed faculty needs for an easy-to-use, dependable repository that accommodates a broad range of formats. It is intended to provide a solid foundation for the collection of digital material from and around the institute. MIT Libraries hold a non-exclusive license to distribute and preserve items but do not own the DSpace content. It is incumbent upon libraries to develop strategic and economic plans for the preservation and usability of those resources over time. (http://www.dspace.org)[6]

4.3 E-prints:

E-Print is developed by University of Southampton and is intended to create a highly configurable web-based archive. The primary goal of e-prints seems to be set up as an open archive for research papers, but it could be easily used for other things such as images, research data, audio archives etc. (http://www.software.eprints.org/)[7]

4.4 Greenstone:

The Greenstone Digital Library (GSDL) Software is developed by university of Waikato and is open source software for building and distributing digital library collections. It provides new ways of organizing information and publishing it on the Internet or on CD-ROMs. (http://greenstone.org/cgl_bin/library)[8]

4.5 Fedora:

Fedora is developed by Cornell University and the University of Virginia. It is based on the Flexible Extensible Digital Object and repository Architecture (FEDORA). (http://www.fedora.info/)[9]

4.6 i-Tor:

It is open-source software that enables to create websites, which may be straightforward web pages or information from a database or some other file. i-Tor can also be used to make modifications. The creator of a web page can manage it directly on the site, either alone or in collaboration with others. Users can search all of the information that is linked to i-Tor. (http://www.i-Tor.org/en/)[10]

4.7 ROADS:

This software is intended to aid in the setting up and day-to-day running of www based catalogues of online resources. Although designed specifically to meet the requirements of the eLib subject gateways, ROADS software may be useful in a variety of other purposes. (http://www.roads.sourceforge.net/)[11]

According to the Directory of Open Access Repositories (The Open DOAR) [12] the usage of open access software worldwide is graphically represented as below.

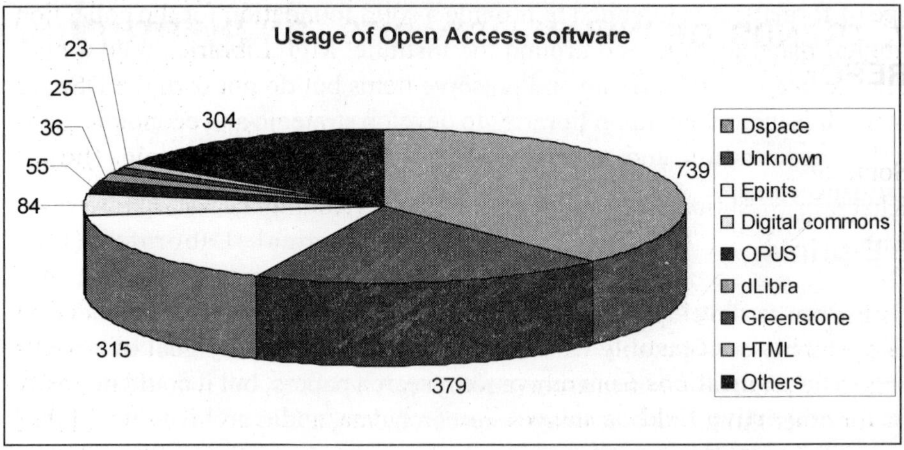

(Graph-1: Worldwide usage of open access software)

5. PROBLEMS IN BUILDING INSTITUTIONAL REPOSITORY

There are a lot of problems in building Institutional Repository. In the opinion of Crow [13], the problems and hurdles which implementation team face in building a repository include the following:

a) Adoption rate by academics,

b) Providing for sustainability,

c) Developing policies,

d) Managing intellectual property rights,

e) University support,

f) Cost management,

g) Digital preservation,

h) Identifying key stakeholders,

6. BENEFITS OF INSTITUTIONAL REPOSITORY

The benefits of Institutional Repository to an institution are many. Some of the main benefits are:

a) It increases the professional visibility of the faculty,

b) Raises the prestige of the institution

c) Lower access barriers

d) Offers wider dissemination of scholarly communication

e) Open access online articles are highly cited,

f) Students can easily access the papers written by the faculty members,

g) Publication in IR can be immediately found in global search service.

7. TRENDS OF INDIAN LIBRARIES ON INSTITUTIONAL REPOSITORIES

The Indian initiative on creation of Institutional Repository is new one. Some of the notable institutions in India, like IISc,Bangalore, IIT (Delhi & Kharagpur), National Institute of Technology (Rourkela), National Aerospace Laboratories (Bangalore), National Chemical Laboratory(Pune), INFLIBNET(Ahemdabad), National Institute of Oceanography(Goa), Raman Research Institute(Bangalore) etc. have created Open Access Institutional Repositories successfully. There are some other repositories, which accept scholarly publications from any professional or the researcher who is working in the respective field or subject area. Librarian's Digital Library (LDL) of DRTC, Bangalore is such a subject- specific repository for the library and information professionals. OpenMEd@NIC is maintained by National Informatics Center, New Delhi and it provides access to biomedical literature. Also some other kinds of digital repositories are established in India which is based on specific type of document collections. Vidyanidhi of University of Mysore is an example of such type of repository, which store and provides access to theses and dissertation collection. It accepts any theses or dissertation from any researcher or from the student, accepted by Indian Universities or the institutions. This indicates towards a positive trends of Indian libraries towards Institutional Repository.

But in world ranking of Institutional Repository, the position of Indian repository is not encouraging. It can be seen for the ranking of the Cybermetrics Lab, a research group belonging to the Consejo Superior de Investigaciones Científicas (CSIC), the largest public research body in Spain as follows [14].The ranking is from the 500 world top Institutional Repositories.

Table-1: World Rank of top Indian Institutional Repositories

World Rank	Name of the repository	Position			
		Size	Visibility	Rich files	Scholars
116	Indian Institute of Science Bangalore e-print	71	235	85	245
222	Indian Institute of Astro physics Dspace	475	198	273	517
248	Openmed National Informatics center India	64	408	216	271
271	Vidyanidhi Digital Library, University of Mysore	252	438	24	742
341	Indian Statistical Institute Digital Library	232	342	532	606
382	National Institute of Oceanography India Digital Repository	247	684	244	276

8. SUGGESTIONS

The LIS professionals play a vital role in acquisition, organization and dissemination of information of all kinds and provision to provide information services in libraries have been a part of library services since early time. Information services through creation of Institutional Repositories is one such services provided by the LIS professionals. During recent years debate is going on that building and maintenance of Institutional repositories is whose responsibility? Some are on the opinion that it is the responsibility of LIS professionals but other opines that it is the responsibility of the Computer science professionals. But basically organization and dissemination of information is the job of LIS professional .Hence the professionals need to possess positive attitude towards these new tools of information storage and dissemination. Also there is every need to acquire necessary skills and knowledge by the LIS professionals to run and maintain the institutional repository.

The common steps which needs to be followed in building an Institutional repository can be summarized as follows:

a) Formulation of clear cut policies for Institutional Repository on the basis of guidelines of parent organization.

b) Formulation of a strategic on the basis of examining the existing IRs of other organizations, need assessment study of own organization, estimation of cost, time and manpower required for building the IR.

c) Selection of hardware and software

d) Collection of materials to be stored in IR

e) Motivate faculty members, research scholars and students to contribute their research outputs (both pre print and post print)

f) Developing a team of LIS professionals to manage the IR

g) Wide publication of the IR to inform users to use the IR

h) Collection of users feedback and necessary modification in the system and services of the IR

i) Adaptation of preservation strategy for digital materials

j) Maintenance and updating the IR regularly.

9. CONCLUSION

Over past few years ,the library environment, particularly information dissemination system has rapidly changed due to changes in the types of library collection ,particularly with the inclusion of electronic resources. Further the tremendous growth of study and research in all fields of knowledge facilitates in the production of a large number of intellectual output. Keeping pace with the impact of ICT on all walks of life, the user's expectations for information have also changed considerably and their preference has increased more towards digital resources. In this changing situation, libraries have no other option than to develop new IT tools and implement new techniques of information organization and dissemination, specifically for digital information. Institutional repository is one of the best solutions to this. Accordingly many academic and research libraries are involved in building Institutional Repositories in their own way for accessing their intellectual outputs in networked environment. The trends of Indian libraries towards this shows to be more positive day by day. However various issues such as sound policy, persuading faculty to participate, rights management, organizational and administrative funding, long-term preservation, accession policy, open access or control, central vs. institutional repositories, metadata, technological etc needs to be addressed .Also a positive attitude needs to be developed by the LIS professionals where their role would be designer, creator, maintainer and promoter of Institutional Repository.

REFERENCES

1. Clifford A. Lynch, "Institutional Repositories: Essential Infrastructure for Scholarship in the Digital Age," ARL: A Bimonthly Report on Research Library Issues and Actions from ARL, CNI, and SPARC. 226 (2003) <http://www.arl.org/resources/pubs/br/br226/br226ir.shtml>.

2. Ware, Mark .Pathfinder Research on Web-based Repositories. London: Publisher and Library/Learning Solutions, 2004. <http://www.palsgroup.org.uk/palsweb/palsweb.nsf/79b0d164e01a6cb880256ae0004a0e34/8c43ce800a9c67cd80256e370051e88a/$FILE/PALS%20report%20on%20In stitutional%20Repositories.pdf.>

3. C.W.Bailey , “Institutional Repositories, Tout de Suite” . < http://www.digital-scholarship.org/ts/irtoutsuite.pdf> .

4. Barton,M.R and Waters,M.M.”Creating an Institutional Repository” LEADIERS Workbook. <http://www.dspace.org/images/stories/leadirs.pdf>

5. http://cdsware.cern.ch/

6. http://www.dspace.org

7. http://www.software.eprints.org/

8. http://greenstone.org/cgl_bin/library

9. http://www.fedora.info/

10. http://www.i-Tor.org/en/

11. http://www.roads.sourceforge.net/

12. Available at <http://www.opendoar.org/onechart.php?cID=&ctID=&rtID=&clID=&lID=&potID=&rSoftWa reName=&search=&groupby=r.rSoftWareName&or derby=Tally%20DESC& charttype=pie&width= 600&height=300&caption=Usage%2 0of%20Open%20Access %20Repository%20Software%20-% >

13. R.Crow.”The Case for Institutional Repositories: A SPARC Position Paper”. <http://www.ifla.org/IV/ifla72/papers/155-Mark_Shearer-en.pdf>

14. Available at <http://repositories.webometrics.info/top800_rep.asp> .

❑❑❑

Chapter - 17

Hybrid Library and Information Services to Agriculture in The Landscape Need to Develop Self-service among Users

S. M. Rokade

INTRODUCTION

Information services are keys to the development of agriculture education, research and extension education in India. The services are rendered by the agricultural department, university, college and ICAR institute libraries. In changing scenario the users of libraries access the information themselves from various sources such as computer, internet, television, e-governance, video-conferencing, call centers, mobile phones and other electronic sources from anywhere, at any time as and when required.

Agricultural trends are changing everyday with the development of new research techniques and technologies and in support of this a heterogeneous knowledge is available in the form of various electronic sources. To make the best of emerging technologies in agriculture, it is vital that agricultural students, scientists, research scholars, academicians, extension workers, agriculturalists receive continuous information on education, research, extension work, training and to the cultivators on topics such as pesticide management, use of better seeds, irrigation and use etc. for the development of farm and farming. With the introduction of new technology that affects both their processes and products, libraries become more and more hybrid organizations. Hybrid libraries are mixes of traditional print material like books and magazines, as well as electronic based material such as downloadable audio books, electronic journals, e-books, etc. Because of this shift, libraries face many challenges, the most important of which is the competition for scarce resources. In this competition libraries have to change the allocation of resources from the more traditional processes like circulation to more value added processes like direct self-services to their patrons. The FAO is also a source of knowledge and information, providing behind the scenes assistance to help people help themselves.

HYBRID LIBRARY

The first identified use of the term hybrid library was by Sutton (1996). However, it was almost simultaneously coined by Rusbridge (1998), then Programme Director of the Electronic Libraries (e-Lib) Programme in the United Kingdom, who popularized the term and with whose name it is now associated (JISC 1997). Although largely confined to higher education, it is likely that the concept will spread to other types of library. The hybrid library is a transitional working pattern between the conventional library and the digital library. With the idea of systematic integration and the methodology of thoughts, the hybrid library should integrate the various formats of information resources and user interfaces, and establish a new model of organizations and staff, which is helpful for, in this way, solving the existing problems in the implementation of digital library projects, such as the separation of the development, management and services of paper-based resources and digital information resources, and improving the overall operation efficiency of the library.

SELF SERVICE

In 1917, the US Patent Office awarded Clarence Saunders a patent for a "self-serving store." Saunders invited his customers to collect the goods they wanted to buy from the store and present them to a cashier, rather than having the store employee consult a list presented by the customer, and collect the goods. Saunders licensed the business method to independent grocery stores. As such the Self service is the practice of serving oneself, usually when purchasing items and has opened the account in library and information services. Self-service is used on the phone, web and email to facilitate users' service interactions using automation.

AGRICULTURAL SYSTEM IN INDIA

Agricultural system in India comprises Ministry of Agriculture and Cooperation - Central and State. Department of Agriculture, Indian Council of Agricultural Research, (ICAR), New Delhi, Agricultural Universities 43, Deemed Universities 5, ICAR Institutes 45, National Research Centers 30, Project Directorates 10, National Bureau 4, All India Coordinated Research Projects 80, Krishi Vigyan Kendras 262, Trainers Training Centres 8, National Research Centre in Agriculture for Women 1, Operational Research Projects 400, and all the related sectors and sections.

PRESENT STATUS OF INFORMATION SERVICES IN AGRICULTURAL LIBRARIES

The ICAR Library functions as the depository of FAO, IDRC and AVRDC publications and also as the National Depository for CGIAR institutes publications. Under **AGRIS project** IARI Library was declared an input Centre for national agricultural research database (NARD). The Library was assigned the job of scanning articles from 10 most important Indian journals. The input was done in ISO format using AGRIN methodology. During the period under report, 392 articles were scanned, processed and sent to DIPA, ICAR for inclusion in AGRIS Index. **C-DAC Project A** memorandum was signed with C-DAC (Ministry of Information Technology) on 4th September 2004 to digitize old documents. During the period, 43, 00,000 pages of 6250 publications published before 1950 and not covered under Copyright Act were scanned. They can be accessed through the software developed by C-DAC.

In India the agriculture university and ICAR institute libraries are rendering information services to their users. The information services in changing scenario rendered normally are internet, modern Cyberary, e-mail, online, OPAC, Online Computer Library Centre (OCLC), on-line Full Text e-journals, e-journals, e-books Theses, Statistical, e-Reference sources etc. as per the requirement of users. The services are provided with the help of sources like Internet, work-stations, Vidyanidhi,e, **KrishiPrabha – Indian Agricultural Doctoral Dissertations Repository, digitization of library document,** access to e-contents, and multimedia. The services are also rendered through CD-ROM Databases: CABCD, AGRICOLA, AGRIS, BIOSIS, CAB, COMPENDEX, FSTA, Abstract and Index, FAO Depository Library, Data-bases on CD-ROM such as CAB-CD. HORT-CD, TREE-CD Multimedia center, provides access to e-contents, e-knowledgebase including multimedia contents; and to establish linkage to ICAR-net, ICAR-e-journals consortium.

There is linkage with NISSAT under DSIR, INFLIBNET, and National Informatics Centre (NIC) under Planning Commission, Informatics Division of UNESCO, Paris and institutes under Consultative Group on International Agricultural Research (CGIAR).

NEED OF NAIS TO DEVELOP SELF-SERVICE IN USER'S COMMUNITY

The application of ICT in research, education and technology transfer in agriculture is at a nascent stage and initiatives introduced by the ICAR such as Intranet and centralized data centre, ICT-mediated knowledge management, Agro web - Digital Dissemination System for Indian Agricultural Research (ADDSIAR), Development of e-courses, KrishiPrabha - Indian agricultural dissertations repository, Consortium of e-Resources in Agriculture (CeRA) through the NAIP will trigger greater interest and activity in this area. It is expected that these are snowball into a national mission and make the NARS system modern, vibrant and responsible to the requirement of all stakeholders. Considering the development in sources, services and technology a survey of agricultural library users was carried out to know about self-service and its importance along with the present status of information services in agricultural libraries. National Agricultural Information Services Project is proposed for the development of 'self-service' among the users.

Table: 1.Needs of users and self service

Sl.No.	Users	Total Quest	response	Self service				Need of self service
				Y	%	N	%	
1.	Students UG	100	82	61	74	21	26	Use of speedy access services Get Privacy, Remove the levels of supportSave the time and money Teaching, research, extensionTo use anywhere, anytime as desiredUp-to-date method To improve self-confidence More use of technologySelf-development & career
2.	Students PG	040	31	31	100	00	00	
3.	Research scholars	020	16	15	94	01	06	
4.	Academicians	080	63	43	68	20	32	
5.	Scientists	020	14	14	100	00	00	
6.	Extension workers	055	34	28	82	06	18	
7.	Agrobased industries	020	13	10	77	03	23	
8.	Cultivators	020	18	14	78	04	22	
		Total	271	216	80	55	20	

SOURCE

The sample survey has been carried out of the users of university, college, ICAR institute and NGO library with the help of questionnaire, personal discussion and visit. It is found that the 100% PG students, scientists and 94% research scholars, 82% extension workers, 77% agro based industry users, 74% undergraduate students and 78% cultivators are interested in self service and accessing information themselves. The users between the ages of 28-45 are interested to access the information themselves. The users are also interested to have a separate integrated national agricultural information services available on single web at any time and any where to save the time and money.

ADVANTAGES OF SELF SERVICE

- To improve the working condition and quality of staff
- To improve the quality of services
- Use of speedy services to the users
- Get Privacy to users
- Up-to-date method of library service
- Building of self-check and return in the users
- Save the time and money of the users & library
- Remove the levels of support, help and advice from library.

INTEGRATED NATIONAL AGRICULTURAL INFORMATION SERVICES

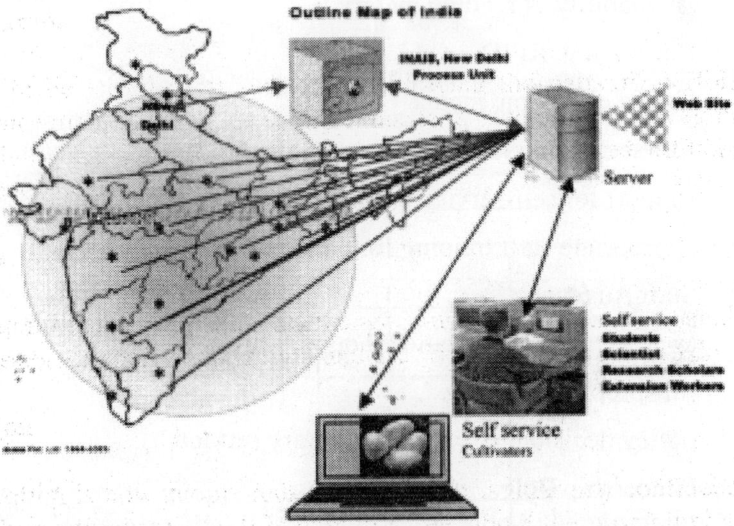

The information generation, dissemination, transfer and communication take place through diverse channels and media in a variety of content environments in the agricultural university and ICAR institute libraries. The students, academic staff, research scientists are the actual users of this knowledge, information and technology. This information technology is to be transferred to the farmers who are at the grass roots and who are the actual beneficiaries directly and through the extension specialists. The diagram depicts a concept where in a network is in place, consisting of a super node at New Delhi and the agricultural university and ICAR institute libraries in all state and union territories connected via network to each other. Similarly, all the central nodes of different states can then be connected to the super-node placed at Delhi. The data servers at each location will then be able to communicate with each other through systematic application of various networking protocols.

For the users a computer search site can be developed that will enable them to access valuable information placed at any of the library locations, through the established network pattern.

SUCCESSFUL SELF-SERVICE DEVELOPMENT PLAN FOR :

- standard equipment, computer
- Proper placement of furniture and equipment
- setting up more service stations
- adequate space for self-service station
- open access for all
- user identification code number
- Self return counter
- Availability of reading materials
- Bar-coding, RFID
- Use of electronic media
- Library staff assistance
- support for self-service users to
- appropriate staff training for better solution
- Staff Advocacy
- appropriate and educational opportunities for users
- full-proof self-service
- policy decision to extend the library service
- Leadership Role
- circulating materials for users to train themselves
- effect on space ship
- Robotized material handling

CONCLUSION

It concludes that users preferred agricultural libraries and volunteering and the desire to develop volunteering in importance due to the change of the landscape is quite useful for their better growth and improved library services to them effectively. To develop the trust, confidence, privacy of users and their information to enhance users' access to information to maintain , full use of technology, services, capacity building for better results, save time for users and staff working help to have the code easier to help users access information anywhere and finally support library staff to develop the image of agricultural commodities to meet the library Modernization such as "National Agriculture Information Services" in agriculture will be useful for all community users.

The agricultural graduate, postgraduate students, and research scholars, 20-30 ages and scientist, extension workers and academic staff 28-50 ages are interested in volunteering desires and other library users find information with the help of subordinate desire.

Increase the use of library services to find information for themselves and their own work routines to reduce the amount of ergonomic stress can teach library staff know and in view of this instructions to users as often as possible to how to use self-service for their better development.

REFERENCES

1. Rusbridge, C (1998). Towards the hybrid library. *DLib Magazine* July/ August
2. Sutton, S (1996). Future service models and the convergence of functions: The reference librarian as technician, author and consultant. ***In*** Low, K (ed.) *The Roles of Reference Librarians, Today and Tomorrow,* New York: Haworth Press.
3. Bundy, A.A (1999). Partner in learning and research: The hybrid university library of the 21st century.
4. www.himss.bham.ac.uk/Documents/OfficialDocs/PBSummary.html
5. www.ariadne.ac.uk/issue26
6. www.library.unisa.edu.au/papers/hybrid.htm
7. www.angrau.net
8. www.gbpuat.ac.in
9. www.pau.edu

❑❑❑

Chapter – 18

Digital Rights Management Issues/Copyright Issues

A. A. Abbas Khan

INTRODUCTION

Andries Van Dam of Brown University, USA coined the term electronic book. E-books are print versions of books, which exist in electronic formats and can be read on a machine. The development of e-book started around 1960s by Alan Kay, called the Dyna Book. Stephen King's 'Riding the Bullet' was one of the most popular electronic books available on the web. The electronic documents are easy to access, easy to search, inexpensive and economy in storage. An e-book can be purchased/borrowed, downloaded, and used immediately, whereas to buy a printed book, one must go to a bookshop, or library etc. It can reduce photocopying activities. The concept of Digital library was created based on the electronic documents.

The transfer of ownership of an e-book author is very difficult, whereas such transfer is possible in printed books. It is cheaper and easier for authors to self-publish e-books when compared to printed form. In electronic format there is no hold on licensing. The problems with e-documents are lack of long term access, dependence on the computer, lack of standardization and less permanent. Digital Right Management system is one of the most important development of electronic publishing. It has control over intellectual property. The e-publishers are more concerned about rights. They are offering limited usage for printing, downloading and copying.

DEFINITION

Digital Rights Management (DRM) refers to technologies used by publishers or copyright holders to try to control access to digital data or hardware as well as to restrictions associated with specific instances of digital works.

Digital Rights Management is anti-piracy technology. DRM is used by digital copyright owners who can control access and copy their work. DRM gives programmers the ability in remote controlling people, who can install and duplicate digital files.

Digital rights management involves the description, identification, trading, protection, monitoring and tracking of all forms of rights usages over both tangible and intangible assets including management of rights holders' relationship.

Digital Rights Management is a broad term describing many different technical formats; it always involves some form of digital lock on the file. These locks are called "licensed encryption keys" (intricate mathematical codes) that prevent anyone from using or copying the file. People who pay for these licensed encryption keys are given the unlock codes to use the file for themselves, but are usually prevented from, than sharing that file with other people.

Analog media inevitably loses quality with each copy generation, and in some cases even during normal use, digital files may be copied a number of times with no degradation in the quality of subsequent copies. The advent of personal computers, the ease of ripping media files from CDs or from radio broadcasts, combined with the internet and popular file sharing tools, has made unauthorized dissemination of copies of digital files, often referred to as digital piracy, much easy.

Although technical controls on the reproduction and use of software have been intermittently common since the 1970s, the term DRM has come to primarily mean the use of these measures to control copyrightable artistic content. DRM technologies enable publishers to enforce access policies that not only prevent copyright violations, but also obstruct legal fair use.

E-publishers have adopted various DRM strategies in recent times. A number of television producers have begun demanding implementation of DRM measures to control access to the content of their shows in connection with the popularity of time-shifting digital video recorder systems.

Microsoft's Windows Vista contains a DRM system called the Protected Media Path, which contains Protected User Mode Audio (PUMA). PUMA implements DRM policies on audio.

WHAT IS COPYRIGHT?

The concept of copyright originally excluded from protection of many new communication technologies. From copyright point of view, printed materials have certain advantages over the digital information:

- Print material is permanent and authenticated.
- Its ownership is easy to ascertain
- It facilitates easy identification of piracy or plagiarism
- However, digital information has certain characteristics, which is perhaps easy for copyright infringement.
- Digital information is not permanent
- It is easily amendable to revise, modify without leaving any resemblance to the original.
- Large volumes of data can be copied and stored in different media without difficulty.

ISSUES OF COPYRIGHT

Computer programs generate abstracts and create databases. The programs are copyrightable, but questions do exist who owns the generated text? The idea that machines are capable of intellectual labor is beyond the scope of copyright.

Although there is difference of opinion with respect to originality and treating a database as intellectual property, the contents and their selection, internal coordination between the structural elements, and the arrangement of elements in a database is generally treated as original intellectual work.

Most important problem in the virtual library environment is copyright in cyberspace. Existing copyright laws do not cope up with the technological developments in cyberspace. Many a times there is no clarity whether the content of electronic resources are free or priced.

For the management of digital copyright several projects have been undertaken, such as:

- Electronic Copyright Management System (ECMS)
- Copyright in Transmitted Electronic Documents (CITED)
- Copyright Ownership in Computer Assisted Training (COPICAT)

DRM AND DOCUMENTS

Enterprise Digital Rights Management (E-DRM or ERM) is the application of DRM technology to control access to corporate documents such as Microsoft Word, PDF, and AutoCAD files, emails and internet web pages rather than to the control of consumer media. E-DRM is generally intended to prevent the unauthorized use of proprietary documents. E-DRM typically integrates with content management system software.

DRM STANDARDS

There are no industry-wide standards for DRM. At this point, many companies in the digital entertainment sector are opting for the crude approach in which users can't copy, print, alter or transfer material. The area of concern regarding DRM is the fact that current DRM trends surpass the protections afforded under traditional copyright law. Libraries and educational institutions that archive and lend digital content have a lot to lose, if highly restrictive DRM software becomes the norm.

A library can't archive a piece of software with a time-limited encryption key, and it can't lend out a machine-specific license for viewing content using its traditional lending structure.

Under copyright law, the fair use doctrine gives a consumer the right to make copies of copyrighted content for their own use. Other doctrines like "first sale," the right of a content purchaser to resell or give away the content he has purchased, and " limited term," the expiration of a copyright after a certain period of time, also afford consumers rights that fall by the wayside in DRM implementation.

The arguments against digital rights management issues are user privacy, technological innovation and fair use.

Berry Sign

It is a sign language video dictionary that contains American Sign Language (ASL) signs, finger spelled words, and other common signs are called Berry Sign.

Docket Number

A court clerk keeps track of cases by using a system known as a docket. Each new case is assigned a number, which it carries for as long as it takes to be resolved. This "docket number" is often abbreviated "docket no." and provides a key to finding out what is happening in a particular case.

SIGNATURE METHODS: DIGITAL SIGNATURE

The digital signature method involves encryption and decryption. Encryption is the standard means of rendering a communication private. The receiver knows the appropriate deciphering function to apply to the received message to obtain the original message. When the message is transmitted the end user hears only garbage which makes no sense, since the end user does not know how to decrypt it. If electronic mail systems are to replace the existing paper mail system for business transactions, signing an electronic message must be possible. The recipient of a signed message has proof that the message originated from the sender. This quality is stronger than mere authentication (where the recipient can verify that the message came from the sender); the recipient can convince a judge that the signer sent the message. To do so, he must convince the judge that he did not forge the signed message himself! In an authentication problem the recipient does not worry about this possibility, since he only wants to satisfy himself that the message came from the sender.

An electronic signature must be message-dependent, as well as signer-dependent. Otherwise the recipient could modify the message before showing the message-signature pair to a judge. Or he could attach the signature to any message whatsoever, since it is impossible to detect electronic "cutting and pasting."

DIGITAL MILLENNIUM COPYRIGHT ACT OF 1998 (DCMA)

The Digital Millennium Copyright Act (DMCA) is an extension to United States copyright law passed unanimously on May 14, 1998, which criminalizes the production and dissemination of technology that allows users to find a way for technical copy-restriction methods. Under the Act, finding a way for technological measure that effectively controls access to a work is illegal, if done with the primary intention of violating the rights of copyright holders.

DCMA ensures the protection of a DRM scheme regardless of whether or not it respects the fair use doctrine. It's not only illegal to get around DRM, but it's also illegal to create, purchase or download any product that enables you to bypass DRM restrictions. Consumer rights' groups are lobbying Congress to amend the section of the Digital Millennium Copyright Act that makes disabling a DRM system against the law, claiming that it gives an improper advantage to copyright holders by not placing limits on the type of DRM schemes they can employ. In essence, according to some, the DCMA encourages anti-competitiveness and makes it increasingly difficult for consumers to easily enjoy their entertainment

The DMCA has been largely ineffective in protecting DRM systems, as software allowing users to circumvent DRM remains readily available over the Internet. However, those with an interest in preserving the DRM systems have attempted to use the Act to restrict the distribution and development of such software.

DRM has been used by organizations such as the British Library in its secure electronic delivery service to permit worldwide access to substantial number of rare documents, which, for legal reasons, were previously only available to authorized individuals.

India's Copyright Act was established in 1857 and was most recently amended in 2010. In the Copyright Bill 2010 there are two proposed provisions to prevent anti circumvention of DMR technologies, and one provision that clarifies what is a DMR technology. The protection of rights management information, suggesting that "Any person who circumvents an effective technological measure applied for the purpose of protecting any of the rights conferred by this Act, with the intention of infringing such rights, shall be punishable with imprisonment which may extend to two years and shall also be liable to fine." Breaking DRM was not prohibited as long as it was encryption research using a lawfully obtained encrypted copy or conducting any lawful investigation or testing the security of a computer system or network, surveillance or identification of a user or for national security.

The idea of DRM is to provide technical means to assure that the creators of content such as artistic works maintain appropriate control of their work, including the ability to obtain compensation for their creative investment. This becomes controversial because of three main factors: the traditions and culture of the web which include free and open access to all information; unintended consequences of DRM in limiting the fair use of legitimately acquired digital media in ways traditionally not restricted in other media and concerns that DRM schemes enormously complicate and may prevent effective archive management and historical research.

HOW DRM WORKS

DRM is a cryptographic system. The medium protected by DRM is encoded in some way to prevent it from being played without the consent of the DRM system. In practical terms, this means that it must be encrypted. A traditional cryptographic system involves sending a message from one person to another without an attacker being able to intercept the message. In the case of DRM, the recipient of the message and the attacker are the same person.

The advent of magnetic tape as a recording medium began to change things, primarily after blank micro-cassettes went on sale. Some recording industry executives took issue with people duplicating cassette tapes, but soon they had bigger problems to worry about — especially when CDs arrived and sound became digital. CD burners allowed people to rip music off of CDs and onto personal computers. Added to this the Internet and peer-to-peer sites (P2P) to the equation, and record executives really started to worry. People were suddenly able to duplicate and share music with end number of users over the Internet, giving many the chances to download songs, albums, even entire discographies without paying a dime. With the value of music changing so rapidly, how would the music industry react?

Soon, record companies began selling "special" music CDs to consumers who were getting ordinary compact discs. When people played these CDs on their computers, it was found to be spyware nightmare, i.e., Programs froze up, applications slowed and a series of hidden files that were the source of the problem proved to be nearly impossible to uninstall.

The digital revolution that has empowered consumers to use digital content in new and innovative ways has also made it impossible for copyright holders to control the distribution of their property. It's not just music, but film, video games and any other media that can be digitized and passed around. **Digital rights management,** or **DRM,** is a general term used to describe any type of technology that aims to stop, or at least ease, the practice of piracy.

DIGITAL RIGHTS MANAGEMENT (DRM): LEGAL ISSUES

DRM has some interesting legal aspects. In many countries, including the USA, copyright includes the principle of fair use. Wholesale copying of a copyrighted work is not permitted without the owner's consent, but limited quoting is allowed. DRM can prevent this.

Inserting a clip from a song into a documentary about music, for example, would usually be considered fair use. Another example comes from the doctrine of first sale. This means that if we have purchased a license to a copyrighted work, we have the right to sell that license to someone else.

Because many Digital Rights Management works cannot be resold, their resale value is effectively zero. If we buy a CD, and later decide we don't like the artist, we can sell (or give) it to someone. If we buy a Digital Rights Management - encumbered version of the same album, however, we can resell it only if the original vendor or Digital Rights Management author decides to allow resale.

It's worth noting that content creators rarely drive technical innovation. Historically, the phonographic and film industries have fought to try to ban the player piano, radio, audiocassette recorders, video recorders, and online music distribution.

DRM OPPONENTS

Many organizations, prominent individuals, and computer scientists are opposed to DRM. They consider "digital rights management' to be a misnomer. They argue that DRM manages rights, the same way prison manages freedom. A common alternative is "digital restrictions management". The use of DRM may also be a barrier to future historians, since technologies designed to permit data to be read only on particular machines, or with particular keys, or for certain periods may well make future data recovery impossible. DRM opponents argue that the presence of DRM infringes existing private property rights and restricts a range of heretofore normal and legal user activities.

A DRM opponent would control a device, a user owns by restricting how it may act with regards to certain content, over-riding some of the wishes. An example of this effect may be seen in Microsoft's Windows Vista operating system in which content is disabled or degraded depending on the DRM scheme's evaluation of whether the hardware and its use are 'secure'. All forms of DRM enabled device like Computer, DVD player, TV, etc. imposing restrictions that cannot be disabled or modified by the user.

CONCLUSION

In the face of technological development, the present copyright laws will not be able to prevent piracy or infringement of rights. The digital environment is to be tightened to assure the creators, prevent piracy and plagiarism, and encourage use. The copyright laws should help in enhancing and not preventing access and usage of electronic information.

Strictly implementing a working Digital Rights Management system is difficult. Digital Rights Management systems impose significant constraints on their users. As the systems become more advanced, these constraints become greater and the illegal version becomes more and more attractive. It is difficult to imagine a situation in which Digital Rights Management has any positive benefits for the content creators, the technical innovators, or society as a whole in the long term. There is a need for research into all the aspects of DRM from the creator and user point of view.

REFERENCES

1. Fernandez, Ben, Digital content protection and fair use: what's the use? Retrieved 19 May 2011, from the World Wide Web: http://www.jthtl.org/content/ articles/
2. Hickok, Elonnai. Privacy and the Indian Copyright Act, 1857 as Amended in 2010, in Blog — Aug 20, 2010 09:30 AM , Retrieved 27 July 2011 from the World Wide web : http://www.cis-india.org/advocacy/ipr/blog/copyright-privacy
3. Iannella,, Renato. Open E-book Digital Rights Management Standards, Open Publish 2001, 30 July- 2 August 2001. Sydney, Australia, Retrieved 1st June 2011, from the World Wide Web http: //www.iprsystems.com
4. Layton, Julia, How Digital Rights Management Works, Retrieved 19 March 2011, from the World Wide Web : http://computer.howstuffworks.com/drm.htm
5. Rajeev Kumar (2003). Electronic books and their academic use: an overview, *University News* 41(13), pp. 1-4
6. Rivest, R.L; Shamir, A and Adleman, L. A Method for Obtaining Digital Signatures and Public-Key Cryptosystems, Retrieved 15 March 2011, from the World Wide Web: http://securespeech.cs.cmu.edu/reports/RSA.pdf

❑❑❑

Chapter - 19

Role of Digital Library in E-Learning: Concept and Challenges

N.P. Ravi Kumar and M. Sandhya

INTRODUCTION

The Digital Library concept has evolved to provide solutions for storage, access, dissemination, content delivery and it paved way to mobile library, as we can browse and share content while on the move. Information and Communication Technology (ICT) has given a new shape to the learning process, which includes reading, understanding and gaining information, which becomes knowledge. As the type of format of information changed from written to e-format, libraries assumed the role of digital libraries.

The library is a place which holds the information resources in print and digital formats. The concept of digital library is a major success as it came out of closed four walls of library and reached readers in their home, workplace and even while traveling, with the help of mobile electronic gadgets like laptop, palmtop, e-Book reader etc. e-Learning technology is a wonderful gift provided by the present day technological advancement and innovations. *e-Learning is the convergence of learning and the Internet'* and it has brought about profound changes around the globe in the way people learn and train, allowing them to do it anywhere, any time. Through the World Wide Web the users can access e-content from any point, off or in campus, through a computer and connectivity.

e-LEARNING : MEANING & DEFINITION

E-learning is defined as an interactive learning in which the learning content is available in electronic format or on-line and provides support to the learning activities. e-Learning covers a wide set of applications and processes, such as web-based learning, computer based learning, virtual class rooms, and digital collaboration. It includes the delivery of content via Internet, intranet/ extranet, satellite broadcast, interactive television, CD-ROM, DVD, audio and videotape, etc. E-learning can be defined as instructional content or learning experiences delivered or enabled by electronic technology. It is a structured, interactive approach to educating and informing the students/learners of formal and informal education.

MEANING

"Online Education or E-Learning refers to any form of learning/teaching that takes place via a computer network. Network can be of any form, viz. LAN, WAN, MAN or WWW".

"E-Learning refers to the use of Internet technologies to deliver a broad array of solutions that enhance knowledge and performance".

e-LEARNING - CONCEPT

The present day libraries are not mere store houses of books, the modern library with the explosion of information technology has lead to paperless society. The traditional libraries occupy more space and require lot of supporting resources, but the alternative is to digitize the collection which occupies less space and instant access from any time any where. Digital and Virtual libraries has opened up electronic information and the users want that information in a refined manner. As the world is contracting and time is reducing, human being wants more information in less time. Internet has come as boon at such a time. As far as teaching and learning is concerned, educators and students, both find it difficult to take out time from their busy schedules to meet and spend time at a place like classroom. Here Internet brings in picture "Online Learning" or "E-learning". Online education is becoming increasingly common in schools, colleges, and the training realm.

e-LEARNING - ROLE OF DIGITAL LIBRARY

Digital libraries are set of electronic resources and associated technical capabilities of creating, storing, searching and dissemination of information. Digital libraries are playing a vital role in online learning education system. Most of the digital libraries are dedicated to support higher education and research and they justify their investment in digital development as a powerful means of realizing the larger institutional goals of the academic community they serve. According to Gary Marchionini (1995), digital libraries serve three roles in the learning process-

- Sharing valuable resources Digital library plays a vital role by allowing several information seekers to access documents simultaneously regardless of their physical location.
- Preserving and organizing artifacts and ideas million books project is a live example of a digital library serving for preserving old artifacts of intellectual importance by archiving their soft copies. The material is digitized with the help of scanning devices.
- Bringing people and ideas together Digital libraries offer diverse information resources shared by groups of learners irrespective of physical space and time.

ADVANTAGES OF E-LEARNING THROUGH DIGITAL LIBRARIES

Digital libraries are set of electronic resources and associated technical capabilities of creating, storing, searching and dissemination of information. Digital libraries are playing an imperative role in online learning education system. Most of the digital libraries are dedicated to supporting higher education and research and they justify their investment in digital development as a powerful means of realizing the larger institutional goals of the academic community they serve.

The reason for using digital libraries in e-Learning is that it can store and manage huge amounts of digital content or databases. Thus it brings together collections, services and people to fulfill the life cycle of creation, dissemination and preservation of data, information and knowledge. By using various electronic tools, learners can search text materials and images easily and quickly which can be applied in all kinds of institutions. Advance inter-communication technology, sophisticated search engines, with an affordable cost, large storage of digital content are the other reasons to implement a digital library in modern education. Other advantages of digital libraries in e-Learning are:

- Full text digital resources contained in a digital library database can be directly linked to its e-learning module. Efficient Digital Library software provides ability to identify access, evaluate, organize and communicate information and knowledge.
- Digital library of an organization or institute is Intranet based, thus providing a readymade framework for e-learning.
- Digital library provides a platform for all information seekers to user interaction, and provides facility for dual role of user as both teacher and learner.
- The library would allow learner to use electronic resources from anywhere, without even knowing where it is stored geographically.

- One copy of the document could be viewed by any number of users simultaneously.
- Study materials need never go out of print, and new editions can easily be created. One can carry several titles at once on a portable reader and, over time, build a personal library.
- It provides faster learning, increased access, clear accountability and equal education for every body; the web is available on the desktop.
- It would be easy for non-specialist to use due to the simplicity of operation.
- Provide links to publisher's web sites for full text journals and books .
- It facilitates online enrolment in study and examinations.
- Search result will be delivered to an e-mail box to the user's choice.
- Protecting rare books that are rapidly deteriorating due to over use and poor storage conditions.
- It is cost effective and cost-efficient for its ability of reuse.
- It provides current information and helps in research work.
- It can be used for increasing course delivery for a large number of clients at any particular point of time.

CREATING E-LEARNING STRATEGY

Implementation of E-learning in an organization needs a well framed strategy and sophisticated technologies. To develop an e-learning module we need to plan on various levels like technology level, policy level and organizational level.

Marc J. Rosenberg, in his book "e-Learning: Strategies for Delivering Knowledge in the Digital Age" has described in detail the various viewpoints required while planning e-learning for an organization. Following are few of the necessary steps for developing an E-learning strategy:

PARTICIPANTS

First and foremost we should identify who all should participate in strategy development. People who should be involved at initial level should include training managers, developers, instructors and administrators. In the second stage all prospective clients like students, organizations (if the project is big one), sponsors and other stakeholders like senior managers should be involved. On the basis of the compiled result of these two discussed stages, IT department should be included to discuss technical aspects. Once whole strategy is clear a small task force should be used further.

CURRENT SITUATION

The first step after identifying all participants is to fully analyze the current situation as it pertains to the ability to launch and sustain e-learning. It includes identifying main objectives of your organization, current state of your overall learning and development efforts, and analyzing how much support you will get from the administration.

DESIRED SITUATION

A vision statement describes a future state as if it were the present. It's more about how you will be recognized and valued internally and through the eyes of your users. Once you agree-upon vision, develop a mission statement, i.e., what will you do to achieve your vision.

- Identify what are the best practices in learning and development, and e-learning.
- What should be your e-learning value proposition?
- Building a vision and mission for learning and development.
- What principles are most important to you in guiding how you will implement your mission and realize your vision?
- How learning and e-learning are defined by you and your organization?
- The support you receive from top management

GAP ANALYSIS

Create detailed specifications of the key disparities between the current and desired situation, along with associated descriptions of root causes.

SWOT ANALYSIS

A SWOT analysis looks at the entire organization to determine its strengths, weaknesses, opportunities and threats, either at the moment or at some future point in time.

ACTION PLAN

Prepare an action plan to implement e-learning on the basis of the findings of the till now done research and studies. This is where the specific tactics are described in enough detail so everyone knows what needs to be done. At this stage

- Identify critical success factors.
- Set and stick to timeliness and milestones.
- Provide adequate funding for implementation.

- Define and implement a change management plan.
- Define and implement a communications plan

CHALLENGES FACED BY THE E-LEARNERS

The development of E-learning has thrown up new problems focused on the copyright implications of electronic text. Students, researchers, staff, employees and other end users affiliated with virtual university or digital libraries should be allowed to print-on-paper excerpts of digitally available works on the same conditions according to which they may make photocopies of print material. The authorities of universities/libraries should take initiative to evolve some solution on this aspect and which may benefit learners, publishers as well as authors.

MAJOR CHALLENGES/ISSUES:

1. There is no mechanism available to establish standards for internet materials, instruction, design and quality of interaction.? Study materials are accessible only by specified students, licensing problems are unlikely to be serious barrier.
2. Since course materials are instructionally designed, it hardly provides for individual variations and further revision.
3. Dangers of increased learner isolation as students learn from the screen, and not through much interaction with their peers and teachers.
4. Crossing national boundaries creates logistical and organizational problems of distance teaching institutions.
5. Operating overseas can also expose one to the all problems of any international business, exchange rate fluctuations, restriction on foreign exchange, and the export of money from the country of operation to pay for services, sources from another jurisdiction, political turmoil, civil unrest and war etc.
6. Information providers are more interested in profit than quality services.
7. Lack of organization of information on Internet.
8. Not all sites are updated regularly.
9. Absence of monitoring mechanism to evaluate the course ware
10. Lack of awareness about the use of electronic equipment.
11. Access to Internet in developing countries may not be easy or widespread, in comparison to the developed countries.

CONCLUSION

Electronic documents offer possibilities for expanding access as well as changing learning behavior and academic research trends. Content can always be accessible, regardless of time or place to be read on PCs. The role of digital libraries in distance learning is still not clear in the country like India. The INFLIBNET has already started networking of different university libraries; on its completion it will be possible to share all available resources for imparting E-learning to far distant places in the country. Digital libraries have proved themselves not only as effective electronic repositories of knowledge and information, but also as effective communication medium between peers and for scholarly discourse. Digital libraries are capable enough to provide an information rich platform to both instructors and students to teach, learn and share knowledge. Thus in future we will witness major role of Digital Libraries in online learning or as we call it "e-learning".

REFERENCES

1. Allan, and Barbara (2002). E-Learning and teaching in library and information services. London : Facet publishing.
2. Debanshu, Karmakar and Suman, S (2002). E-Learning Trends of CMS and the role of Digital Libraries .Workshop on Information Resource Management, DRTC, Bangalore.
3. Gill, S.S. and Dabas, K.C. (1998). Digital Library : Its emergence and challenges. *INFLIBNET: Caliber*, Bhuvaneswar, pp. 348-351.
4. Girish Kumar, P and Abedin, Sainul (2000).. Content management for E- Learning in Digital Libraries. *IN IASLIC.*
5. http://www.aazad.com/abdul-kalam.html *http://www.abdi.org/conf-seminar-papers/2004/10/13/692*
6. Jayaprakash, A and Venkatramana, R (2006). Role of Digital Libraries in E-Learning. DRTC Conference on ICT for Digital Learning Environmnet, DRTC, Bangalore.
7. Kant, Ravi. E-learning program in India.
8. Prachi Singh (2005). Role of Digital Libraries in E-Learning. 3rd International CALIBER, INFLIBNET, Ahmedabad.
9. Rathinasabapathy, G. (2005). E-Learning and E-content development opportunities in library and information science. *XXII IATLIS National Conference*, Tiruchirapalli.
10. Rosenberg, Marc J. e-Learning: Strategies for Delivering Knowledge in the Digital Age. New York: McGraw-Hill, pp. 20-30 & 291-303.

11. Rosenberg, Marc Jeffery (2001). E-learning: Strategies for delivering knowledge in the digital age. McGraw Hill.

12. Schank, Roger C. Designing World-Class E-Learning: How IBM, GE, Harvard Business School, and Columbia University are succeeding at e-Learning. New York: McGraw-Hill, pp. 187-188.

❑❑❑

Chapter – 20

Safeguarding Digital Library Materials: A Study

M. Tholkappian, M. Suresh Babu, Doraswamy Naick and D. Chandran

INTRODUCTION

Libraries are social institutions bestowed with the responsibility of storing preserving the cultural heritage of accounting and making them available for use to the community. The inherent characteristics of artifacts, the storage conditions and the type; intensity and amount of the processes of monitoring the physical condition of the library's materials and taking action to prevent future deterioration are critical issues. Preservation issues can be defined as those that relate to the longevity of materials, while conservation issues include handling and storage. Ironically, books published since the beginning of the 20th century are more likely to decay than the older books. Other modern materials such as microfilm, photographs, videotapes, and films have unique preservation need.

DIGITAL PRESERVATION

Digital preservation means taking steps to ensure the longevity of the electronic document in terms of the following.

- Data text, image, video or audio stored in variety of formats and standards)
- Index to the data

- Link to other data
- Metadata
- Software (relies upon hardware and operating system)
- Storage medium, etc

Hence, in preservation of digital objects the following measures are taken into account

- Integrity of digital materials
- The physical presence
- The preservation format
- The digital materials functionality
- The location and reference of digital materials
- The authenticity of that materials
- The context of preserved materials
- The provenance

There are three distinct but not mutually exclusive preservation applications of digital technologies, defined in part by the possible purposes that the product may serve for end users.

- Protect originals
- Represent originals
- Transcend originals

STANDARDS FOR DIGITAL PRESERVATION

For preservation of digital document / information over time, the following types of standards are mentioned (Dempsey; 1998)

Standards for Architecture

In a distributed digital environment the management of digital collection cannot be the responsibility of just one central organization. In such an environment it is important to agree on concepts, definition and procedures. For this there are several standards for records management architecture.

- ISO / DIS 15489
- AS 4390
- DOD 5015.2-STD
- OAIS (Open Archived Information System)

Standards for Preservation Content

Standards for preservation content should be depending upon ageing process of the semantic and physical recoverability of the document that is being preserved. A standard can only provide such longevity when the standard itself does not change and backward compatibility is provided. Therefore for future preservation, standard should be slected depending upon the technical obsolesce. More often XML and put forward as two rivals to preserve a document for long – term preservation (Hage: 2002)

- PDF (Portable Document Format)
- XML (Extensible Markup Language)

Standards for Preservation Access

Preservation of the bit-stream of the document in some standard format is not enough to preserve a digital document over an indefinite period of time. So, it is necessary for the description of the digital, objective of various parts into one object means file/formats stored in different physical places in the information system, and by linked by cross references. Such types of description are called metadata , which include the contextual infoamtion to mange, retrieve and interpret the electronic information over time (Dempsey 1998)

Metadata for preservation and access carried out in different projects much as CEDEARS or PANDORA or NEDLIB or by RLG. The infoamtion involved in long term preservation metadata gives information about both preserved document and information about the data processes of the digital objectives that are to be preserved by information about format name strucute, application etc. (Lupvici and Masanes ;2000). There are several existing metadata schemes that have been standardized, each having some specific goal.

- Dublin core
- MARC
- ISBD
- Z39.50

Standards for Interoperability

Interoperability is the ability of multiple systems with different hardware / software platform, data structure, and interface to exchange data with minimum loss of content and functionality (understanding metadata). Therefore Interoperability is a critical problem in the network environment with increase of diverse computer systems software applications, file formats, information and users. But, it is important for digital preservation in digital library and archives. In fact digital conservation of traditional print based resources and standards pertaining to Interoperability are very so important.

- ODMA (Open Document Management Application)
- DMA (Document Management Alliance)
- Web Dav (World Wide Web Distributed Authoring and Versioning)

CONCLUSION

Preservation of traditional library materials needs lot of care in terms of material shelving, handing and managing the environment. But in the case of preserving electronic digital materials the management of libraries are forced to think about different period options and strategies. Long term preservation of the content and its access for indefinite period of time has a lot of requirement concerning content, law, organization and techniques, etc. These standards and strategy have ensured the slow down of ageing process of the digital materials.

Like rapid growth of digital objects, standards and format are also proliferating. It creates a messy situation to choose standards for digital preservation. Therefore, in order to facilitate digital preservation in standardized way it is necessary to merge groups of standards into specific "standards domain" and this will provide domain communication, acceptance and use of such groups of standards (Lorist:2002). Such "domain" standards would facilitate interoperability among the discrete storehouses of digital information .

REFERENCES

1. Conway, Paul. (1994). Digital Preservation: paper and Mircofilms Go Electronic. *Library Journa*l 119, pp.42-45
2. Conway, Paul. (1994). The implication of Digital imaging for preservation, in Preservation of Library and Archival Materials. 2nd Edited by Sherelyn Ogden Andover AM: Northest Document Conservation Center Technical Services, 40, pp. 67-77
3. Dempsy, L. etal. (1998). e – lib standards guidelines, version 2. http://www.ukoln.ac.uk/ services/elib/paper/ other/standards/version2
4. Lorist, J (2002). Standards for digital libraries and archives : digital longevity.
5. Lupvici, C and Masanes, J (2002). Metadata for long–term preservation. http://www.kb.nl/ loop/nedlib/result/

❑❑❑

Chapter - 21

Metadata Encoding And Transmission Standards (METS) in Digital Libraries : Indian Scenario

K. Kumar, D. Konappa and D. Chandran

INTRODUCTION

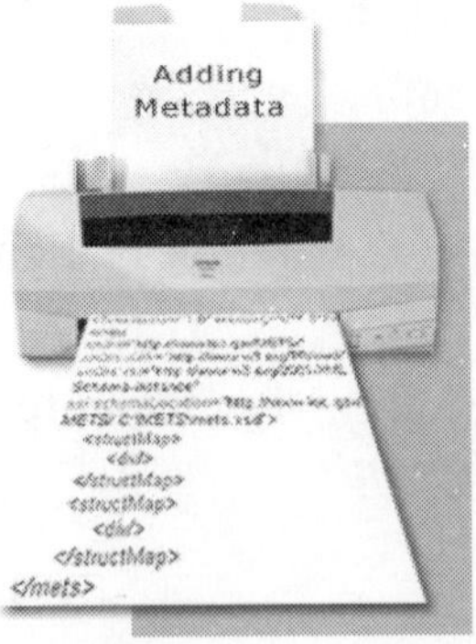

Digital resources are growing at an exponential rate and uncountable stacks of resources are available on the web. Semantic based search engines and meta-search engines stimulate resource discovery on digital collections[1]. During recent years an increasing quantity and variety of digital material has been created or held by libraries, and consequently many standards have been developed to encode different catego-ries of metadata for specific object types. Metadata today is an essential phenomenon for electronic cataloguing, federated searching, and open URLs. Selecting metadata is perceived to be essential for the librarians in pursuing long-term management and preservation of digital objects in digital library. Metadata is also important for digital archivists, database developers, resource authors, web-page designers, aggregators, system designers, as well as seekers of electronic information. In fact, metadata is inevitable for digital resource management and for discovering information from a large distributed environment. Metadata is expected to improve matching by standardizing the structure[2] and content of indexing or cataloguing information. The Metadata Encoding and Transmission Standards (METS) were developed to deal with diverse metadata is-sues. It is an XML Schema designed as an overall framework[3] within which all the metadata associ-ated with a single digital object can be stored or referred to. It enables effective management of digital objects within the repository; acts as a standard for transferring metadata within repositor-ies, facilitates access and navigation by the researcher, and links the digital object and its meta-data inextricably together.

REVIEW OF LITERATURE

METS – International Scenario

Morgan (2004)[4] in his research paper provides an overview of the METS. The article is very useful for librarians and technical staff who are encountering METS for the first time. The article contains a brief history of the development of METS, a primer covering the basic structure and contents of METS documents, and a discussion of several issues relevant to the implementation and continuing development of METS including object models, extension schema, and application profiles. **Michael Day (2005)**[5] discusses the increasingly important role of metadata for digital curation, some practical applications for metadata, issues of interoperability between metadata schemas, the topic's place within the OAIS reference model and the issues associated with preservation metadata. **Peter Cao (2006)**[6] discusses three issues related to implementation of a HDF5 Archival Information Package (AIP) in METS file viz extracting metadata from a HDF5 (Hierarchical Data Format) file; organizing the metadata and creating a tool to generate metadata from the HDF5 AIP. According to **Rebecca S.Guenther (2008)**[7] many institutions use METS to implement metadata in digital library application, and adds that many implementers of PREMIS are looking at METS as a container to include PREMIS metadata along with other information about and links to the digital objects. **Angela Dappert and Markus Enders (2009)**[8] reports on the use of METS structure, PREMIS Preservation and MODS descriptive metadata for the British Library's e-journal system. **Mc Donough, Jerome. P (2009)**[9] examines the Metadata Encoding and Transmission Standards (METS) and the issues that arise when trying to map from a localized structural metadata schema into the OAI-ORE data model and serialization syntaxes.

METS - Indian Scenario

M. G. Sreekumar (2005)[10] reports the experience of IIMK (Indian Institute of Management, Kozhikode) in setting up a multimedia digital library using the open source Greenstone digital library software, He suggests that multimedia digital libraries indeed require the strong footings of RDF (Resource Description Framework) supplemented with descriptive metadata standards such as METS or MODS. **Biswajit Saha (2006)** [11] suggests that new metadata sets can be defined using Greenstone's metadata set editors. He adds that "plug-ins" is used to ingest forms and plug-ins exists for XML, MARC and METS. The author states that based on the OAIS (Open Archival Information System) ISO standards and utilizing the METS, the digital archive brings context, accessibility and longevity to the fast shifting and often ephemeral world of digital assets. **Ajay Kumar et al (2008)**[12] have tried to present the Indian scenario of the Institutional Repositories. They discuss about the softwares that are easily available to create and maintain institutional repositories. They have stated that Greenstone software produced by the New Zealand Digital Library Project at University of Waitako and developed and distributed in cooperation with UNESCO and the Human Info: An NGO (http://www.greenstone.org) software. Apart from serving and harvesting documents and collections over OAI-PHM, the collections may also be exported to or imported from METS. **Devika and Dimple (2009)**[13] discuss various issues involved in Indian languages computing, particularly Telugu, like creating, displaying, searching and retrieving digital content. The authors stress the importance of presenting grammar, syntax and morphology of Indian language while creating metadata in Indian languages.

WHAT IS METADATA ENCODING AND TRANSMISSION STANDARD (METS)?

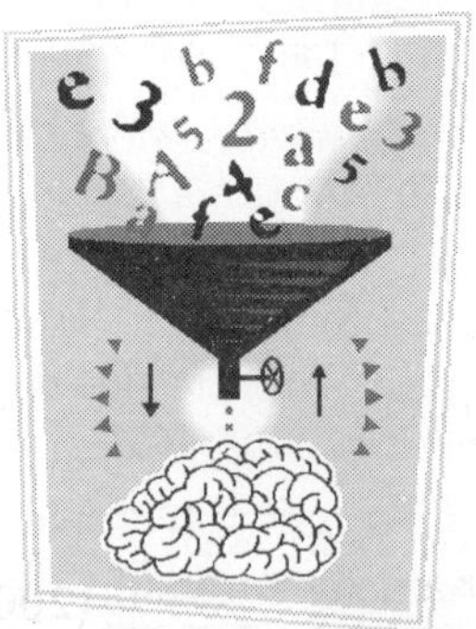

In the late 1990s a digitization initiative called the Making of America II (MOA2) Tested Project identified categories for descriptive, structural and administrative metadata[14] types. An XML Docu-ment Type Definition (DTD) was developed for the project. In 2001, this DTD was reviewed and re-vised under the sponsorship of the Digital Library Federation; the outcome was Version 1.0 of the METS XML Schema, which inherited the broad metadata structure set out by the MOA2 project. The Library of Congress is the maintenance agency for METS[15]. does not include descriptive metadata. However, it can accommodate any transmitting and or exchanging digital objects. It forms a standard basis descriptive metadata schema like Dublin Core, VRA Core etc. In brief, METS is a standard for providing end users with the ability to view and navigate digital content and its associated metadata. It is governed by the METS Editorial Board, which also promotes the standard, endorses best practice and supports the METS com-munity. The standard has been widely practice and supports the METS com-munity. The standard has been widely adopted by institutions and projects worldwide. The METS Imple-mentation Registry[16] contains information about METS projects both planned, in progress and fully implemented, which have been registered with the METS Board. The metadata necessary for successful management and use of digital objects is both more extensive than and different from the metadata used for managing collections of printed works and other physical materials.

CREATING METS FOR DIGITAL LIBRARY

The METS schema provides a flexible mechanism for encoding descriptive, administrative, and structural metadata for a digital library object, and for expressing the complex links between the various forms of metadata. It makes available a useful standard for the exchange of digital library objects between repositories. In addition, METS provides the ability to associate a digital object with behaviors or services. The figure 1 illustrated below highlights the major features of the schema, but a thorough examination of the schema[17] and its included documentation is necessary to understand the full range of its capabilities.

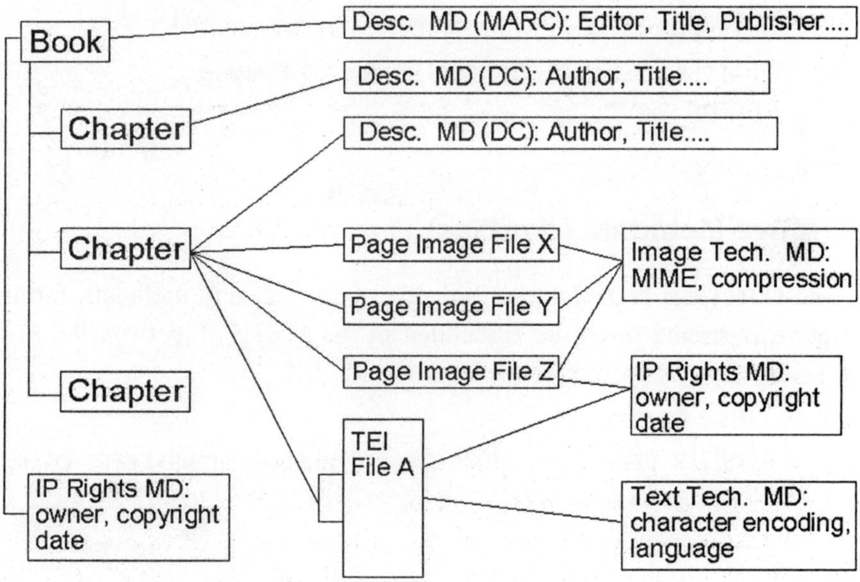

Figure 1: Structure of METS

COMPONENTS OF METS

A METS document contains seven[18] major sections, which are mentioned in figure 2:

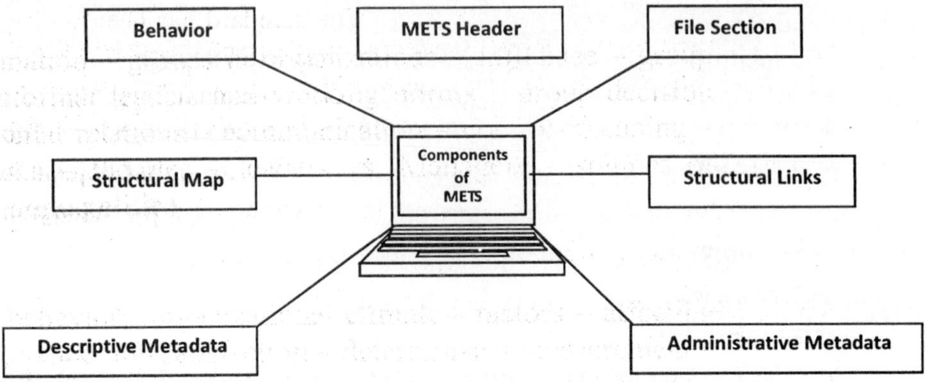

Figure 2: Components of METS

Header (*metsHdr*)

Contains metadata describing the METS[19] document itself, including such information as creator, editor, etc.

```
<METS:metsHdr ID="BOOK1" CREATEDATE="2010-12-20T06:32:00"
    LASTMODDATE="2010-12-20T06:32:00" RECORDSTATUS="A">
    <METS:agent>ROLE="CREATOR" TYPE="ORGANIZATION">
        <METS:name>University Digital Library</METS:name>
    </METS:agent>
</METS:metsHdr>
```

Descriptive Metadata (*dmdSec*)

One or several records describing the work - in any metadata format. Descriptive metadata might be embedded in the METS object (*mdWrap*) or stored externally and pointed to (*mdRef*).

```
<METS:dmdSec ID="DMD1">
    <mdRef LOCTYPE="URL" MIMETYPE="application/xml" MDTYPE="OTHER"
        LABEL="MAB record"></mdRef>
        </METS:dmdSec>
<METS:dmdSec ID="DMD2">
  <mdWrap MIMETYPE="application/mab" MDTYPE="OTHER" LABEL="MAB
Record">
  <binData>
00471nM2.01010024           h001 66230�002 19941207000000.0�003
20070608000000.0�030 zz5d||rz||||7�050 |||||||||||||�051 n||||||�077 �c0�100
```

```
Oertel, Christian Gottfried�331 VollstÉandiges corpus gravaminum evangelicorum�359 An das Licht gestellet von Christian Gottfried Oertel�410aRegensburg�412aNeubauer �501 Erschienen: 1 (1771) - [8] (1775). -Bd. [8] im Verl. Montag, Regensburg, erschienen �710 Corpus Evangelicorum / Gravamen�902 |Corpus Evangelicorum�902 |Gravamen��
            </binData>
        </mdWrap>
</METS:dmdSec>
<METS:dmdSec ID="DMD3">
        <mdWrap MIMETYPE="text/xml" MDTYPE="DC" LABEL=" METS Metadata">
          <xmlData>
            <dc:title>Vollständiges corpus gravaminum evangelicorum</dc:title>
            <dc:creator>Oertel, Christian Gottfried</dc:creator>
            <dc:date>1 (1771) - [8] (1775)</dc:date>
            <dc:publisher>Montag, Regensburg</dc:publisher>
            <dc:type>text</dc:type>
          </xmlData>
        </mdWrap>
</METS:dmdSec>
```

Administrative Metadata (*amdSec*)

A group of administrative metadata accessible for a METS document and/or its components. This can be:

- Technical metadata: information regarding the file, e.g. compression, bit depth, etc.
- IPR metadata: copyright and/or license statement.
- Source metadata: "expressive and organizational metadata regarding the analog source from which a digital library[20] object derives".
- Digital attribution metadata: "information regarding source/destination relationships between files".

Again, the information can be embedded (*mdWrap*) or just pointed to (*mdRef*).

```
<METS:amdSec>
    <METS:techMD ID="TMD1">
        <METS:mdWrap MDTYPE="OTHER" MIMETYPE="text/xml"
        OTHERMDTYPE= "TECHMD">
```

```
<METS:xmlData>
<techmd:compression NAME="LZW"/>
<techmd:image>
<techmd:bitDepth>24</techmd:bitDepth>
<techmd:storage PLANARCONFIGURATION="UNKNOWN" SEGMENT=
"STRIP"/>
[......]
</techmd:image>
</METS:xmlData>
</METS:mdWrap>
</METS:techMD>
<METS:rightsMD ID="RMD1">
<METS:mdWrap MDTYPE="OTHER" MIMETYPE="text/xml" OTHERMDTYPE=
"RIGHTSMD">
<METS:xmlData>
<rightsmd:versionStatement>Copyright by MPIeR</rightsmd:versionStatement>
</METS:xmlData>
</METS:mdWrap>
</METS:rightsMD>
<METS:rightsMD ID="ADMRTS1">
<METS:mdWrap MDTYPE="OTHER" OTHERMDTYPE="METSRights">
<METS:xmlData>
<rts:RightsDeclarationMD RIGHTSCATEGORY="PUBLIC DOMAIN">
[...]
</rts:RightsDeclarationMD>
</METS:xmlData>
</METS:mdWrap>
</METS:rightsMD>
</METS:amdSec>
```

File List (*fileSec*)

The file list is the inventory of all files which comprise the digital object. This section is not repeatable, thus each file is listed once and then referenced from the structural map. The inventory arranges the files into groups (*fileGrp*), which may represent the hierarchy of the document. Every file element (*file*) may optionally reference descriptive as well as administrative metadata. The content data streams may be referenced (*xlink:href*) or embedded in the METS document.

```
<METS:fileSec>
  <METS:fileGrp ID="DATASTREAMS">
   <METS:fileGrp ID="DS1" USE="MASTER IMAGE">
    <METS:file ID="DS1.0" CREATED="2007-05-20T06:32:00" MIMETYPE="image/tiff" SIZE="8238866"
          ADMID="TMD1 RMD1" DMDID="DMD1" OWNERID="E">
          <METS:FLocat LOCTYPE="URL" xlink:href="http://www.escidoc.mpg.de/virr/12433.tiff"/>
          </METS:file>
          [......]
          </METS:fileGrp>
          <METS:fileGrp ID="DS2" USE="text/tei">
            <METS:file ID="DS2.0" CREATED="2007-10-20T06:32:00" MIMETYPE="text/xml" SIZE="7343"
          ADMID="RMD1" DMDID="DMD1" OWNERID="X">
            <METS:FLocat LOCTYPE="URL"
xlink:href="http://www.escidoc.mpg.de/virrbeame.xml"/>
          </METS:file>
          [.....]
       </METS:fileGrp>
    </METS:fileGrp>
</METS:fileSec>
```

Structural Map (*structMap*)

A representation of the complete object modeled as tree structure. The structural map is the heart of a METS document, defining the hierarchical arrangement of a primary source document which has been digitized. This hierarchy is encoded as a tree of *div* elements. Any given *div* can point to another METS document[21] via the *mptr* element, or to a single file, to a group of files, or to segments of individual files or groups of files through the *fptr* and subsidiary elements." Maps may focus on the physical composition of the digitized work (e.g. book->pages) or the intellectual structure of the work (e.g. book->table of contents->chapter->references, etc.). The type attribute specifies which kind of structural map is provided. The *div* element supports parallel number via the ORDER, ORDERLABEL, and LABEL attributes. "[...] imagine a text with 10 roman numbered pages followed by 10 Arabic numbered pages. Page iii would have an ORDER of '3', an ORDERLABEL of 'iii'; and a LABEL of 'Page iii'; while page 3 would have an ORDER of '13'; an ORDERLABEL of '3'; and a LABEL of 'Page 3'".

```
<METS:structMap TYPE="physical">
  <METS:div TYPE="multiVolume" LABEL="Vollstaendiges corpus gravaminum evangelicorum">
```

```
<METS:div TYPE="book" LABEL="Vollstaendiges corpus gravaminum evangelicorum, Band 1" ORDERLABEL="Band 1" ORDER="1">
    <METS:div TYPE="page" LABEL="Blank page" ORDER="1"></METS:div>
    <METS:div TYPE="page" LABEL="Page i: Half title page" ORDERLABEL="i" ORDER="2">
    <METS:fptr FILEID="DS1.0"/>
    <METS:fptr FILEID="DS2.0"/>
  </METS:div>
  <METS:div TYPE="page" LABEL="Page ii: Blank page" ORDERLABEL="ii" ORDER="3"></METS:div>
    [...]
 </METS:div>
</METS:div>
</METS:structMap>
```

One digitized work may have several structural maps, e.g. one to describe the physical and one to describe the logical structure. The METS Profile used by the DFG Viewer[22]http://colab.mpdl.mpg.de/mediawiki/Metadata_Encoding_and_Transmission_Standard - cite_note-mets_dfg-5 describes both structures independently from each other and connects them via entries in the strucLink section:

```
<METS:structMap TYPE="LOGICAL">
 <METS:div ID="log0000" TYPE="Multivolume" LABEL="Vollstaendiges corpus gravaminum evangelicorum">
 <METS:div ID="log0001" TYPE="Book" LABEL="Vollstaendiges corpus gravaminum evangelicorum, Band 1">
   <METS:div ID="log0002" TYPE="Section" LABEL="Blank pages"/>
   <METS:div ID="log0003" TYPE="Chapter" LABEL="Kapitel 1">
    <METS:div ID="log0004" TYPE="Chapter"/>
   </METS:div>
  </METS:div>
 </METS:div>
</METS:structMap>
<METS:structMap TYPE="PHYSICAL">
 <METS:div ID="phys0000" TYPE="physSequence">
  <METS:div ID="phys0001" TYPE="page" ORDER="1" ORDERLABEL="I">
   <METS:fptr FILEID="DS1.0"/>
  </METS:div>
  <METS:div ID="phys0002" TYPE="page" ORDER="2" ORDERLABEL="II">
   <METS:fptr FILEID="DS2.0"/>
```

```
      </METS:div>
      <METS:div ID="phys0003" TYPE="page" ORDER="3" ORDERLABEL="Seite 1">
        <METS:fptr FILEID="DS2.0"/>
      </METS:div>
      <METS:div ID="phys0004" TYPE="page" ORDER="4" ORDERLABEL="Seite 2">
        <METS:fptr FILEID="DS2.0"/>
      </METS:div>
    </METS:div>
  </METS:structMap>
  <METS:structLink>
    <METS:smLink xlink:from="log_0001" xlink:to="phys_0000"/>
    <METS:smLink xlink:from="log_0002" xlink:to="phys_0001"/>
    <METS:smLink xlink:from="log_0003" xlink:to="phys_0003"/>
    <METS:smLink xlink:from="log_0004" xlink:to="phys_0004"/>
  </METS:structLink>
```

Structural Link (*structLink*)

Allow METS creators to record the nodes in the hierarchy outlined in the Structural Map.

Behaviors

Associates executable behaviors with content in the METS object.

DIGITAL LIBRARIES USING METS IN INDIA

INFLIBNET, the Inter University Centre of UGC under Ministry of HRD has initiated Institutional Repository and archive its publications, proceedings etc using DSpace (DSpace @ INFLIBNET).DSpace[23] is a groundbreaking digital repository system that captures, stores, indexes, preserves, and redistributes an organization's research data. Developed by MIT Libraries & Hewlett-Packard Labs, the DSpace software platform[24] serves a variety of digital archiving needs. Devika P. Madalli (2003) [25] discusses the DSpace digital library software of MIT-HP, and explains the implementation of DSpace to build a digital library of Library and Information Science, where she mentions that METS format is included in DSpace software in version 1.2 and Fedora. DSpace 1.4 includes a package disseminator and matching ingester for the DSpace METS SIP (Submission Information Package) format. They were created to help end users prepare sets of digital resources and metadata[27] for submission to the archive using well-defined standards such as METS, MODS, and PREMIS. The plug-in name is METS by default, and it uses MODS for descriptive metadata. The

DSpace METS SIP profile is available at:http://www.dspace.org/standards/METS/SIP/profilev1p0/met sipv1p0.pdf. configuration of DSpace is represented[26] in Table 1.

Table 1. Configuration of Dspace

Sl.No.	Configuration	Dspace
1	Creator	MIT libraries and Hewlett-Packard
2	Open Source and Free	Yes
3	Operating System	Unices, Linux Windows
4	Language	J2SDK v.1.4
5	Database	Postures 7.3
6	Resource Identifier	CNRI Handles
7	Dublin Core	Qualified Dublin Core
8	**METS**	**Implemented in Version 1.2**
9	OAI-PMH V 2.0	Yes
10	Subscription	No
11	Supported File formats	MS-Word, PDF, PPTs, JPEG, GIF

DSpace software is implemented in various organizations of India in their digital library. As previously mentioned, METS rooted in DSpace software for management of digital objects within the repository. Table 2 outlines various[28] Universities and Institutions using METS standard in their digital libraries.

Table 2. METS Using Universities and Institutions for Digital Library in India

Universities			
S.No	**Name**	**Location**	**URL**
1	Anna University	Chennai	http://www.anna-university.in/
2	Cochin University of Science and Technology	Cochin	http://dspace.cusat.ac.in/dspace/
3	GB Pant University of Agriculture & Technology	Pantnagar	http://www.gbpuat.ac.in
4	Guru Gobind Singh Indraprastha University	Delhi	http://dspace.ipu.ernet.in:8080/
5	Pandit Deendayal Petroleum University,	Gandhinagar	http://203.77.192.116:8080/xmlu
6	Thapar University	Patiala	http://dspace.thapar.edu:8080/dspace
7	University of Hyderabad	Hyderabad	http://www.digilib.uohyd.ernet.in/dspac
8	University of Mumbai	Mumbai	http://mum.digitaluniversity.ac/
9	University of Mysore, Vidyanidhi	Mysore	http://dspace.vidyanidhi.org.in:8080/dspace/
10	University of Sumatera	Utara	repository.usu.ac.id

Contd.

11	Veltech University	Chennai	http://dspace.veltechuniv.edu.in
12	North-Eastern Hill University	Shillong	http://dspace.nehu.ac.in/jspui
Technological Institutions			
13	Indian Institute of Science	Bangalore	http://etd.ncsi.iisc.ernet.in/
14	Indian Institute of Technology	New Delhi	http://eprint.iitd.ac.in/dspace/
15	Indian Institute of Technology	Bombay	http://dspace.library.iitb.ac.in/dspace/
16	Indian Institute of Technology	Allahabad	http://eprint.iita.ac.in/
17	National Institute of Technology,	Rourkela	http://dspace.nitrkl.ac.in/dspace
18	Indira Gandhi Institute of Development Research	Mumbai	http://oii.igidr.ac.in:8888/dspace
19	Vidya Academy of Science & Technology	Kerala.	http://dspace.vidyaacademy.ac.in/
20	Sree Narayana Gurukulam College of Engineering	Kerala.	http://dspace.sngce.ac.in
21	R. K. College of Engineering & Technology	Gujarat	http://www.rkcollege.com/
22	Thejus College Engineering	Kerala.	http://www.thejusengg.com/
23	B N M Institute of Technology	Bangalore	http://www.bnmit.org/placementportal.aspx
24	University Institute of Engineering and Technology	Chandigarh	dspace.uiet.net
25	Federal Institute of Science And Technology	Kerala.	http://www.dspace.fisat.edu:8080/jspui

Figure 3 represented below indicate usage of METS in digital libraries of diverse Universities (30.77%), Technological (33.33%), Management Institutions (23.08%) and Research Centres (12.82%) respectively.

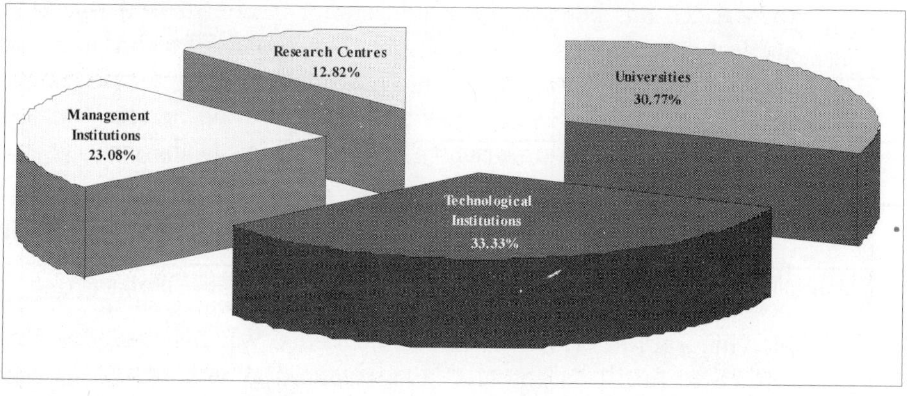

Figure3: Digital Libraries of Educational Institutions Using METS in India

FEATURES OF METS

METS allows

- To point to external descriptive metadata or for including metadata[29] internally. It provides a way for linking this metadata to the digital content of the digital object.
- To link to external administrative metadata or used for with metadata internally. It provides a way for linking this metadata to the digital content of the digital object.
- To specify the structure of a digital object i.e. how the files and parts of files of a digital object are linked.
- To provide a way for linking digital content with external software capable of disseminating that content, as well as an interface file that defines the specific dissemination and the required parameters for each through its behaviors section.

IMPORTANCE OF METS IN DIGITAL LIBRARY

- Digital library technology is now well established, and the number of major collections coming online is increasing daily. Much time has been expended over the last decade in getting to grips with the requirements of imaging technology, and discovering how it may sensibly be applied to library materials. Comparatively little attention, however, has been paid to the needs of metadata, an omission which has resulted in a confusing array of approaches to dealing with this vexed question.
- Often digital library metadata is not up to the standard that is the norm in traditional library cataloguing; no agreed format, analogous to MARC, has been applied, and authority control for names and subject descriptions is often absent. The choice of technology used for digital library projects has often been dictated by the presence of an accepted software package within an institution, and the format of metadata is held in proprietary formats which in the case of older packages may no longer be readable.
- To make effective use of METS and its associated schemas, digital library projects[30] do need to adopt cataloguing rules governing the content of their metadata: AACR2 will in most cases suffice for this, as it incorporates rules for electronic media. What is needed to allow METS to fulfill its potential as a standard akin to MARC in more traditional library practice is the widespread adoption of agreed cataloguing rules to complement standardization it offers as a container for this content.

ADVANTAGES OF METS

- METS is a standard maintained by the Network Development and MARC Standards[31] Office of the Library of Congress, and is non-proprietary. Any system capable of handling XML docu-ments can be used to create, store and deliver a METS file, thereby mitigating problems of software obsolescence.
- It is written in XML, which is robust as an archival medium and is readily interchangeable because it uses standard ASCII code rather than a binary format to encode its data.
- As an XML Schema it has certain advantages over a DTD. Schemas are generally richer and more powerful than DTDs: they provide greater control of the content and usage of elements and attributes; they are extensible to future additions, meaning that METS can accommo-date new standards as they are developed in the future; and they support the use of multiple XML namespace, which allows different kinds of metadata to be encoded in the same docu-ment.
- METS has the ability to deal with a wide variety of materials; this is particularly useful in the context of personal archives which typically contain a wide range of object types – including text documents, images, email directories, websites and blogs.
- METS was specifically designed to act as an OAIS Information Package: it can deal with all categories of OAIS metadata; it packages this metadata with the digital object it describes, ensuring that the object is self-documenting over time; and it intellectually links together all the categories of metadata for an object, even if they are stored in separate locations.
- It was developed by the library community and has been widely adopted in preservation re-positories, although its use in the context of personal digital archives has been little explored to date.
- It effectively expresses the hierarchical structure of digital objects. This is very useful in the case of personal archives, as it enables the creator's original structure of directories and folders to be maintained.
- Whilst METS has the capability to deal with large and complex digital objects which might be comprised of many files, it is also useful for dealing with individual files (e.g. a single word-processed document). The !atter is useful for digital archives, where long-term digital preser-vation requires that extensive metadata be recorded for each individual digital object.
- The possibility of creating multiple structural maps in a METS document means that whilst it is invaluable for preserving original hierarchical relationships between objects, archivists can also take

advantage of its capacity for sorting and reordering records in varied ways for researcher access.

- It is relatively easy for archivists familiar with XML to pick up: it copes well with the kind of hierarchical structures archivists are used to dealing with, and the mark-up will be relatively familiar to archivists who are used to encoding archival finding aids in EAD.
- It is extensible: new versions of metadata may be incorporated alongside older versions of metadata, thus providing an audit trail.

DISADVANTAGES OF METS

- The very flexibility of METS can raise interoperability problems. It does not ensure standardization because it does not operate as a metadata standard, rather as a framework within which metadata can be stored.
- While using METS Profiles can mitigate these problems to an extent and facilitate manual cross-mapping, this still does not allow the automatic transfer of files between systems.
- At present, and certainly in the case of personal digital archives, METS documents largely have to be generated manually; this is unfeasible in the long-term, and solutions will have to be found.
- METS relies on the effective use of unique identifiers. This can be difficult to administer.

CONCLUSION

This article has attempted to discuss the concept of METS and indicate its general relevance to digital library. It has provided some definitions and has outlined certain merits and demerits that METS intended to support. METS is in its early stages, but is already sufficiently well established amongst key digital library players. It can reasonably considered the only viable standards for digital library objects in the foreseeable future. The evolution of a unified approach to METS and ontology is of paramount importance. In the evolutionary process, some of the existing METS schema may be further developed and refined and some may get extinct.

REFERENCE

1. Ding, W and Marchionini, G. (1996). A Comparative study of web search service performance. In Proceedings of the American Society for Information Science, Baltimore: 21-24th October.p.135-142.
2. Milstead, J and Feldman, S. (1999). Metadata: Cataloging by any

other name. Online (Information Today Inc.). January issue 1999. Available at: http://www.infotoday.com/onlin /OL1999/milstead.html.

3. XML Security Library. URL: http://www.aleksey.com/xmlsec/index.html

4. Morgan, V. Cundiff (2004). An Introduction to the Metadata Encoding and Transmission Standard (METS). Library Hi Tech, Vol.22. Issue.1.p52-64. Available at:http://www.emeraldinsight.com/journals.htm? articleid=861404&show=html

5. Michael, Day (2005). DCC Digital Curation Manual Installment on Metadata. UKLON University of Bath. November, 2005. Version-1 Available at: http://www.dcc.ac.uk/resource /curation-manual/chapters/metadata.

6. Peter, Cao (2006). HDF5 Archival. Information Packages (AIP) A METS Implementation. NCSA, University of Illinois at Urbana Champaign. 26th April 2006 Available at: http://www.hdfgroup.org /projects/hdf5_aip /hdf5_aip_wp.html.

7. Rebecca S.Guenther (2008). Battle of the Buzzwords. Flexibility vs. Interoperability when Implementing PREMIS in METS. D-Lib Magazine, Vol.14, No.7/8. July/Aug 2008. Available at: http://www.dlib.org/dlib/july08/guenther/07guenther.html.

8. Dappert, Angela and Enders, Markus (2008). Using METS, PREMIS and MODS for Archiving e-Journals. D-Lib Magazine. Volume 14 Number 9/10 September/October. Available at: http://www.dlib.org/dlib/september08/dappert/09dappert.html.

9. McDonough, Jerome P (2009). "Aligning METS with the OAI-ORE Data Model" in Proceedings of the 9th ACM/IEEE-CS Joint Conference on Digital Libraries, Austin, TX, June 15-19, 2009. New York: Association for Computing Machinery.

10. Sreekumar, M.G. (2005). Building a Multimedia Digital Library of Audio/Video Resources Using Open Source Software and Open Digital Library Standards. In Jaginder Singh Ramdevon Festschrift.

11. Biswajit, Saha (2006). Digital Archiving and Preservation: Present Scenario.PLANNER-2006 available at: http://hdl.handle.net/1944/1258

12. Ajay Kumar Sharma et al. (2008). Institutional Repositories and skill requirements, A New Horizon to preserve the Intellectual output: An Indian Perspective. PLANNER- 2008.p.336-353. Available at: http:/ /ir.inflibnet.ac.in/dxml/handle/1944/1145.

13. Devika, P.M. and Dimple, P (2009). Issues in Indian languages

computing in particular reference to search and retrieval in Telugu Language, Library Hi Tech, 27 (3).

14. Network Development and MARC Standards Office, 'METS Extension Schemas', Metadata

Encoding & Transmission Standard Available at: http://www.loc.gov/standards/mets/mets- extenders.html

15. Network Development and MARC Standards Office, Metadata Encoding & Transmission

Standard Available at: http://www.loc.gov/standards/mets/

16. Network Development and MARC Standards Office, 'METS Implementation Registry', Metadata Encoding and Transmission Standards Available at: http://www.loc.gov/standards/ mets/mets-registry.html.
17. METS structure diagram Available at:http://sunsite.berkeley.edu/mets/diagram/
18. METS: An overview & Tutorial Available at:http://www.loc.gov/standards/mets/METS Overview.v2.html
19. METS Structure Available at: http://colab.mpdl.mpg.de/mediawiki/Metadata_Encoding_and_Transmission_Standard
20. Administrative Metadata Available at:http://www.loc.gov/standards/mets/METS Overview.v2.html
21. Metadata Structure Map http://www.loc.gov/standards/mets/mets.xsd.
22. Rahmen and Projects. DFG Viewer METS/MODS – Profile Available at:http://dfg-viewer.de/profil-der-metadaten.
23. INFLIBNET Intuitional Repository Available at: http://dspace.inflibnet.ac.in/handle/1944/283
24. DSpace with MIT Library Available at:http://dspace.mit.edu/
25. Devika,P. Madalli (2003) A Digital Library of Library and Information Science using DSpace. National Workshop on Building Digital Libraries Application of DSpace (DELNET). 22-25th April, 2006. Available at: https://drtc.isibang.ac.in/bitstream/handle/1849/56/G_Devik_Dspac.pdf? Sequence=2.
26. Biswas, Goutam and Paul, Dibyen (2010). An evaluative study on the open source digital library softwares for institutional repository: Special reference to Dspace and greenstone digital library International Journal of Library and Information Science Vol. 2(1) p. 001-010, February, 2010.Available online http://www.academicjournals.org/ijlis
27. DSpace using METS Available at http://www.dspace.org/

1_5_2Documentation/ch09.html#N 13775.

28. Using METS in India Available at:http://www.dspace.org/whos-using-dspace.

29. Prasad., ARD and Devika, P Madalli (2009). Metadata Standards for Textual and Multimedia Content Open Access to Textual and Multimedia Content: Bridging the Digital Divide, January 29-30, 2009 © INFLIBNET Centre, Ahmedabad and CEC, New Delhi. Available at: http://hdl.handle.net/1944/1467.

30. Gartner, Richard (2002). METS: Metadata Encoding and Transmission Standard.TSW 02-05, October, 2002. Available at: http://www.jisc.ac.uk/media/documents/techwatch/tsw_02-05.pdf

31. METS Editorial Board (2007) Metadata Encoding and Transmission Standard: Primer and Reference Manual. Available at: http://www.loc.gov/standards/mets/METS%20Documentation%20final%20070930%20msw.pdf.

❑❑❑

Chapter – 22

Anthropology Online: A Review of Opencourseware Content of MIT on Anthropology

Shriram Venkatraman, V. Seetha Lakshmi and P. Govinda Reddy

INTRODUCTION

Education, as is widely argued is a method of knowledge sharing and distance education is a concept in education that is widely prevalent. Several people around the world qualify themselves through this mode of education. Though widely popular, it has its limitations with respect to production, reproduction and distribution costs, however, the role of distance education is shifting (Caswell et al. 2008). This shift is accomplished with the help of technology, which reduces and almost nullifies the reproduction costs (Caswell et al. 2008). This is a step towards making the quality of life of learners around the world improve (Caswell et al. 2008). Further as Caswell et al. (2008), rightly quote that, this is also the beginning of a movement to ensure the Universal Declaration of Human Rights article 26, which declares that everyone has the right to education and "technical and professional education shall be made generally available" (United Nations, 1948).

Distance learning made possible through the help of technology specifically the internet or e-learning is not a new concept. Several individual course materials are available online (Baldi et al. 2003). However, systematically organizing and structuring the academic course materials from different disciplines and easy retrieval of such information is a sign of innovation (Baldi et al. 2003). This innovation which is currently made possible through initiatives of different Universities, institutes of learning and organizations is popularly titled Open Course Ware (OCW).

As an initiative in the Open Educational Resources movement (Hewlett, 2005; Caswell et al. 2008), Open Course Ware is a testament to the adage that 'knowledge has no boundaries.' The Open Course Ware Consortium defines Open Course Ware as "...a free and open digital publication of high quality university level educational materials."(Open Course Ware Consortium, URL: http://www.ocwconsortium.org/en/courses). From this definition, we can derive that Open Course Ware (OCW) is not charged, has open access, and is a publication of real undergraduate and graduate level course material of top ranked universities. Thus, Open Course Ware is not a formal course; rather it's a compilation of course material for independent perusal.

Open Course Ware (OCW) is different from online resource sites like Wikipedia, Wise geek etc. in concept as it is a systematized presentation of information in a format appealing to a student seeking knowledge about a particular subject. Often, the materials are from real undergraduate and graduate courses from universities across the world and may include syllabi, lecture presentations, assignments, readings and other resource material. The presentation style may make it seem similar to distance learning or online courses. However being Open source, OCW is free and there is no course duration or interaction with the faculty or facilitator. Also, unlike online or distance education courses, OCW does not offer credit or a 'degree' at the end of the course. Instead, OCW is a technological innovation that enables independent knowledge acquisition at one's own pace with the help of top class resources (Baldi et al. 2003; The Hindu, 2011).

RATIONALE FOR CHOOSING MIT OPEN COURSE WARE

Massachusetts Institute of Technology (MIT), USA was the first institution to come up with the concept of Open Course Ware back in 2001. It was announced in 2001, that most of MIT's course materials would be made available online (through internet) free of cost in the next ten years. This concept was named the MIT Open Course Ware (MIT, 2001; Caswell et al. 2008). With a dual mission of providing free access to educators, students and independent learners all around the world and at the same time popularizing the concept of Open Course Ware, MIT launched its pilot version of Open Course Ware in 2002 with 50 courses (MIT, 2006; Caswell et al. 2008).

Wikipedia, Project Gutenberg, the Internet Archive and other such websites had already been running when MIT went live in 2002 (Caswell et al. 2008). However, the idea of Open Course Ware was conceptualized by MIT (Caswell et al. 2008). An aspect that stood out with MIT's Open Course Ware (MITOCW) was that it provided a structure, that included materials used to teach in MIT free of cost during the dot.com boom, when the general feeling was that the cost of online education will be used by the University. This came as a surprise (Caswell et al. 2008).

The year 2005 saw the Open Course Ware movement move beyond MIT with the formation of Open Course Ware Consortium. Within a short span of time, hundreds of universities joined the consortium and hosted their own course material in the Open Course Ware format (Abelson, 2008). Currently, the consortium website offers search facilities for courses based on subjects, institutes, languages etc and has universities as members from various countries of the world.

According to Abelson (2008), MIT began a series of experimentations with technological innovations in education in 1999. The most significant outcome of these experiments was the emergence of MIT Open Course Ware in 2001 that made available undergraduate and graduate MIT course materials for global users. As of 2008, MITOCW published materials on more than 1600 courses taught in MIT with more courses being added every year. Today, the Open Course Ware site of MIT boasts of 2000 courses (MITOCW, URL: http://ocw.mit.edu/index.htm).

MITOCW has a global reach with people around the world exploring its various subjects for courses of interest. Abelson (2008) stated that in 2007, it was found that only 43% of the visitors were from North America. The remaining 57% was distributed across Asia (24%), Europe (18%) and Latin America (5%) and others (10%). One can find evidence of this global reach today by a simple keyword search ("MIT Open Course Ware") in Google Trends. The result showed many Asian countries being among the most prolific searchers for MITOCW. The following is a snapshot image of the result.

Figure 1: Snapshot Image of search traffic for the key word "MIT Open Course Ware" according to Google Trends

Figure 1 shows the traffic volume from top 10 countries that search for MITOCW using the keyword MIT Open Course Ware as of July 17th 2011. It also becomes evident that India is one of the countries that record the highest traffic for such a search, even surpassing USA. This graph also provides an understanding that the top five countries that generate traffic through this keyword search are Asian countries.

However, the description section of MITOCW (URL: http://ocw.mit.edu/about/) quotes that though the facility is a free publication of MIT course materials, it does not provide a certificate or a degree, it does not reflect the entire course materials or content of the course nor does it give access to any faculty. Hence, it must be remembered that MITOCW is a platform for learners, with an appetite for continuous learning; faculty who wish to benchmark their courses; and students who wish to refer materials other than the limited resources that they have.

As Anthropologists we have chosen Anthropology Section of MITOCW for review

Anthropology is a holistic study of different facets of human beings (Ember et al. 2007). Anthropologists explore physical, social, cultural and intellectual progress of human societies since the time of evolution in an integrated manner. *The International Encyclopaedia of Social Sciences* (Sills, 1968) mentions that Anthropology has four basic disciplines namely, 1) Physical anthropology 2) Archaeological anthropology 3) Social- cultural anthropology & 4) Linguistic anthropology. However, currently these broad topics have diversified into sub-specializations like medical anthropology, anthropological genetics, psychological anthropology, forensic anthropology, media anthropology, visual anthropology, environmental anthropology, nutritional anthropology, physiological anthropology, political anthropology, economic anthropology, business/ organizational anthropology, ethnography, ethnology, ethnomusicology, anthropology of war and peace etc. Therefore, as a study of humanity, Anthropology offers exciting, interesting and innovative insights into human life, learning through technology being one such aspect.

Anthropology is a popular field in the West, though still a little known subject in India. Given the paucity of formal Anthropology courses in India, the need of the hour is to bring to light other options like OCW for those interested in studying Anthropology. Also, as researchers in the field of Anthropology, making the internet resources such as OCWs known to the world becomes imperative.

To further, rationalize and experiment if MITOCW was the best structured OCW resource available online for courses in Anthropology, a simple keyword search in the OCW Consortium Webpage for 'Anthropology' was performed. The search returned the availability of 39 Anthropology related courses through different Universities, institutes and organizations which are all a part of OCW

Consortium, out of which 28 courses were offered by MITOCW. Almost 71.79 percent of the courses on Anthropology on OCW were being offered by MITOCW. However, an analysis of trends for keyword search of Anthropology in MIT Open Course Ware on Google Trends reported a rather surprising result, that the traffic of such a search did not have enough volume to generate a trend analysis chart. Also, the listing of the most visited courses on MITOCW website (URL: http://ocw.mit.edu/courses/most-visited-courses/) reveals that Anthropology was not a subject of high preference.

These results catalyzed a thought process that as one of the most structured resources of Anthropology available online, MITOCW was not known much for Anthropology as other subjects of Engineering. Hence, it was deemed appropriate that the Anthropology section of MITOCW be taken up for review to benefit the community of Anthropology students.

This article is designed to be a review of the different features of the Anthropology section of MITOCW. An in-depth study of the technical aspects of the website or detailed critiques of individual courses presented in the website is beyond the scope of this paper.

The Anthropology Section of MITOCW can be accessed in the following manner.

Figure 2: A screenshot image of the MITOCW web page listing Anthropology as an OCW course

Description of MITOCW Anthropology section

The Anthropology section of MITOCW is divided into two distinct sections namely undergraduate and graduate. A total of 41 courses that includes both undergraduate and graduate courses are listed. Of these 41 courses, there are 36 undergraduate courses and 5 graduate courses. Since MIT offers only an undergraduate program with Anthropology specialization, it follows that there are more undergraduate courses listed. The graduate courses are offered for advanced study of specialized topics.

The following pages list out the different programs offered by the Anthropology department for MITOCW.

Figure 3: Screenshot image of the MITOCW Anthropology section

Undergraduate Courses

	Course #	Course Title	Term
	21A.100	Introduction to Anthropology	Fall 2004
	21A.110	Anthropological Theory	Spring 2003
	21A.112	Seminar in Ethnography and Fieldwork	Spring 2008
	21A.113J	The Supernatural in Music, Literature and Culture	Spring 2009
	21A.211	Magic, Witchcraft, and the Spirit World	Fall 2003
	21A.212	Myth, Ritual, and Symbolism	Spring 2004
	21A.215	Medical Anthropology: Culture, Society, and Ethics in Disease and Health	Fall 2008
	21A.216J	Dilemmas in Bio-Medical Ethics: Playing God or Doing Good?	Spring 2005
	21A.217	Anthropology of War and Peace	Fall 2004
	21A.218J	Identity and Difference	Spring 2010
	21A.219	Law and Society	Spring 2003
	21A.224J	Introduction to Latin American Studies	Fall 2005
	21A.225J	Violence, Human Rights, and Justice	Fall 2004
	21A.226	Ethnic and National Identity	Fall 2009
	21A.230J	The Contemporary American Family	Spring 2004

Contd.

	Course #	Course Title	Term
	21A.231J	Gender, Sexuality, and Society	Spring 2006
	21A.235	American Dream: Exploring Class in the U.S.	Spring 2007
	21A.240	Race and Science	Spring 2004
	21A.245J	Power: Interpersonal, Organizational and Global Dimensions	Fall 2005
	21A.260	Culture, Embodiment and the Senses	Fall 2005
NEW	21A.270	Anthropology Through Speculative Fiction	Fall 2009
	21A.336	Marketing, Microchips and McDonalds: Debating Globalization	Spring 2004
	21A.337J	Documenting Culture	Spring 2004
	21A.338J	Gender, Power, and International Development	Fall 2003
	21A.340J	Technology and Culture	Fall 2006
	21A.342	Environmental Struggles	Fall 2004
	21A.344J	Drugs, Politics, and Culture	Spring 2006
	21A.348	Photography and Truth	Spring 2008
	21A.350J	The Anthropology of Computing	Fall 2004
	21A.355J	The Anthropology of Biology	Spring 2009
	21A.360J	The Anthropology of Sound	Spring 2008
NEW	21A.380J	People and Other Animals	Fall 2010
	21A.430J	Introduction to Latin American Studies	Fall 2006
	21A.441	The Conquest of America	Spring 2004
	21A.453	Anthropology of the Middle East	Spring 2004
	21A.460J	Medicine, Religion and Politics in Africa and the African Diaspora	Spring 2005

Figure 4: Screenshot images of Anthropology Undergraduate Courses offered at MITOCW

Graduate Courses

	Course #	Course Title	Term
	21A.337J	Documenting Culture	Spring 2004
	21A.750J	Social Theory and Analysis	Fall 2004
	21A.830J	History and Anthropology of Medicine and Biology	Spring 2009
NEW	21A.835J	People and Other Animals	Fall 2010
	21A.850J	The Anthropology of Cybercultures	Spring 2009

Figure 5: Screenshot images of Anthropology Graduate Courses offered at MITOCW

MITOCW Anthropology Undergraduate Courses

The 36 undergraduate courses can be classified into 6 broad areas of Anthropology based on faculty interests and areas of research. These are as follows (MITOCW Anthropology section URL: http://ocw.mit.edu/courses/anthropology/#undergrad)

1. Introduction To Anthropology
2. Social Anthropology
3. Technology In Cultural Context
4. Historical Studies
5. Special Topics In Anthropology
6. Advanced Graduate Topics

Some of the courses offered are very innovative to the Anthropology field. For example – the course Anthropology of sound studies the various influences on sound patterns and cross-cultural differences perceptions of sound ('Anthropology of Sound' Course Description URL: http://ocw.mit.edu/courses/anthropology/21a-360j-the-anthropology-of-sound-spring-2008).

Another course, Photography and Truth studies uses, meaning and influences of still photographs from a historical and social perspective ('Photography and Truth' Course Description URL: http://ocw.mit.edu/courses/anthropology/21a-348-photography-and-truth-spring-2008/).

An interesting fact about the array of undergraduate courses in Anthropology is the number of courses that deal with aspects of technology and Anthropology. Examples include "Anthropology of Computing", "Technology and Culture" etc. This could be because a strong forte of MIT is their background and footing in technology.

Further, there is a very specific mention in the first lecture of the Course Introduction to Anthropology by Howe (2004) (MITOCW, URL: http://ocw.mit.edu/courses/anthropology/21a-100-introduction-to-anthropology-fall-2004/lecture-notes/Ses1_OPENER.pdf), that the Introductory course on Anthropology at MIT concentrates specifically on Social and Cultural Anthropology, rather than on Archaeological Anthropology or Physical Anthropology. This seems to be the case with respect to all the courses listed under the undergraduate curriculum of the University.

Trend Analysis of Undergraduate Courses

The course offering web page specifies that these courses have been uploaded onto OCW across a span of 7-8 years. Some interesting facts come to light by conducting a simple analysis of the years in which the courses were actually taught and were later uploaded. A graphical depiction of the same is presented below:

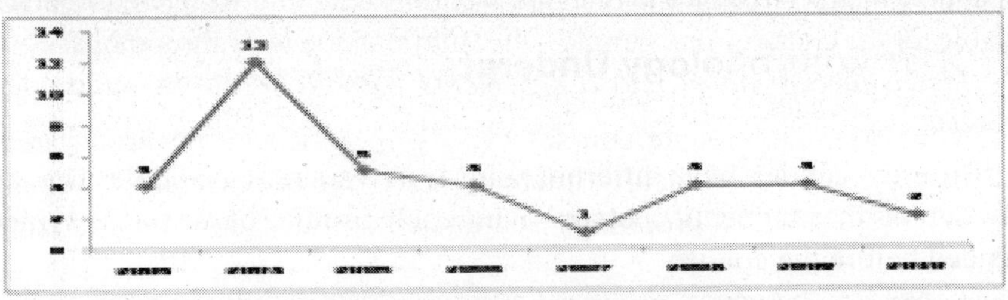

Graph 1 – Number of courses taught and later uploaded every year during 2003-2010

The graph reveals that maximum number of courses were taught and later uploaded during 2003-2006 with 2004 being the year with the highest number of courses - 12 courses being taught and uploaded. This could be due to the fact MITOCW was started in 2001 with a pilot offer of courses in 2002 (MIT, 2006; Caswell et al. 2008) and 2003-2006 were the initial years which usually is a period of high growth. Post 2006, the number of new courses taught and uploaded was comparatively lower with 2010 having only 2 courses. Though six months have passed in 2011, there has not been an update regarding new courses. The reasons for this decline in uploading more recent courses are not known. Such a decline could challenge MIT's position as a leader in providing Open Course Ware in the future.

Resources Analysis of Courses

MITOCW provides different kinds of resources for the various undergraduate courses. These include selected and full lecture notes, assignments, exams, readings, projects etc. The image below is a screenshot of the various resources available.

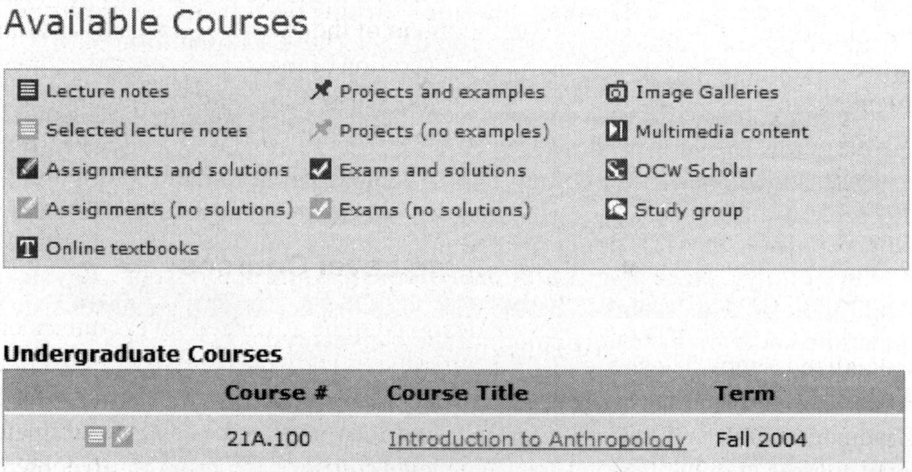

Figure 6: Screenshot image depicting the various resources that may be available for each course

As seen in the image above, these resources are depicted by symbols and each course is preceded by the relevant symbols denoting which resources are available for the course. For example – the 'Introduction to Anthropology' course has *selected lecture notes* and *assignments without solutions* available as resources.

Different courses have different number of resources available. The table below depicts the number of courses having each resource based on the symbols appended before the course.

Table 1: Number of courses with resources based on symbols in MITOCW Anthropology section

Complete Lecture Notes	2
Selected Lecture Notes Only	11
Selected Lecture Notes with Assignments (No Solutions)	5
Assignments (No Solutions) Only	3
Assignments (No Solutions) with Exams (No Solutions)	1
Exams with Solutions	1
Image Gallery with Multimedia Content	1

Other than these 24 courses, some of the remaining 12 courses also offer assignments/readings without any symbols being appended.

One reason why some courses do not have certain resources could be prevention of copyright violation. Since MITOCW is available to all, there could be unintended copyright violations if the contents are used for commercial purposes (example – multimedia clips, readings etc) (Lerman and Miyagawa, 2002). Further, the description section of MITOCW clearly provides a disclaimer that "materials may not reflect entire content of the course". Also, as this is an entirely voluntary action resting on the discretion of the Professors, the content might be a choice driven content. The authors also think that this might be due to the fact that once everything is available online; this will make no difference in studying at MIT except for the certificates and direct interaction with the faculty.

MITOCW Anthropology Graduate Level Courses

The graduate level courses are designed to be advanced level courses on specialized topics. These topics seem interdisciplinary drawing from fields like History, Society and Science & Technology. However, as MIT does not offer a Graduate course in Anthropology, the site does not boast of many graduate level courses. It only offers five graduate level courses. However, not all content is uploaded as OCW materials, although syllabus and reading materials are mentioned as a part of the graduate courses offered. Due to the low volume of courses offered as Graduate courses and a lack of resource materials available in the MITOCW website on Anthropology graduate courses, an in depth review or analysis is challenging.

CONCLUSION

MIT's OCW and Open Course Ware in general benefit multiple stakeholders in the education sphere. For a student or even a layperson seeking to enhance knowledge on a particular subject, OCW offers a systematic presentation of information without the constraints of cost, time or coursework.

For educators around the world, OCW offers high class course components that may be used as a basis for the former's own courses. For universities like MIT, OCW is an ideal way to bring education to the world without the burden of high operating costs. Finally, for society, OCW is a good supplementary to formal education without the necessity for heavy infrastructure investment and training of educators.

This article specifically presented a review of the Anthropology section of MIT's Open Course Ware initiative. An overall description of the undergraduate and graduate courses available was presented and the organization of the website in terms of when the courses were uploaded and the resources available for readers was discussed. The benefits of Open Course Ware including MITOCW for various stakeholders involved were also discussed in the article.

This review will help students of Anthropology in exploring a source for further knowledge on the subject. As newer content is uploaded, it will also help keep them updated on new thoughts and trends in the field. For non-Anthropology students not aware of Open Course Ware, this review will be a springboard to utilizing a vast repository of high class material from top universities. Finally, for educators in India, this review will be an introduction to OCW as databases of education material of global institutions and also introduce a model OCW like MIT that can be emulated if they choose to create their own Open Course Ware.

REFERENCES

1. Abelson, H. (2008): The Creation of Open Course Ware at MIT. *Journal of Science Education and Technology*, 17 (2): 164-174.
2. Baldi, S., Heier, H., and Mehler-Bicher, A. (2003): Open courseware and open source software. *Communications of the ACM*, 46: 105–107.
3. Caswell, T., Henson, S., Jensen, M., and Wiley, D. (2008): Open Content and Open Educational Resources: Enabling universal education. *The International Review of Research in Open and Distance Learning, 9*(1), Article 9.1.1.
4. Hewlett (2005): *Open Educational Resources Initiative Overview.* William and Flora Hewlett Foundation.
5. Howe, J. (2004): Introduction: Anthropology and Its Divisions. *Introduction to Anthropology*. MITOCW: URL: http://ocw.mit.edu/courses/anthropology/21a-100-introduction-to-anthropology-fall-2004/lecture-notes/Ses1_OPENER.pdf
6. Lerman, S. R., and Miyagawa, S. (2002): Open Course Ware. A Case Study in Institutional Decision Making. *Academe Online, 88*(5).

7. MIT (2001): *MIT to make nearly all course materials available free on the World Wide Web.*

8. MIT (2006): *2005 Program Evaluation Findings Report. Press Kit.*

9. MITOCW: URL: http://ocw.mit.edu/index.htm.

10. MITOCW (About OCW): URL: http://ocw.mit.edu/about/

11. MITOCW (Anthropology section): URL: http://ocw.mit.edu/courses/anthropology/#undergrad

12. MIT OCW ('Anthropology of Sound' (Course Description)): URL: http://ocw.mit.edu/courses/anthropology/21a-360j-the-anthropology-of-sound-spring-2008/

13. MITOCW (Most Visited Courses): URL: http://ocw.mit.edu/courses/most-visited-courses/

14. MIT OCW ('Photography and Truth' (Course Description)) URL: http://ocw.mit.edu/courses/anthropology/21a-348-photography-and-truth-spring-2008/

15. Murali, J. (2011): A Decade of open courseware movement. *The Hindu,* May 8, 2011.

16. Open Course Ware Consortium: URL: http://www.ocwconsortium.org/en/courses

17. Sills, D. (ed.), (1968): International Encyclopedia of the Social Sciences. New York : MacMillan

18. United Nations General Assembly (1948): Universal Declaration of Human Rights.

❑❑❑

Chapter – 23

A Survey of E-Library Environment in IITs

Usha M Dangre and Ashwini P Paradkar

INTRODUCTION

Libraries are undergoing rapid changes due to the developments in Information Communication Technology (ICT). Paper based resources are giving way to electronic resources. The dynamic linking capability of web has provided users unrestricted access to information. ICT has brought massive changes in distance mode of education. ICT has helped to introduce many virtual universities in the world, which are operated through Internet and other telecommunication technologies. The e-learning library should organize and present the e-learning resources and services in a way that help users to locate and retrieve materials needed efficiently.

At present e-portals of various organizations come across as gateway for the websites that aggregates information from variety of sources, providing access to information network and set of services through the web. For examples the libraries of National Research Centers of India, Indian Institutes of Technology (IIT), Indian Institute of Science (IISc) and Indian Institute of Management (IIM). The approach of learning of these institutes doesn't mean composed, organized and packaged e-information resources in a blogging pattern but it is comprehensive and fully accessible to the user as reader and writer. Undoubtedly, a study of e-library environment of these institutes immensely helps us in evaluate the potential of proliferation of digitalization of libraries in India.

INDIAN NATIONAL DIGITAL LIBRARY IN SCIENCE AND TECHNOLOGY (INDEST) CONSORTIUM

In 2002 the Department of Secondary and Higher Education of the Ministry of Human Resource Development has set up a "Consortia-Based Subscription to Electronic Resources for Technical Education in India" based on the recommendations of the expert group appointed by the Ministry. 37 centrally-funded Government institutions including IITs, IISc Bangalore, NITs, IITs and IIMs are core members of the INDEST Consortium. The Ministry provides funds required for providing differential access to electronic resources subscribed for the core members through the Consortium Headquarters set-up at the IIT Delhi.

NATIONAL PROGRAMME ON TECHNOLOGY ENHANCED LEARNING (NPTEL)

NPTEL has been initiated by Indian institutes of Technology (IIT Bombay, Delhi, Guwahati, Kanpur, Kharagpur, Madras and Roorkee) and Indian Institute of Science (IISc) for creating course contents in engineering and science with financial support from the Ministry of Human Resource Development (MHRD.) The basic idea of NPTEL was to introduce multimedia and web technology (online courseware) to enhance learning of basic Science and Engineering concepts. It provides E-learning through online Web and Video courses in Engineering, Science and Humanities streams.

LIBRARY E-RESOURCES AND E-SERVICES IN IITS

IIT Delhi

Central Library of the Institute (IIT Delhi) supports the teaching, research and development programs of the Institute for the users through e-services. E-services available with this library are e-books, e-journals, e-databases, e-repositories etc. The leading Abstracting and Indexing databases in the field of Engineering & Technology are also available on Intranet and Internet. It has developed a number of databases in-house using Micro CDS/ISIS packages of UNESCO. These databases have now been ported to www is interface so as to facilitate simultaneous access to users on Internet and Intranet. These databases are:

- Database of Research Articles by the IIT Delhi Faculty
- Database of Ph.D. Theses Submitted to IIT Delhi, and
- Back files of e-Journals are accessible from the Library.

The library subscribes Journals in e-version as its own subscription excluding INDEST subscription. Ph. D. theses have been digitized in-house under the project funded by the Department of Biotechnology and MHRD. The faculty, student and researchers at IIT Delhi have been provided access to electronic journals and bibliographic databases through INDEST-AICTE Consortium. Links to electronic journals are available through the Library web site as well as through the Libsys WebOPAC. The institutional repository, called Eprints@IIT Delhi, provides a platform for faculty and researchers to submit, reuse and share their research publications. The Library also maintains a web-enabled database of research articles published by the faculty and researchers of the Institute. The database consists of research articles and their abstracts that appeared in international peer reviewed journals indexed by Science Citation Index (SCI). The database is being updated regularly for new records that are added to the SCI.

The Library website serves as an integrated interface for all computer and web-based service networks available in the institute.

The Library is committed towards fully web-based digitalization of resources available with them. Some of the following measures has initiated by the library for digitalization are given below:

- Digitized collection consisting of bibliographic records
- Online integrated library information system
- Libsys/WebPAC
- Web based access to the Materials Science Collection from CSA
- Online interactive courseware in Information Technology (IT)
- CD-ROM based search services through a CDNET System
- Website for specialized collections
- Online access to journal subscriptions in print
- Home page and subject gateways for Web resources
- IIT Delhi's website provides FAQ and downloads facility
- Electronic Thesis & Dissertation (ETD)

IIT Bombay

In IIIT Bombay the Library Home Page is an integrated interface for all computer and web-based services available in the Central library. The Central Library of IIT Bombay has taken several initiatives to provide Digital Library Services to the users. It has its own homepage providing web-based access to its collection of books and other reading materials, electronic full-text journals, and databases, and has set up an institutional repository of all publications brought out by IIT Bombay community. It has its own homepage providing web-based access to its collection of books and other reading material, and procures electronic full-text journals, and databases, and has set up an institutional repository of all publications brought out by IIT Bombay community. The library is a part of the institute-wide network and has adequate computing infrastructure to cater to the needs of the users. Two multimedia workstations have been added to provide DVD viewing facility to the users. The Wi-Fi facility in the campus is the additional advantage to the users as they are able to use their laptops inside the library without a cable connection to the Internet.

Library Homepage provides a single window to all the resources and services of the Central Library. It allows to:

- Search/Browse the material in the library (Search Library Catalogue, OPAC)
- Check the materials borrowed by a user and their due date
- Know the recent arrivals
- Access E-Resources (books, journals, theses, databases and multimedia products)
- Submit dissertation / thesis (IIT Bombay students only)
- Download library membership form, Book suggestion form, library guide (Know Your Library)
- Locate library material (Collection organization)
- Ask the librarian
- OPAC (On-line Public Access Catalogue): The OPAC is one of the most heavily used databases of the library and is accessible 24 X 7 via library web page. Besides listing all the documents available in the library, it allows on-line reservation, circulation, fine collection, and indicates status of a particular book. OPAC is searchable by author, title, accession number, subject and several other fields.
- e-resources –usage policy and user undertaking
- Library video
- INDEST Consortium

ELECTRONIC THESES & DISSERTATIONS

Central Library of IIT Bombay is support electronic submission of Ph.D. theses and dissertations by the students. The library has also developed a database (providing bibliographic details and abstract) is accessible through the library homepage.

INSTITUTIONAL ARCHIVE

Central Library has installed open source software, D-space to set up an archive of all publications brought out by the faculty and the institute. The archive facilitates on line submission of the publications by their authors which are permissible within the copyright regulations. The archive is expected to evolve into a major database of all publications produced by the IIT Bombay community and will be accessible on the Internet through the library homepage.

IIT Madras

Realizing the importance of digital library in academic and research activities, Central Library of IIT Madras has implemented Library Management Software, named VTLS which has facilitated the integrated workflow ensuring various value-added services. Users are able to conduct search for the books through i-portal at their desktops. They can also see their transactions, search history, renew and reserve books on-line. Users can also request for Inter Library Loan through Document Delivery Service webpage. Website provide IPR-Patent, Standards, Reference sources to encyclopedias, Newspapers, Yellow pages Atlases, Transaction Citation guides, Dictionaries, Associations, ISO 9001, List of New Addition, Ph. D. Theses.

Web based Document Delivery Service

The website of the Central Library of IIT Madras is very interactive and comprehensive. List of Library Advisory Committee and staff directory is the unique feature of this website. Web based Document Delivery Service (DDS) is provided through the Central Library website. A separate link and page have been created for DDS wherein users can go to DDS page and fill-up the necessary bibliographical details for the paper or publications they need. The details can be submitted online which are received and responded immediately. The users can also see the holdings of the journals subscribed at IIT Madras through the separate page of the Central Library website under Journals at IIT Madras. The main e-services featured in Library website are:

- The Central Library being a member of INDEST Consortium.
- Children library corner
- Virtual Reference Desk
- Suggestion box
- Feedback-user online feedback form
- Media Resource Center
- Central Library Virtual Tour

IIT Kanpur

The central library of IIT Kanpur is named after P. K. Kelkar. The Central Library has CD Server network, ETD search facility, Library Catalogue Search facilities and Periodical search facility. Other facilities are provided by the Digital Library are:

- Computer Aided Reference Service
- OPAC
- Access to Online service comprising online journals, databases and CD collection
- Alert/ Awareness service consisting of new arrivals of books.
- It has ISI Standards

IIT Roorkee

Mahatma Gandhi Central Library of IIT Roorkee is providing information through e-resources. Cyber room, Online Catalogue Internet and wi-fi environment are some of the main features of the library. Besides printed books and journals, CD-ROMs, E- databases, audio-video materials, E-standards, E-Books, E-journals, E-repository, specifications, theses, reports etc. The e-collection in the library is mainly related to Sciences and Technology.

The library has access to electronic journals which is available through the campus wide fiber-optic network to all computers in the institute. The Library is currently in the process of digitizing its archival collection and theses and dissertation. Library subscribes to e-journals through the INDEST and its own arrangement. NPTEL Course ware is available on website. The Library Repository, named Bhagirithi is an archive for conference proceedings and manuals. Website of the institute also provides virtual tour, links for IIT Mandi.

IIT Kharagpur

The Central Library, IIT Kharagpur has initiated as modern in-house Electronic Library. It has involved various digitization activities of the old documents for digital archiving. It has a large number of electronic resources (e-Books, e-journals & e-databases, Bibliographic Databases), INDEST Consortium. NPTEL A large number of video courses produced by the Centre for Education Technology is made available to the users. The digital library contains CD-ROM databases; Online Video Lectures; SCIFINDER Scholar; Book CD-ROM Database; User Education guide; Institutional Repository etc IIT's website have other services for the user like Trial Access ,Library FAQ, May I help you, Notice Board.web mail, Ask a Librarian.

Institutional Archives on technical Education, Books, Articles, Institutional profile, speeches, and list of engineering institution in India are also available.

IIT Guwahati

The Central Library of IIT Guwahati is one of the important central facilities of the Institute including textbooks, reference books, conference proceedings, back volumes, standards, and non-book materials such as CDROMs, audio tapes, video tapes, and slides. Database for the entire collection has been created and made available through On-Line Public Access Catalogue (OPAC) to the users via campus network. Now this facility is also available through Institute's Intranet as a Web enabled OPAC.

The Central Library being a member of INDEST Consortium (Indian National Digital Library in Science and Technology Consortium) under the aegis of the MHRD, provides online access to few important Science & Engineering abstracting database services, such as COMPENDEX & INSPEC, MathSciNet, SciFinder Scholar, Web of Science etc and several full-text journals and Indian Standards. The Central Library Intranet Page provides the IP based online access to these resources. The Central Library Web-page of IIT Guwahati provides the basic information about the activities of the library, its collections and links to its Web-OPAC and other associated services. The library web-page provides links to all subscribed online journals. It also provides links to all E-resources available through the INDEST Consortium. The publishers'/service providers' URLs are linked through the library web-page. It provides download links to different client software.

CONCLUSION

This paper has mainly focused on the websites of all IITs for e-resources and e-reference services carried out in IITs as they are the pioneer in the e-library. It is found that all the IITs are fairly advanced in digitization activities. The library web-page provides links to all subscribed online journals. It also provides links to all e-resources available through the INDEST Consortium. The Implementation of INDEST Consortium has acted as a catalyst for the digital library initiatives in IIT system. IITs have established CD-ROM Networking. Open source software is the important instrumental for creation of Institutional Repositories (IRs), electronic theses and dissertations (ETDs). Most of the IITs have facility of e-submission of theses. They provide e-reference services and Webmail service for its clients. Information about library like brief history, staff directory, contact details, services provided, rules and regulations, etc are also posted on the websites of the IIT's.

The libraries of IITs are quite advanced as they are institutes of national importance and form club of higher education comparable to best in the world. They have generous grants and projects from Government bodies (AICTE) and Ministry of Human Resources Development.

WEBLIOGRAPHY

1. http://library.iitk.ac.in/index1.html (accessed on 27th July 2011)
2. http://www.cenlib.iitm.ac.in/ docs/library/index. php (accessed on 27th July 2011)

3. http://www.iitb. ac.in/facilities/library. Html (accessed on 27th July 2011)
4. http://web.iitd.ac.in/~library/ (accessed on 27th July 2011)
5. http://www.iitr.ernet.in/centers/ library/ pages/About_.html (accessed on 27th July 2011)
6. http://www.library.iitkgp.ernet.in/ (accessed on 27th July 2011)
7. www.iitg.ernet.in/rs/lib/public_html/card.html (accessed on 27th July 2011)

❑❑❑

Chapter – 24

Library Network and Consortia

Amit Dhar, Ajay Kaundal and Dev Walia

INTRODUCTION

Library networks and cooperatives were formed to provide support among libraries, leveraging staff and resources to provide cost-effective and efficient services that the libraries individually could not afford. By 1960s, the networks and cooperatives were focusing on automation; it was through them that library automation was introduced and pioneering efforts in resource sharing began. As the world of libraries changed, other services became the business of networks and cooperatives. Frequently, services initiated by networks were later integrated into the daily operations of individual libraries. Examples of such pioneering services included Internet connectivity and training; teleconferencing; services to special populations; distance learning; database licensing and training. Hence the discipline of LIS meant to manage and provide information service may not be taught effectively and practiced perfectly through a framed curriculum in the formal education stream alone. Driven by the market demands and user needs, the discipline is embracing other disciplines like computers, communication technology research etc. Library consortia and networking are not new to the library community as it is the latest phrase of the so-called library cooperation, library networks and so on. We have talked a lot about the issues that caused the lack of successful implementation of library networks in India. Of them, technology and economics are very important factors for realizing a successful cooperation. We talked about the solutions that are of global in nature but never suited Indian environments with its economic background.

The result is that we developed library networks, but nothing to share. And then we realized that we need to develop information resources in the electronic form so that library networks become effective for the purposes they were setup. We have had number of conferences, meetings, publications etc on discussing the bibliographic formats, standards and the software to host these resources. There was a lot of initiatives by networks such as INFLIBNET, DELNET and other library networks supported by NISSAT to formulate bibliographic standards and formats that is suitable for Indian environment. And the database development activities started. Union catalogs of serials, thesis and dissertations were developed followed by catalog of books. Web enabled search interfaces were also developed for searching. However, union catalog system will be effective only when they are supported by efficient and timely document delivery system.

LIBRARY NETWORK

Library and information networking is the area with a direct impact on information services, their efficiency and effectiveness. Networking technology (sharing of resources) which has met, multi-directional, multiform, format of information needs of users, irrespective of geographical boundary and language. Information scientists / librarians are the matchmaker of the information resources and information seekers. Due to networking technology the concept has totally changed towards the access of information, rather than possess the documents. The concepts of digital and virtual library are already taking the shape and are reality. The range of services provided by many resource sharing networks include storage and retrieval of data such as factual, physical and bibliographic data, document ordering and delivery services, general computer and support of group communication and decision making. The most widely used network can be described by four major types of services:

- Shared cataloguing
- On-line reference
- Shared circulation
- Interlibrary loan

The different types of networks that have been evolved share a set of common objectives:

- Connectivity to permit different hardware and software products.
- Simplicity to permit easy installation
- Modulating to enable building a wide variety of network devices.
- Flexibility to permit the network to as new needs arise.

INDIAN SCENARIO

The growth of library and information networks in India is of recent origin. The growth can be traced to some of the policies that Govt. of India pursued during the last decade. In 1984 the Planning Commission constituted a working group which recommended the need for the modernisation of library services and in 7th plan period during 1985-1990 the same report given by working group also recommended the interlinking of library systems in the country using modern information technology at national level to improve the library and information services in the country for more result oriented and more purposive. Some of the significant data communication networks functioning in the country are :-

- DELNET (Developing Library Network)
- PUNET (Pune Library Network)
- ADINET (Ahmedabad Library Network)
- BONET (Bombay Library Network)
- MALIBNET (Madras Library Network)
- INFLIBNET (Information and Library Network)
- ERNET (Education and Research Network)
- NICNET (National Informatics Centre)
- CALIBNET (Calcutta Library Network)

LIBRARY CONSORTIA

Consortium is a resource-sharing organization formed by libraries also described as co-operatives, network collectives, alliances or partnership. Library consortia consists of a number of libraries, preferably with some common features by subject, institutional affiliation or branch / unit of libraries that come together with common interest and objectives to certain job collectively. Services which are covered under consortium may vary but comprise cooperative collection development, education and training, preservation, centralized services and network alliance features library automation services, system support, inter library lending, retro conversion, consultation and cooperative purchasing. The consortia for library can be considered as a major step towards library cooperation in sharing electronic resources. The consortium should take lead role in the development of a national strategy for information provision for research in higher education. The overall motto of consortia is to achieve what the member of group cannot achieve individually.

Need

- Shortage in library budget
- Information explosion
- Increasing cost of journal
- Excessive demand of users
- Decrease in print subscription
- Variation of pricing models

Leading library consortia

Some of the important and successful library consortia in India are:

- INDEST (Indian National Digital Library in Engineering Science and Technology by IIT Delhi)[http://paniit.iitd.ac.in/indest/]
- CSIR e-Journal consortia by (NISCAIR) New Delhi [http://www.niscair.res.in/ActivitiesandServices/MajorProjects/majproj.htm#ejournalcons ortia]
- UGC-INFONET e-journal consortia managed by INFLIBNET[http://www.inflibnet.ac.in]
- CeRA by IARI New Delhi
- IIM Consortium[http://www.iimb.ernet.in/]
- Health Science Library& Information Network (HELINET)
- Indian Council of Medical Research
- [http://www.jccc-icmr.informindia.co.in/about/about.asp]
- Tata Institute of Fundamental Research (TIFR Bombay)

Strengthening of Digital Library and Information Management under NARS e-GRANTH. Heading towards formation with lead centre IARI New Delhi

IMPACT IN FUTURE

In the evolution of library networks, it can be observed that in the beginning, networks were established with the limited and well defined objectives. As the use of networking has become more pervasive due to the easy availability of the infrastructure, the scope of the networks became broader and a number of interconnected consortia of network and members has become possible. This has enabled the end-user to choose more than one route through the maze of networks in order to locate a given document or piece of bibliographic information. In other words access barriers have become less and less. Another reason could be that networks allow users to exchange data and communicate with each other using e-mail or bulletin boards irrespective of their location. In other words, networks can be considered as the information roads and highways over which data and information are transported to support different application in different locations. In fact, it is technological developments that paved the way for realization of the concept information superhighway. The ultimate aim of the information superhighway is to provide a global universal communication network to provide information to the users across the globe.

CONCLUSION

Network and consortium are an important way of extending access to information for our patrons. The success and survival of libraries depends on how much and to what extent the libraries cooperate with each other in future. It is rightly seen that due to change in ICT the world of library through network and consortia is spreading rapidly around the world and along different lines with the motive being the same cooperation. Now hundreds of OPAC (Online Public Access Catalogues) are available for global access via the internet. The explosion of networked information has contributed to an age of vast transformation. The flood of information and duplication create the problem in front of the scholars but due to e-resources it becomes very easy to cope with the respective field. It is costly to procure all e-resources by a single library and under one roof. Library network and consortia have gradually reduced the monopoly of publishing community. Through consortium and networking among the libraries offer opportunities for providing access to broader and deeper range of collection. A healthy percentage of use of network facility by greater number of users may also be very helpful in justifying the financial burden and paved way for enormous amount of saving of time and manpower.

REFERENCES

1. Khatri, N. K. (2010). Enhancing usage of e-Resources at Indian Statistical Institute Delhi Centre Library through consortia based subscription. In Madan Kumar Stanley, et al (Eds) National Conference on Knowledge Management in the Globalized era: Lead papers, April 21-23, 2010, New Delhi, *AALDI:* (254-260.)
2. Kumar, Manish (2010). Library Consortium : Panacea to Libraries Financial Crunch. In Madan Kumar, Stanley, et. al. (Eds). National Conference on Knowledge Management in the Globalized era: Lead papers, April 21-23, 2010, New Delhi. *AALDI:* (247-253.)
3. Kumar, P. S. G. (2004). A Students Manual of Library and Information Science New Delhi : B R Publishing Corporation.
4. Pandey, Ravindra (2010). University Grants Commission Junior Research Fellow / Lectureship Exam LIS, New Delhi : Ramesh Publishing.
5. Saini, Surbhi. (2010). Electronic Resources in Libraries and Education. In Madan Kumar, Stanley, et. al. (Eds). National Conference on

Knowledge Management in the Globalized era: Lead papers, April 21-23, 2010, New Delhi. *AALDI:* (282-286.)

6. Singh, Surya Nath (2002). Trends and impact of networking technology on biomedical information and library science professionals in India : A survey XXth National Seminar of IASLIC : Digital Information System and Services December 2002, Patiala: (111-120)
7. Singh, Vinod Kumar (2010). DeLcon consortium Boon for Researchers in the field of biotechnology. In Madan Kumar, Stanley, et. al. (Eds). National Conference on Knowledge Management in the Globalized era: Lead papers, April 21-23, 2010, New Delhi. *AALDI:* (267-276.)
8. NAIP/ ICAR project document on "Strengthening of digital library and information management" under NARS 2009 : (56)
9. http://ir.inflibnet.ac.in/dxml/bitstream/handle/1944/201/03cali_32.pdf?sequence=3 (Accessed on 12-1-2011)
10. http://www.ala.org/ala/research/librarystats/cooperatives/lncc/Final%20report.pdf (Accessed on 12-1-2011)
11. http://eprints.rclis.org/bitstream/10760/8393/1/Maitraye_2.pdf (Accessed on 12-1-2011)
12. http://ir.inflibnet.ac.in/dxml/bitstream/handle/1944/1299/370-379.pdf?sequence=1(Accessed on 13-1-2011)
13. http://nopr.niscair.res.in/bitstream/123456789/829/1/ALIS%2055%281%29%20%282008%29%2045-51.PDF(Accessed on 13-1-2011)
14. http://ir.inflibnet.ac.in/dxml/bitstream/handle/1944/204/03cali_35.pdf?sequence=2 (Accessed on 17-1-2011)
15. http://www.lsu.com/ocsweb/louishome.nsf/$Content/Bibliography/$File/Recent%2BTrends%2BinStatewide%2BAcademic%2BLibrary%2BConsortia.pdf (Accessed ib 17-1-2011)
16. www.icast.org.in/staff/ejconsortia-rvce1.ppt (Accessed on 12-1-2011)
17. http://www.gndec.ac.in/~librarian/sveri/dbit1602003.pdf (Accessed on 12-1-2011)
18. http://www.icmr.nic.in/library_bull/jan_2005.pdf (Accessed on 13-1-2011)
19. http://dspace.knust.edu.gh/dspace/bitstream/123456789/1908/1/Library%20Consortia.....pdf (Accessed on 18-1-2011)

20. http://www.bookaid.org/resources/downloads/advocacy/sharing-resources-research-paper.PDF (Accessed on 17-1-2011)

21. http://digitalcommons.unl.edu/cgi/viewcontent.cgi?article=1029&context=libphilprac (Accessed on 13-1-2011)

22. ir.inflibnet.ac.in/dxml/bitstream/handle/1944/1299/370-379.pdf?...1 (Accessed on 17-1-2011)

❑❑❑

Chapter – 25

Consortia and Prospects of Libraries in Academic Environment: An Outline

M. K. G. Rajev

INTRODUCTION

Library Consortia is the sharing of resources among the libraries based on a number and utility over their respected areas. The resources that are shared in today's consortia atmosphere are largely in electronic form such as electronic journals and databases. The aim of consortia is to accomplish what the members of the group cannot achieve individually, and its intention is sharing of resources, manpower and money, etc. It is regarded as a valuable strategy to increase the buying power and risk-sharing capacity of academic libraries over a short term. It is also a chance to maximize the opportunities for joint collection development and resource sharing over the long term. A consortium has the ability to share resources without forfeiting the individuality of member library. As a result, the end-users can collect the benefits of more resources than would be accessible through one library, while staff can adapt the system to meet their individual library's needs. It can be a single agency with multiple locations around the world, all sharing one name, or the consortia members can retain their own name, but use the name of the consortia to recognize that they are the part of a larger, often worldwide, organization. It acts as director for the electronic resource sharing at the national, regional and local levels. The accessibility of IT-based electronic information products put forth portions of their budgetary allocation for either acquiring or accessing web-based online full-text search services, online databases shared services, on the one hand, permits flourishing consumption and desktop access to electronic resources at highly increasing users demands and growing cost of journals.

WHAT IS LIBRARY CONSORTIA?

A library consortia is a group of two or more libraries that have agreed to collaborate with each other in order to fulfill definite related needs, frequently resource sharing. Collaboration among libraries is not a new perception. It has subsisted in many forms, in many countries, for many years. Some collaboration was, and still is, informal while other types include multifaceted processes to share collections or services. Traditionally, library collaboration meant sharing collections in some way, but it could also include sharing of services, or of processes such as joint classification of materials, or of staff and user training. However, most libraries kept their sovereignty and consortia involvement as a peripheral library service. Accommodating efforts frequently had an economic enthusiasm, and that encouragement continues today. Recent improvement in library funding, and the growth in importance of electronic materials have led to a change in thoughts about how libraries collaborate, and the growth of formal supportive entities.

DEFINITION OF LIBRARY CONSORTIA

A Consortium could be expressed as a group of organizations who come together to fulfill a combined intention that beneficially requires co-operation and the sharing of resources and need to have a clear communal goal in order to ensure their achievement. A library consortium formation can be regional, state, national and inter institutional level. The way by which the users belong to different institutions or university, joined mutually and purchasing the costly electronic products and sharing its cost creating a common infrastructure is called " Library Consortia".

As we all know academic libraries presently subscribe only to those journals that they can manage to pay for on any explicit time of date, and there will be a number of other journals of the precise publisher the library infrequently will have to interline as well. Such a consortium agreement will give the library, and therefore also the user, comprehensive access that is better service and reduces the cost, i.e., staff costs and document deliverance costs in inter-lending procedures.

NEED OF LIBRARY CONSORTIA

The yearly cost of academic libraries to uphold information access is growing faster than library budgets and publishers keep on asking libraries to spend on new publishing proposals while still maintaining or intensifying the existing publications. Thus, consortia wish to accomplish greater value for money by acquiring the titles that receive authentic use, by discontinuing less use or unused titles and to arrive at some lesser costs, and to some more cost-effective or more available models.

1. Due to the developments in pricing policies of the publishers, the academic libraries are facing new challenges in acquiring the serials, either electronic or print resources. In order to reduce the cost it is essential to go for a library consortia.
2. The continuous price inflation in scientific information and the lack of funds availability has led to enormous cancellations of scientific journals. Because of this it is very difficult to purchase all the necessary information resources, hence the need of library consortia arises.
3. The technological developments are also in need of new supporting devices in the field of hardware and software and also the training and education for library staff have resulted in the need of library consortia.
4. The users are building up their expectations in order to get the needed information in the quicker and immediate access through various electronic resources such as databases, for this purpose. The library consortia will be best effective one in order to satisfy the needs of the users.
5. The library consortia is very much needed for the traditional libraries to stick together with the modern libraries in order to provide more resources to their users at the affordable cost.

CONSORTIA MODELS

A multiplicity of organizational models of consortia have appeared in India based on their objectives, participants, sources of funding, etc.

Open Ended Model: In this model, the libraries can join at any point of time and at the same time in a group. If they are not interested they can quit at any point of time from the group. There is no fixed term for joining or quitting and moreover the member numbers are not fixed. It just flexible. Example – FORSA and INDEST (partly).

Closed Group Model: In this model, based on certain criteria and the essential members are uniformed and where the needs are common and the resources shared are in specific area. So, the administration and guidelines are easy and simple. Example – CSIR consortium (institutional affiliation) and IIMs Consortium (homogeneity)

Shared-Budget Model: In this model, the participating members have to share the funds which is controlled through the Memorandum of Understanding for better and strong consideration. Example – IIM, HELINET, FORSA.

Centrally Funded Model: In this model, survival of the consortium exclusively depends on the central funding agency, eventually obligatory regulations by the funding authority. Here spring of funding often state the structure of the consortium. Example - UGC-InfoNet.

Publisher Initiated Model: In this model, the publisher can quote the consortia price and will provide the attractive discount for the participating libraries with the precondition that there should not be any discard in their print subscriptions. Such pricing practices by the distinguished publishers are coming up for countries - like India. Example: Consortia price for ScienceDirect (from Elsevier Sc. & Associates), for MathSciNet (from AMS).

National Venture Model: This is a national level proposal, but in India it is partially initiated through UGC-InfoNet (national license for Encyclopedia Britanica) and INDEST (national prices for various e-resources). A national consortium can greatly decrease repetition of efforts/ resources and also offer greater acquiring power.

Headquarter Executed Model: In this model, the consortia is motivated by the Headquarter of a particular organization. Here the head office of the branches or institutes which individually carry on the financial liability of the consortium and the consortium is fully directed and implemented by the head quarter. Example: Consortia subscriptions among the centers of ISI.

BENEFITS OF LIBRARY CONSORTIA

- Possibility of huge and complete collection of materials.
- Communication construction can be developed among different libraries.
- Resource Sharing can be enhanced.
- More Time can be saved.
- Introducing of more services can be done in a professional way.
- Competitive professionalism can be developed among librarians.
- Duplication of same collection of core serials can be avoided
- Prompt and efficient document delivery system is possible.
- Electronic Archives also can be developed in a perfect manner.
- Cost of Information can be reduced

- Information can be accommodating within the budget.
- Scope for developing a Union Catalogue.

BARRIERS OF CONSORTIA INITIATIVES

A consortium has its own intrinsic benefits and those benefits can be maximized, while minimizing the harmful aspects. Helmer distinguishes that the benefits of consortia could be susceptible by several issues, results the breakdown of a consortia. As far as the Indian libraries are concerned, it has been established that some of the consortia proposals could not materialized properly and some others are besieged with multiple hurdles. Authors have identified a few common barriers that are unique to India, which interrupt proper accomplishment of consortia initiatives in a real situation, as specified below.

Budget Allocation and Funding: This is an important barrier which always occurs at the time of budget allocation. Since it is rarely possible to know the consortia subscription cost, the libraries cannot fix up the exact price for consortium in the budget. Sometimes, the cost may vary according to the pricing and allocation of resources and it results in lack of funds for participation in library consortia.

Decision making and Control: There is a panic that if a library joins in a consortium then local autonomy, decision making and control will be unfavorably affected. The library authorities sometimes convey their negative attitudes towards consortia. Moreover the libraries will not have the liberty to drop any title which once committed and to include the other title on replacement of it.

Fund Transfer and Audit Problems: Normally while transferring the funds, the shared subscription cost will be sent to the publisher and the publisher will be sending a consolidated invoice. At auditing time, this invoice may not be matching with the consortium prices with the participating libraries paid amount. Hence, the audit panel may question and reject the invoice, and it is hardly acceptable of the payment allotments and this results in creating problem of transferring of funds in the auditing time.

Legal Entity: The participating libraries should have the proper legal entity with permission and authority to covenant with institutions like banks, since the membership amount involved in collection of subscription fees in making the payments to the publisher, The banking organization like Reserve Bank of India has make a deal with consortium in arranging the foreign exchange prices and transfers on behalf of libraries participating in consortium.

Understanding and Awareness : In India some of the librarians do not fully understand the concept of consortia based subscription to electronic resources and are not very enthusiastic to go whole- heartedly for the development of consortia among libraries Sometimes they don't have good perceptive about consortia benefits and often fail to get the prospects. Even many libraries believe to think that their financial contribution may not be appropriate with the benefits they get from a consortium.

·**Multiple Consortia Memberships:** Individual libraries with multiple consortia membership can be a barrier to summarize actions and to regulate with variant consortia cultures. Hence, Multi partnership may cause the inconsistency and cultural gap, is an indisputable barrier to library consortia.

Geographic Distance: Due to the distance the participating libraries in the consortia, might not have the proper communication, regular meetings, face to face discussions. This may cause difference of opinion and may affect the successful consortium among the participating libraries.

Consortia Agreement: Agreement between members can have a major collision on the consortium's efficiency. It has been found that some libraries did not join in consortia simply for the reason that of the agreement was not of their preference.

Specific Library Problems: Every library has its own specific problems related to environmental differences, work culture, compromising attitudes, policies and procedures, etc. These behaviors of individual libraries can be a big restraint of a consortium.

Technology & Security: The technology and communication systems of the members of the consortia should have the proper and needed compatibility of equipments to meet the effectiveness and achieve the benefits of the information technology. For an instance, if the consortium provides access to ten users at one point of time, then the speed of the net is based on the dialup and broadband status of it. If the dialup is slow and the other member has the broadband the compatibility will become a barrier to the consortia setup. The same thing arises in the security systems too, hence, it is suggested to have proper and latest configured system and necessary technological advancements should be implemented in all the participated libraries.

LIBRARY CONSORTIA ISSUES

- Technology development and communications
- Finding out the resources.
- Financial Plan and budget.
- Issues on Cost and Funds availability.
- Subscription and imbursement issues

- Access related issues.
- Copyright and Licensing issues
- Issues on Archival Systems.
- Convention and usability issues.
- Coordination among participating libraries
- Availability of professional staff.
- Overcoming political objections
- The character and opinion of individuals and institutions
- Need of adequate professional training in ICT for the librarians.

CONCLUSION

In order to achieve the goals of perfect resource sharing, prompt document delivery systems, integrating collection and development process, access to the variety of reliable and enormous sources of electronic information, the best and foremost solution for the academic libraries in India is Library Consortia. Of course, the Indian LIS professionals need proper professional training in make use of library consortia for maximizing usage of resources at the minimum cost, time and space. Particularly, academic libraries are facing lot of issues in static budget and the day by day increasing price of collection and management of electronic resources. Hence, the Consortia is very much a needed one and it plays a vital role in collaboration of various academic libraries on the basis to achieve the remarkable improvements and developments for the growth of the building up of huge number of collections, management, maintenance and providing a wide range of access to all its users at an affordable cost in order to satisfy them at a maximum level.

REFERENCES

1. Bostick Sharon L (2001). Academic Library Consortia in the United States : An Introduction. *LIBER Quarterly,* pp. 6-13.
2. Pandian M. Paul and Karisiddappa , C. R. Technology Issues for Library Consortia in India. Available at: http://ir.inflibnet.ac.in/dxml/bitstream/handle/1944/204/03cali_35. pdf?sequence=2 (Accessed on 20 May, 2011).
3. Thamaraiselvi, G and Kaliammal, A (2005). E-Journal Management in Academic Libraries with Special Reference to INDEST Consortia in India. In Proceedings of 3rd Convention Planner -2005, Assam University, Ahmedabad, Nov 10-4, pp. 331-332.
4. Kumar, Manish. Library Consortium : Concept and Licensing models.

Available at : http://dlis.du.ac.in/RC%20IN%20LIS/pdf/Presentations/Manish%20Kumar.pdf (Accessed on 22 May, 2011).

5. Pal Jiban K and Das Prabir Kumar. Progressive through Partnership - Consortia based e-resource Subscription Initiatives in India. Available at :http://www.isical.ac.in/~serial/ consortia/CBSOR-08.pdf (Accessed on 22 May, 2011).

6. Singh Kunwar, Rao and Bhaskar, V (2008). An Overview of the library consortia in India. In Proceedings of 6th Convention Planner -2008, Nagaland University, Nagaland, Nov 6-7 : INFLIBNET: 140-149.

7. Ramesh, Yernangula and Kelkar, P.K. Library Consortia : benefits and models of E-Journals. Available at http://www.isical.ac.in/~serial/consortia/CBSOR-11.pdf (Accessed on 24 May, 2011).

8. Jagdish Arora (2003). The International Information & Library Review, Volume 35 (March), pp. 1-17.

9. Borke, Rick. Library Consortia and the future of Academic Libraries. Available at : http://www.neal-schuman.com/academic/Burke2010.pdf (Accessed on 23 May, 2011).

10. Lancaster, F.W (1995). The evolution of electronic publishing. Library *Trends 43(4)*, pp. 518-27.

11. Janakiraman, S (2002). Thoughts on Library Consortium', Proceedings of the Round Table on Sharing of E-journals through Consortia in Indian Libraries, Bangalore.

12. Hirson, Arnold (1999). Libraries, consortia, and change management. *Journal of Academic Librarianship,* Vol.25 (2), pp.124-126.

13. Shoaf, Eric (1999)."The effects of consortia membership on library planning and budgeting. *Library Administration and Management* 13(4), pp 196-20.

14. Helmer, John F (1999). Epidemiology of the consortial spore. *Information Technology and Libraries.* 18 (3), pp.119-120.

15. Asare-kyire Afia Den si, Hassan Helena R. Asamoah. Library consortia and the enhancement of education and research in Ghana. Available at http://dspace.knust.edu.gh /dspace /bitstream/123456789/1908/1/Library%20Consortia.pdf (Accessed on 25 May, 2011).

16. Sreekumar M.G. et al. (2005). Library capacity building though E-Journal Consortia. 7th MANLIBNET ,.Digital Libraries in Knowledge Management: Indian Institute of Management Kozhikode.

17. Rahman Md Ansur; Nahar Mahmudan and Akhtar Razina (2006). Resource sharing, Networking and Library Consortia: Problem and Prospects in Bangladesh". *In Proceedings of 4th Convention Planner.*

2006. http://www.infolibrarian.com(Accessed on 24 May, 2011).

18. Goudar, IRN and Poornima, Narayana (2004). Emerging pricing models for E-Journals Consortia and Indian initiatives. *Proceedings of the International Conference on Digital Libraries* (ICDL 2004), New Delhi.

19. Aroral , Jagdish (2001).Indian National Digital Library in Engineering Science and Technology (INDEST) – a proposal for strategic co-operation for consortia-based access to electronic resources. *International Information & Library Review,* Vol.33 (2-3), p.149-165.

❑❑❑

Chapter – 26

Information Literacy Skills for LIS Professionals

B. Ramesh Babu

INTRODUCTION

Information literacy has been the subject of many studies over many years. The originating concept of information literacy is generally attributed to Paul Zurkowski, in 1974 (Spitzer, Eisenberg & Lowe 1998). Indeed, since 1974 information literacy has been an area of increasing interest to librarians and information professionals and there is a huge amount of literature on the topic. However, the majority of publications have come from the industrialised, English-speaking countries, especially from the United States and Australia. Information literacy is related to information technology skills, but has broader implications for the individual, the educational system, and for society. Information literacy is a natural extension of the concept of literacy in our information society. Information literacy education is the catalyst required to transform the information society of today into the learning society of tomorrow. IL is generally seen as pivotal to the pursuit of lifelong learning, and central to achieving both personal empowerment and economic development. Information literacy is a key component of, and contributor to, lifelong learning. Information literacy is increasingly important in the contemporary environment of rapid technological changes and proliferating information resources. Because of the escalating complexity of this environment, individuals are faced with diverse and abundant information choices—in their studies, in the workplace, and in their personal lives. It is common to all disciplines, to all learning environments, and to all levels of education. It enables learners to master content and extend their investigations, become more self directed, and assume greater control over their own learning.

The phrase "information skills" (rather than information literacy) is used, for example, by the Standing Conference of National and University Libraries (SCONUL) in the name of its Task Force, and was used by the Joint Information Systems Committee (JISC) when tendering for a project looking at training in UK further and higher education.

Information literacy competency ensures maximum utilization of the information resources as well as optimization of information handling capabilities.. Information literacy competency extends learning beyond formal classroom settings and provides practice with self-directed investigations as individuals move into internships, first professional positions, and increasing responsibilities in all arenas of life. Because information literacy augments students ' competency with evaluating, managing, and using information, it is now considered by several regional and discipline-based accreditation associations as a key outcome for college students and for "on campus " students..

INFORMATION LITERACY: DEFINITIONS AND MEANING

"Information literacy is an intellectual framework for recognizing the need for, understanding, finding, evaluating, and using information. These are activities which may be supported in part by fluency with information technology, in part by sound investigative methods, but most importantly through critical discernment and reasoning. Information literacy initiates, sustains, and extends lifelong learning through abilities that may use technologies but are ultimately independent of them." (Bundy, A. ed. 2004)

"Information literacy - the ability to find and use information – is the keystone of lifelong learning."

Information Literacy is the ability to access, evaluate, and use information from a variety of sources. Information literacy is a set of abilities requiring individuals to "recognize when information is needed and have the ability to locate, evaluate, and use effectively the needed information.". Information literacy in terms of a set of competencies that an informed citizen of an information society ought to possess to participate intelligently and actively in that society.

Most current definitions of information literacy are built on that issued by ALA's Presidential Committee on Information Literacy (1989): 'To be information literate an individual must recognise when information is needed and have the ability to locate, evaluate and use effectively the information needed... Ultimately information literate people are those who have learned how to learn...' (ASLA/ALIA 2001: 1).

Information literacy

- Encompasses the effective use of multiple information technologies and formats.

- Enables individuals to develop skills for learning throughout life.
- Supports skills for workplace enterprise and for community participation

An information literate individual is able to:

- Determine the extent of information needed
- Access the needed information effectively and efficiently
- Evaluate information and its sources critically
- Incorporate selected information into one's knowledge base
- Use information effectively to accomplish a specific purpose
- Understand the economic, legal, and social issues surrounding the use of information, and access and use information ethically and legally

In a nutshell, Information literacy has five broad abilities within the context of this continuum and a lifelong learning context :

- Recognizing the need for information
- Knowing how to access information
- Understanding how to evaluate information
- Knowing how to synthesize information
- Being able to communicate information

NEED FOR INFORMATION LITERACY

Information literacy is required because of proliferating information access and resources. Individuals are faced with diverse, abundant information choices – in their studies, in the workplace, and in their lives. Information is available through community resources, special interest organizations, manufacturers and service providers, media, libraries and the Internet. Increasingly, information comes unfiltered. This raises questions about authenticity, validity and reliability. In addition, information is available through multiple media, including graphical, aural and textual. These pose special challenges in evaluating, understanding and using information in an ethical and legal manner. The uncertain quality and expanding quantity of information also pose large challenges for society. Sheer abundance of information and technology will not in itself create more informed citizens without a complementary understanding and capacity to use information effectively.

Information literacy is a prerequisite for lifelong learning and is common to all disciplines, to all-learning environments, and to all levels of education. It enables learners to engage critically with content and extend their investigations, become more self-directed, and assume greater control over their own learning

(CAUL, 2004). In the changing environment, every library grows in terms of reading materiais, equipments, space, staff, readers etc. The library and information scenario is changing at a dynamic speed and there is a paradigm shift from print media to web media; from ownership of documents to access to information; intermediary to end user model of services and location of specific libraries to digital/virtual/hybrid libraries. Similarly there is a chânge in the needs and interests of the readers. In accordance with this emerging scenario, the library and information professionals' role is also subjected to dramatic changes. To meet the current requirements, library professionals must be able to perform various tasks coping up with the changes in technological environment.

Therefore, library and information professionals are required to acquire knowledge and skills in Information and Communication Technology as the library of to-day centered round highly IT influenced service, especially educational institutions in developing countries. In recent years, the libraries in the engineering education in India are increasingly adopting Information and Communication Technology.

SEVEN FACES OF INFORMATION LITERACY

Christine Bruce, in her book Seven Faces of Information Literacy (1997) identifies seven categories of IL as experienced by Australian educators in two universities:

1. *Information technology conception*

   - using information technology for information retrieval and communication

2. *Information sources conception*

   - finding information

3. Information process conception

   - executing a process

4. *Information control conception*

   - controlling information

5. *Knowledge construction conception*

   - building up a personal knowledge base in a new area of interest

6. *Knowledge extension conception*

   - working with knowledge and personal perspectives adopted in such a way that novel insights are gained

7. *Wisdom conception*

   - using information wisely for the benefit of others.

SCONUL Seven Pillars Model for Information Literacy

© Society of college, National and University Libraries

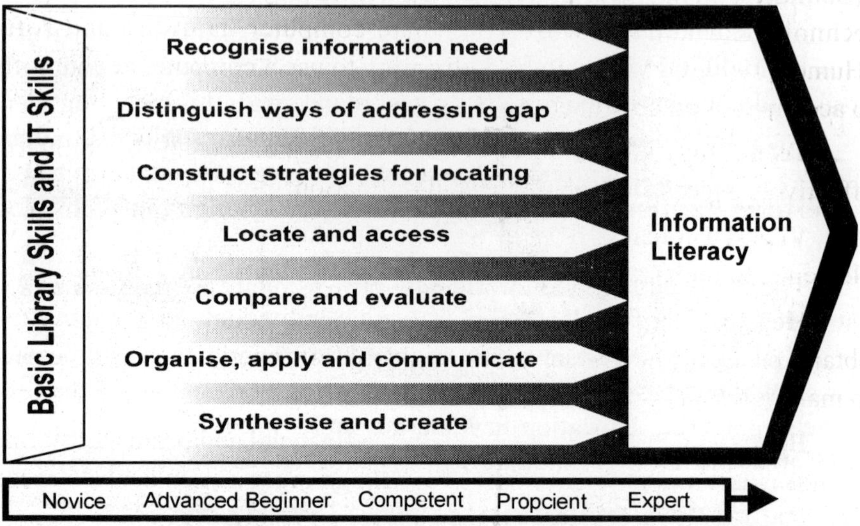

INFORMATION LITERACY RELATED TERMINOLOGY

Information Literacy: Ability to know when there is a need for information, to be able to identify, locate, evaluate, and effectively use that information for the issue or problem at hand.

Functional Literacy Skills needed to survive and prosper in the workplace. It refers to the ability to function in an advanced society - the OCED has used a three-fold definition (Organization for Economic Cooperation and Development, 1995).

Prose Literacy - the knowledge and skills required to locate and use information contained in various formats including job applications, pay roll forms, transportation schedules, maps, tables and graphics.

Quantitative Literacy - the knowledge and skills required to apply arithmetic operations, either alone or sequentially, to numbers embedded in printed materials, such as balancing a chequebook, figuring out a tip, completing an order form or determining the amount of interest on a loan from a advertisement.

Library Literacy refers to competencies in the use of libraries (collections and services), the ability to follow a systematic search strategy to locate and evaluate the most relevant information on a given topic (Humes, 1999).

Media Literacy refers to critical thinking in assessing information made available through television, radio, newspapers, magazines and increasingly the Internet (Bawden. 2001, p. 225). The ability to decode, analyze, evaluate, and produce communication in a variety of forms.

Computer Literacy is the ability to understand and use computer. "(Summers, Della;1995, p. 828). Computer literacy is usually associated with technological know-how to manipulate computer hardware and software (Humes, 1999, Oxbrow, 1998). The ability to use a computer and its software to accomplish practical tasks.

Technology Literacy: The ability to use media such as the Internet to effectively access and communicate information.

Visual Literacy: The ability, through knowledge of the basic visual elements, to understand the meaning and components of the image.

Health Literacy: The degree to which individuals have the capacity to obtain, process, and understand basic health information and services needed to make appropriate health decisions.

Business Literacy: The ability to use financial and business information to understand and make decisions that help an organization achieve success.

- Library literacy;
- Media literacy;
- Computer literacy (synonyms-IT/information technology/electronic/ electronic information literacy);
- Network literacy (synonyms-Internet literacy, hyper - literacy); and
- Digital literacy (synonym - digital information literacy).

Doyle (1992) defined an information literate person as one who:

- recognizes the need for information;
- recognizes that accurate and complete information is the basis for intelligent decision making;
- identifies potential sources of information;
- develops successful search strategies;
- accesses sources of information, including computer-based and other technologies;
- evaluates information;
- organizes information for practical application;
- integrates new information into an existing body of knowledge, and;
- uses information in critical thinking and problem solving.

ROLE OF LIBRARIAN IN IMPARTIY INFORMATION LITERACY

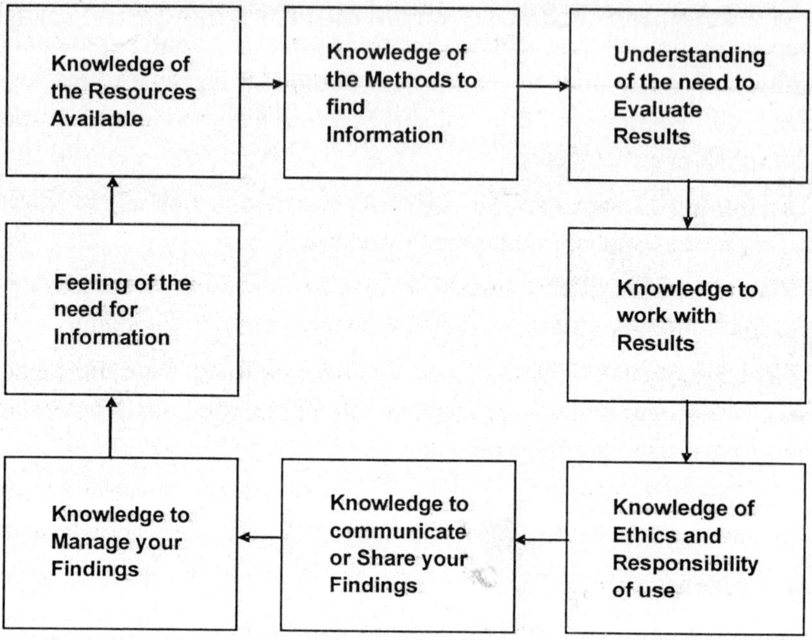

Implications for Librarians and Libraries

Librarians led the way in the early 1970s in conceptualizing the idea of information literacy and its relationship to lifelong learning. Early development of the concept of information literacy frequently focused on the future role of libraries and librarians in helping with the use and application of information (Beherens 1994).

The impact of moving from text-based learning to resource-based learning will involve heavier use of library materials and a demand for more and varied media resources, including print and nonprint. Consequently, school administrators will need to re-evaluate how funds are distributed between the textbook budget and the budget for their library media resources. Public libraries will have to coordinate more closely with schools and other learning sites to ensure sufficient access to information resources and technology for all ages and abilities and to remain a strong community resource for lifelong learning. As information specialists, librarians will be called upon more frequently to consult with teachers and learners, and to provide training and guidance toward the sharpening of information literacy skills not only in school and academic libraries but in public and special libraries as well. These are important considerations for all types of libraries given the range of patrons who use these libraries and given that the linking of library holdings and the stepped up demand for resource sharing among libraries escalates the importance (and costs) of interlibrary loans.

Information Literacy: Academic Libraries

Why is Information Literacy Important for Academic Libraries?

Students need their own internal navigation system to manage the information-rich environment that now surrounds them. Incoming students have far more experience with the Internet and far less experience with print than most of their professors. This often results in a mis-match between academic expectations and student behavior. Academic librarians are the natural in-house experts for teaching both students and faculty colleagues how to find, evaluate and use information effectively.

What's New?

- Moving away from the 50 minute instruction session towards class-integrated instruction, quarter-long research classes and self-directed online learning.
- Moving away from librarian-as-expert towards librarian as teacher.
- Moving away from librarians as the "handmaidens to research" towards librarians as partners with faculty in creating critical thinkers and competent researchers.

Advantages of Academic Libraries in the Shift to Information Literacy

- Academic libraries often have established instruction programs of some kind.
- Academic libraries often enjoy access to advanced information technology.
- Academic librarians are often encouraged to research, explore new issues and create new programs.
- Faculty concerns about Internet use can be used to encourage a curriculum-wide focus on evaluation and critical thinking.

Challenges for Academic Libraries in the Shift to Information Literacy

- Faculty often underestimates their students' need for help in learning the research process.
- Faculty and administrators often remain stuck in their conception of the library as a collection and of librarians as research assistants.
- Academic librarians are often bound to their self-image as experts and often resist any form of teaching.

- Lower student use of the library and librarians makes them hard to reach.
- Often have established instruction programs of some kind.
- Academic libraries often enjoy access to advanced information technology.
- Academic librarians are often encouraged to research, explore new issues and create new programs.
- Faculty concerns about Internet use can be used to encourage a curriculum-wide focus on evaluation and critical thinking.

Challenges for Academic Libraries in the Shift to Information Literacy

- Faculty often underestimate their students' need for help in learning the research process.
- Faculty and administrators often remain stuck in their conception of the library as a collection and of librarians as research assistants.
- Academic librarians are often bound to their self-image as experts and often resist any form of teaching.
- Lower student use of the library and librarians makes them hard to reach.

CORE COMPETENCIES FOR LIS PROFESSIONALS

Competencies are the -

- Skills
- Technical knowledge and
- Personal attributes that enable individuals to contribute positively to their organizations and the library profession.

These Core Competencies apply to all librarians.

- Technical Skills (ICT Skills)
- Management Skills
- Subject Skills
- Information Skills
- Soft Skills

Recognizing this, the Association of College and Research Libraries (ACRL) has identified seven **skills** need to do good research and create knowledge in this information-rich society. These are the ability to :-

1) Access information effectively and efficiently;
2) Determine the extent of information needed;
3) Critically evaluate information and its sources;
4) Incorporate information into knowledge base;
5) Use information purposefully;
6) Understand the economic, legal and social issues surrounding information use;
7) Access and use information ethically and legally **(ACRL, 2000).**

ESSENTIAL SKILLS AND VALUES FOR INFORMATION LITERACY

1. **Generic Skills**
   - Problem solving
   - Collaboration and teamwork
   - Communication
   - Critical thinking
2. **Information Skills**
   - Information seeking
   - Information use
   - Fluency with ICT
3. **Values and Beliefs**
   - Using information wisely and ethically
   - Social responsibility and community participation

Information literacy knows when and why one need information, where to find it, and how to evaluate, use and communicate it in an ethical manner. This definition implies several skills. We believe that the skills (or competencies) that are required to be information literate require an understanding of: (CILIP,2004)

- a need for information
- the resources available
- how to find information
- the need to evaluate results
- how to work with or exploit results
- ethics and responsibility of use

- how to communicate or share your findings
- how to manage your findings

Competencies are the skills, technical knowledge and personal attributes that enable individuals to contribute positively to their organizations and the library profession. These Core Competencies apply to all librarians.

- Demonstrates a strong commitment to excellent customer service.
- Recognizes and addresses the diverse nature of the library's patrons and community.
- Understands and supports the culture and context of the library and, if applicable, its parent institution.
- Demonstrates knowledge of the library system and the library profession.
- Understands the social, political, and economic context in which the library exists.
- Demonstrates knowledge of library and information science theory, information creation, organization, and delivery.
- Adheres to the Code of Ethics.
- Exhibits leadership skills including critical thinking, risk taking, and creativity, regardless of position within the management structure.
- Demonstrates commitment to working with others to achieve common goals.
- Acts within the organization to implement the principles of knowledge management.
- Exhibits an understanding of the importance of a multidisciplinary and cross-functional approach to programs and projects within the organization.
- Monitors and implements changes in technology and information systems.
- Shares knowledge and expertise with users and colleagues.
- Displays excellent communication skills and is able to promote the library and advocate for its needs.
- Communicates effectively with publishers and other information providers to advance the interests of the library.
- Recognizes the value of professional networking and actively participates in professional associations.
- Actively pursues personal and professional growth through continuing education. (Ramesh Babu and Ramesha, 2007)

IFLA's ROLE IN INFORMATION LITERACY IN THE 21st CENTURY

The role of IFLA in defining information literacy in the future is one of balance and inclusiveness. IFLA has a role in broadening the practical definition to include all forms of information literacy for all people. IFLA has included information literacy statements in many of its policy documents, including The IFLA Internet Manifesto, The IFLA/UNESCO School Library Manifesto, and The UNESCO Public Library Manifesto. More recently, one can see the impact of IFLA's activities in section C4 of the World Summit of the Information Society Plan of Action, which reads, "Everyone should have the necessary skills to benefit from the Information Society" and goes on to refer to ITC (Information and Communication Technology) literacy and later e-literacy. However, there is much more work to be done in specifying how ITC literacy and e-literacy will be developed and implemented in tandem with the delivery of the Information and Communication Technologies.

In addition to continuing its information literacy related lobbying efforts and partnerships with other organizations, IFLA has a role in supporting the creation of standards against which librarians and libraries can evaluate all forms of information literacy, in supporting and valuing all forms of information literacy, and in continuing to provide various forums in which all interested parties can share their successes in defining information literacy in their own environments.

Information Literacy Standards.

The **information literacy standards** to become effective learners include three basic components: access, evaluation and use of **information**. These core goals are found in most of the **standards** created by library associations, and individual educators (Byerly/Brodie/ Kuhlthau), such as the relevant contributions of AASL, ACRL, SCONUL and the Australian and New Zealand Institute for **Information Literacy**, followed by the work of other countries, like Mexico.

The **IFLA information literacy standards** are based on these international experiences and contributions.

The **IFLA standards** are grouped under the three basic IL components.

A. ACCESS. The user access **information** effectively and efficiently

1. **Definition and articulation of the information need**
   - Defines or recognizes the need for **information**
   - Decides to do something to find the **information**
   - Express and defines the **information** need
   - Initiates the search process

2. **Location of information**
    - Identifies, and evaluates potential sources of **information**
    - Develops search strategies
    - Accesses the selected **information** sources
    - Selects and retrieves the located **information**

B. EVALUATION. The user evaluates **information** critically and competently

1. **Assessment of information**
    - Analyzes, and examines, extracting **information**
    - Generalizes and interprets **information**
    - Selects, and syntheses **information**
    - Evaluates accuracy and relevance of the retrieved **information**
2. **Organization of information**
    - Arranges, and categorizes **information**
    - Groups and organizes the retrieved **information**
    - Determines which is the best and most useful **information**

C. USE. The user applies/uses **information** accurately and creatively

1. Use of **information**
    - Finds new ways to communicate, present and use **information**
    - Applies the retrieved **information**
    - Learns, or internalizes **information** as a personal knowledge
    - Presents the **information** product
2. Communication and ethical use of **information**
    - Understands ethical use of **information**
    - Respects the legal use of **information**
    - Communicates the learning product with acknowledgement of intellectual property
    - Uses the relevant acknowledgement style **standards**

INFORMATION LITERACY SCENARIO AT GLOBAL LEVEL

Information literacy has become a global issue calling for greater attention. As a result several countries have taken initiatives in starting National and International programmes. The UNESCO, IFLA, ALA and host of other organisations and associations have developed ample number of plans and strategies. One such worth mentioning attempt is by the UNESCO. Its famous

Prague declaration entitled, '**Towards an Information Literate Society**,' is an outcome of the Information Literacy Meeting of Experts (20-23 September 2004, Geneva) that highlights the immediate actions to be taken for the promotion of information literacy by all the countries in the world. The significant aspects listed in the document are given below:

(i) The creation of Information Society is key to social, cultural and economic development of nations and communities, institutions and individuals in the 21st century and beyond.

(ii) Information Literacy encompasses knowledge of one's information concerns and needs, and ability to identify locate, evaluate, organize and effectively create, use and communicate information to address issues or problems at hand; it is a prerequisite for participating effectively in the information society, and is part of the basic human right of life long learning.

(iii) Information Literacy, in conjunction with access to essential information and effective use of information and communicating technologies use of information and communicating technologies, plays a leading role in reducing the inequalities within and among countries and peoples and in promoting tolerance and natural understanding through information use in multicultural and multilingual contexts.

(iv) Governments should develop strong inter disciplinary program to promote Information Literacy nationwide as a necessary step in closing the digital divide through creation of an information literate citizenry an effective civil society and a competitive workforce.

(v) Information Literacy is a concern to all sectors and should be tailored by each to its specific needs and context.

(vi) Information Literacy should be an integral part of education for all, which can contribute critically to the achievement of the United Nations Millennium Development Goals, and respect for the Universal Declaration of Human Rights.

In the last decade information literacy has become a global issue and many information literacy initiatives have been documented throughout the world, with particularly strong efforts and examples in North America, Australia, South Africa and Northern Europe .These programmes addressed many concerns relative to ICT and information skills. In education, teachers, librarians and others are working to integrate information skills instruction within the curricula to achieve relevant learning outcomes.

In the US and Australia, government recognition of information competencies has been informed by high-profile information literacy led by the profession. Examples include the ALA Presidential Committee on

Information Literacy (1987), US Forum on Information Literacy (1989), Association of College and Research Libraries Institute for Information Literacy (1997) and Information Literacy Competency Standards (2000), Australian Library and Information Association Information Literacy Task Force (1997), Australia and New Zealand Institute for Information Literacy and Australian Universities Librarians Information Literacy Standards (2000). There is also a Nordic Information Literacy Institute and IFLA Sectional Committee on Information Literacy which is being established.

INFORMATION LITERACY IN INDIA

In India concept of information literacy begins to appear in the library and information science (LIS) literature is very recent, but related terms, concepts and services are present in research and practice in India during the 1990s. Information literacy cuts across many different disciplines and across professional and even political agendas: librarians, teachers and faculty, experts in educational technology, learning facilitators, all contribute to the training in information literacy of citizens, even while unaware of the concept and its implications. In recent reviews in primary and secondary compulsory education and the higher education sectors, all these are related in several ways to the IL experience. Recording the evolution and achievements of IL in India is not an easy task because of its great variety, but in recent years LIS institutions in India have gone through an accelerated pace in development which certainly has had a strong positive influence for all IL-related activities and services and for the widespread acceptance of the concept itself **(C.R. Karisiddappa, 2004)**

Initiatives at various universities or institutions of higher learning are in process but at different levels and there is a need for awareness and networking of these initiatives. Creating digital libraries, building institutional repositories of the institution's research / scientific output, compiling subject gateways linking to global resources, organizing Information Literacy programmes to utilize all of them are some of the major initiatives in India being a developing country.

An international Information Literacy workshop was organised in India by Punjabi University with the support of UNESCO in Oct 2005 to promote Information Literacy in South and South East Asia. They resolved that Information Literacy should be introduced within national curricula at all levels including life long learning programmes to make the stake holders independent learners and critical thinkers. There is a need for social responsibility to leverage the benefits of higher education for the under privileged.

Recently the Department of Library and Information Science, University of Kerala proposed to implement an Information Literacy programme in colleges affiliated to its university. (Oct 2006). A number of seminars and workshops are being conducted in India, thanks to the generous grants from UNESCO. In addition to this universities are conducting seminars and symposia (University of Madras, 2007).

Role of LIS Schools

The library schools should assume the role of leadership and responsibility to produce competent manpower for the present as well as future needs of different kinds of libraries.

To quote Lancaster, "We must shift the focus of our professional concern away from the library as an institution and towards the skilled professionals, who will become a professional practitioner on par with medical and legal practitioners"

CONCLUSION

Information literacy guidelines can be reviewed, and changed adapted by librarians according to the priorities of their institution, so that IL elements can be better suited to local or national needs. Local budget, policies, procedures, and priorities need to be taken into account in their application. The guidelines are a checklist of subjects to keep in mind during the planning and implementation of IL program or to reinforce previous information literacy work. Information professionals must keep in mind that they need to do whatever they can with the resources that they may have. It is better to do something than to wait for the crafting of the perfect information literacy program. Information literacy is the necessity of the information age. It is an understanding to find way through many sources of information without becoming overwhelmed and overloaded. Information skills further helps to acquire, manage and utilize the information for the benefit of the individuals and the society.

Information literacy demands a new way of thinking about learning and teaching which may be in conflict with cultural standards and expectations concerning the roles of students and educators. Incorporating information literacy across curricula, services, the collaborative efforts of faculty, librarians, lectures and by leading discussions. Faculty also inspire students to explore the unknown, best to fulfill information needs, and monitor students ' programs and services; organize, of access to information; who seek information and staff development among faculty, librarians, initiate information literacy programs, those programs, and provide ongoing resources to sustain them.

Information literacy programme is well positioned to develop these skills, thanks to its learning-how-to-learn framework which is fully articulated in the information literacy standards devised by various associations (ACRL, IFLA, ALA, ALIA, ANZIIL etc.). There is little recognition of the learning-how-to-learn or the knowledge construction approaches in the Indian education system, and these omissions should be addressed through the development of an information literacy policy that is embedded in Indian national learning agenda.

Incorporating information literacy across curricula, services, the collaborative efforts of faculty, librarians, lecturers and by leading discussions. Faculty also inspire students to explore the unknown, best to fulfill information needs, and monitor students ' programs and services; organize, of access to information . There is little recognition of the learning-how-to-learn or the knowledge construction approaches in the Indian education system, and these omissions should be addressed through the development of an information literacy policy that is embedded in Indian national learning agenda. It is better to do something than to wait for the crafting of the perfect information literacy program. We are living in one of the most exciting and challenging times for the information industry. As the information professionals, we take seriously our responsibility to deliver services including disseminating information, facilitating access to and sharing of scientific information, providing forums to create and share new knowledge, enabling collaboration and connecting scientists and students. Information Literacy skills are enabling us to take such services to a new level and make them more interactive and participatory for our users.

Although it is hard to list or document every thing exactly, a successful Information / Library professional needs to have a lot of important IL skills. Without possessing or acquiring them the LIS professional will not be able to fulfil his role in any Information centre. Unless you have the IL skills, you can't get to the hard skills.

"Arise, Awake, and Stop not until the goal is reached"

— Swami Vivekananda

REFERENCES

1. American Association of School Libraries (2003). The nine information literacy standards for student learning. Available at http: //www.ala.org/ aaslTemplate.cfm?Section= Information Power & Template = / ContentManagement/ContentDisplay .cfm&ContentID = 19937
2. ACRL (2000). Information Literacy Competency Standards for Higher Education. Chicago: Association of College and Research Libraries.
3. http://www.ala.org/ala/acrl/acrlstandards/standards.pdf
4. Alaska Association of School Librarians (AkASL). Library/ Information Literacy Standards Board Approved - December 10, 1999
5. Andretta, S. (2005): Information Literacy: A Practitioner's Guide, Chandos Publishing, Oxford.
6. Andretta, S., Cutting, A. (2003): *Information literacy: a plug and play approach*, *Libri*, 53, 3, 202-9.

7. Arp, L and Woodard, B. S. (2002): Recent trends in Information Literacy and instruction. *Reference and User Services Quarterly*, 42(2), Pp.124-132.

8. Association of College and Research Libraries (ACRL) (2000). Information literacy Competency Standards for Higher Education. ACRL, available at : www.ala.org/acrl /ilcomstan.html

9. Bruce, C (1997) *The seven faces of information literacy* Blackwood, South Australia: Auslib

10. Bruce, C. (1995). Information Literacy: A Framework for Higher Education. *Australian Library Journal, No.*44, pp.158-169.

11. Bundy, A. ed. (2004) *Australian and New Zealand Information Literacy Framework: principles, standards and practice.* Second edition Adelaide: Australian and New Zealand Institute for Information Literacy .p4

12. Bruce, C. (1997). Seven Faces of Information Literacy. Adelaide: AUSLIB Press Eld, C. (2001).

13. Byerly, Greg and Brodie, Carolyn S. "Information literacy skills models: defining the choices. In: Stripling, Barbara K. *Learning and Libraries in an Information Age: Principles and Practice. Littleton,* CO: Libraries Unlimited, 1999.

14. Cavalier, R. (1993). Information Literacy: Why Worry? In: D. Booker (Ed.), *Information literacy: The Australian agenda* Adelaide: University of South Australia, pp.17-27.

15. CAUL Information Literacy Assessment Research Project (2002): http://www.caul.edu.au/ meetings/caul20012info-lit-assess.doc

16. CILIP (2004) A short introduction to information literacy. Retrieved January 1 2007 from http://www.cilip.org.uk/professionalguidance/informationliteracy.

17. Council of Australian University Librarians: Information Literacy standards (2004). Australia: CAUL, 2004.

18. IFLA. IFLA/UNESCO School Library Manifesto, rev. Feb.16, 2000. (http://www. ifla.org/VII/s11/pubs/manifest.htm)

19. IFLA. UNESCO Public Library Manifesto, rev. July 16, 1998. (http://www.ifla.org/ VII/s8/unesco/eng.htm)

20. Information Literacy Standards for Student Learning. Prepared by the AASL/AECT National Guidelines Vision Committee Draft #5 October 7, 1996

21. Karisiddappa, C. R. (2004). Information Literary and Capability

Building. In: World Social Forum-2004: International Workshop on Democratization of Information: Focus on Libraries. Proceedings Ed. by Muttayya Koganurmath et al.. Organised by NIGD and TISS.

22. Karisiddappa, C. R. (2004). Literacy Concepts in LIS Curriculum: Perspective from India. Paper presented at 70th IFLA World Library and Information Congress held at Buenos Aires, Argentina, 21st – 28th August 2004.

23. Karisiddappa, C. R. (2004): Literacy Concepts in LIS Curriculum: Perspective from India. Paper presented at 70th IFLA World Library and Information Congress held at Buenos Aires, Argentina, 21st – 28th August 2004.

24. Martin, A. (2003). *Towards e-literacy.* Martin, A. and Rader, H. (Eds.) *Information and IT Literacy*, Facet Publishing, London, pp.3-23.

25. Ramesh Babu B (2008). "Information Literacy Competence standards and performance Indicators: An overview" *DESIDOC Bulletin of Information Technology*. 28(2), 2008: 56-65.

26. Ramesh Babu B, Vinayagamoorthy P and Gopalakrishnan S (2007) "ICT Skills among Librarians in Engineering Educational Institutions in Tamil Nadu" *DESIDOC Bulletin of Information Technology*, 27(6) November 2007.

27. Ramesh Babu, B, and Ramesha (2007) "Soft Skills for LIS Professionals in the Knowledge Society" (Prof. C.R. Karisiddappa festschrift) IN: Library and Information Science Profession in the Knowledge Society, edited by M. M. Koganuramath, B.D. Kumbar and B.S. Kademani. New Delhi: Allied, pp.331-339.

28. Ramesh Babu, B (2006) "Information literacy competency standards, performance indicators and UNESCO/IFLA School/Public Library manifesto." IN: UNESCO sponsored Workshop on Information Literacy Competency Development for Library and Information Professionals and Special Educators (Southern states) organised by SALIS and Madras School of Social Work during 6-10 Nov.2006

29. Senn, Breivik P. (1993). Information Literacy: What's it all about? *In.* Information Literacy: The Australian Agenda: Proceedings of a Conference held 2-4 December 1992, Adelaide, University of South Australia Library, p.8

30. Spitzer, K L, Eisenberg, M B & Lowe, C A (1998) Information literacy: Essential skills for the information age Syracuse, New York: Eric Clearinghouse on Information and Technology.

31. Snavely, L. (2001). Information Literacy Standards for Higher Education: An International Perspective, Paper presented at the 67th IFLA Council and General Conference, *Libraries and Librarians:*

Making a Difference in the Knowledge Age, Boston, MA, 16-21 August, 2001, pp. 1-4.

32. UNESCO Public Library Manifesto. (1994, November).
33. www.ifla.org/documents/libraries/policies/unesco.htm .
34. Thompson, H M & Henley, S A (2000) Fostering information literacy: connecting national standards, Goals 2000, and the SCANS Report, Englewood, Colorado: Libraries Unlimited, Inc.
35. World Summit on the Information Society (2004). Declaration of Principles, IFLA *Journal*, 30(1), p. 72. http://www.state.gov/documents/organization/27778.doc

❑❑❑

Chapter – 27

Knowledge Management in Academic Libraries

Dipak Krushnarao Bhalekar and Prashant P. Deshmukh

INTRODUCTION

In the current climate of rapid change, whether political, economical, social or technological, the importance of knowledge cannot be ignored. Knowledge plays a crucial role in the development of the society which is based on the development of the individual person of that society. Once society is developed automatically the nation will develop. Developed countries have already realized the importance of knowledge and accordingly collected and organized properly. The developing countries like India are now realizing its importance. It has been felt that without knowledge society and then nation cannot be developed.

On this backdrop someone has to come forward and act as a broker between those who have knowledge and those who may use it. No doubt, knowledge cannot be well managed until some organization or professional takes the clear responsibility of it. Library professionals are the right persons to shoulder this responsibility.

Knowledge is action. It is a value-added behavior and activity. It provides the ability to respond to a novel situation. The person having knowledge can take right decision at right time in any critical situation. Such decisions will definitely get fruitful results. Therefore it should not be neglected. It must be focused and shared.

TYPES OF KNOWLEDGE

Available knowledge in the universe is of the two types viz. Explicit and Implicit or Tacit. Explicit knowledge is traditional form of knowledge and is available in the documented form. It is formal, systematic and easily disseminated or communicated as and when required. It can also freely and easily shared amongst its users. Realizing the value of this knowledge, the Librarians and Information professionals have already been engaged in the collection, organization and dissemination of it. On the other hand the implicit knowledge is available with the individuals. It is a personal knowledge based on the individual experience. It is a personal asset. Such knowledge vanishes with the person. It is also known as Tacit Knowledge. It is something not easily visible and expressible.

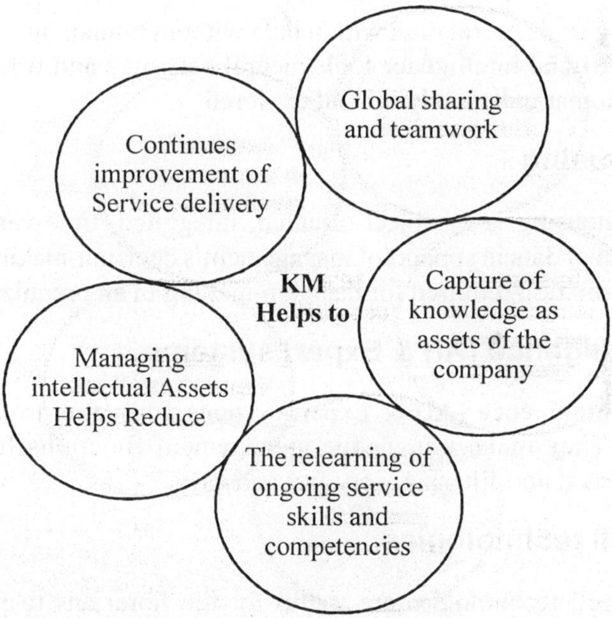

Fig. Expected benefits from Knowledge Management

TECHNOLOGICAL TOOLS

Though technology is not the do-all and end-all of knowledge management, it offers powerful tools for the same. The technologies that enable knowledge management are

- Internet, Intranet and Extranet
- Data Mining
- Data Warehousing

- Artificial Intelligence (AI) & Expert systems
- Push and pull technologies
- Electronic publishing
- DBMS
- Groupware

Internet, Intranet and Extranet

Internet provides a strong collaborative platform for knowledge management. Intranets and extranets help to efficiently share resources. There can be efficient document transfer, exchange, conversations and discussions.

Data Mining

Data mining finds correlation within data without human intervention or effort. It uses artificial intelligence tools, neural networks and fuzzy logic in which data is automatically analyzed and explored.

Data Warehousing

Data Warehousing is a subject-oriented, integrated, time-variant, non-volatile collection of data in support of management's decision-making process. It stores the information required for decision-making in an organization.

Artificial Intelligence (AI) & Expert systems

Artificial Intelligence (AI) & Expert systems add value to knowledge management . They make knowledge management functions like search information retrieval and filtering, very fast and easy.

Push and Pull technologies

Push and pull technologies are useful for the librarians to make their searches more efficient and effective. They help in sending the right information to the right reader at the right time Pull technology provides tools for navigation like directories, search engines or web browsers. They locate and deliver information very fast. They refine searches and give us focused results. Customized search engines and directories use metadata. Push technology alerts the searcher to information and information sources he is not aware of E-mail and voice mail are two examples of push technology. Thus, push technology helps in information capture, whereas pull technology helps in navigation.

Electronic publishing

Electronically publishing the material and providing hyperlinks for the same helps in sharing knowledge. The blogs published through intranet or

Internet help in publishing experiences and thoughts of the persons and thus help in knowledge management.

Groupware

Groupware helps knowledge workers share their expertise. This is a hypertext system having e-mail, computer conferencing and shared screen editing. It allows user to use bulletin board, and going to the file the user can add ones own notes. Lotus Notes is an ideal example of a groupware product.

Knowledge Management Packages

Several readymade Knowledge Management packages like IBM Domino, Hummingbird, Novell Groupwise are available in the market today. There are also portals for development of knowledge management tools.

KNOWLEDGE MANAGEMENT IN ACADEMIC LIBRARIES

Many librarians claim that they already perform knowledge management activities for a long time but KM (1999) said that "Knowledge Management is not about managing or organizing books or journals, searching the internet for clients or arranging for the circulation of materials. However, each of these activities can in some way be part of knowledge management sectrum and processes. Knowledge management is about enhancing the use of organization knowledge through sound practices of knowledge management and organizational learning. Thus, knowledge management is a combination of information management, communication, and human resources. How to manage knowledge will become an important subject facing libraries in near future. Knowledge management in libraries should be focused on effective research and development of knowledge, creation of knowledge base, exchange and sharing of knowledge between library staffs (including its users), training of library staff, speeding up explicit processing of the implicit knowledge and realizing of its sharing (Shanhong,2000). In many ways knowledge management incorporates principles that academic librarians have developed and used with scholarly information for many years. It then applies these principles, and others, to organizational information in ways that create new knowledge to improve organizational effectiveness (Hirshon, 1999). With the help of the knowledge management processes, libraries convert data and information stored in various sources into knowledge and deliver only relevant knowledge to users.

Knowledge management within libraries involves organizing and providing access to intangible resources that help librarians and administrators carry out their tasks more effectively and efficiently (Jantz, 2001). Knowledge Management is one way to develop and apply the organizational knowledge needed to improve library operations and ultimately, library effectiveness. It also enables libraries to generate organizational knowledge for higher education institutions (Townely,2002). Thus Knowledge management in the academic library is the combination of different processes such as acquisition of knowledge from different sources (print, electronic and human) and classification, storing, indexing and dissemination of that knowledge using people, process and technology in such a way by which library could fulfill the mission of the parent organization in term of users, satisfaction. In academic libraries, knowledge management is about encouraging library staff and users to communicate their knowledge and experience by creating environments and systems for capturing, organizing, learning, enhancing and sharing knowledge for the benefit of the organization and its users. The libraries are moving from collection management to knowledge management and digital technologies offering new information services and products.

LOCATION OF KNOWLEDGE

Every library has internal and external knowledge resources for their users. Internal knowledge resources include librarian and staff, books and journals in-house developed database, CD-ROMs, encyclopedias, projects reports. External knowledge resources can include experts and librarians of other libraries, Online journals and books; users, suppliers, membership of other library and Information Centers.

ROLE OF LIBRARIANS IN KNOWLEDGEMENT MANAGEMENT

Role of librarians in KM is not a new role but a continuation of many of the roles that the librarians have played already with the help of information technologies. Reardon (1998) stated that "There is a need for significant changes in thinking, attitudes, education and training before we can confidently face the knowledge management future that awaits in many important areas of the information and library profesions"

The librarians should have following types of knowledge:

1. Knowledge about library's information sources or assets, products and services.
2. Knowledge about where these sources are stored and what is its use.
3. Knowledge about users including teaching staff and researcher and who is using these information sources.
4. What are the current usage of these sources and how to increase its uses?.
5. Knowledge about the library's own competencies and capabilities.
6. Knowledge about the emerging library trends and technologies.

(TPFL,1999) has described following personality attributes for Knowledge Manager:

- Creativity.
- Ability to learn and adapt
- Will and ability to create, share, harness and utilize knowledge
- Understanding of knowledge creation processes
- Understanding of the impact of knowledge
- Information literacy skills – creating, finding, sharing and using:
- Understanding of the knowledge process;
- Understanding of the principles of the "organization of knowledge" is key.

Anyone working in the field of knowledge and information management will require a range of skills, some of which can be grouped in the following categories which are related to knowledge and information management (Webb. 1998):

- Knowledge of sources: print/electronic, internal/external, whom to ask, how to look, evaluation.
- Subject knowledge and understanding.
- Information and records management: indexing methods, database development, thesaurus construction, retrieval/delivery methods, electronics storage, retention policy, structuring records, legislation, standards and controls.
- Internal and external networks.
- Users/patterns of usage: needs analysis, satisfaction measures.
- Current awareness services: monitoring/updating. Abstracting, new services.
- User advice and training.
- Contribution to knowledge and information strategy.

CONCLUSION

The concept of Knowledge Management is as old as the library. Though the terminology is new previously this activity was so simple to perform. However, with the emergence of interdisciplinary and multidisciplinary knowledge it is not possible to accomplish manually. In the process of retrieving and dissemination the knowledge from the well-organized knowledge, at certain places the manual techniques fail to satisfy the demands of seekers Information Technology can do this job effectively and efficiently. Therefore the Knowledge Manager must be master in both fields i.e. Library and Information Science and Computer Science.

As mentioned earlier, development of a nation as based on the richness of the knowledge bank it possesses. Moreover this knowledge bank should be well organized so that the knowledge stored in it should be transmitted to the knowledge customers any time without wasting their valuable time. Today's Library Professionals/Knowledge Managers are capable to manage it.

REFERENCE

1. Al-Hawamdesh, S (2002). Knowledge management: re-thinking information management and facing the challenge of managing tacit knowledge. Information Research, 8(1). [Available at http://informationR.net/ir/8-1paper143.html].
2. Duffy, Jan (2001). The tools and Technologies Needed for Knowledge Management. *Information Management Journal* 5(1), p. 64
3. Koskinen,Kaj U (2004). Knowledge management to improve project communication and implementation. *Project Management Journal* 135(2), pp. 13-19.
4. Khode subhash and Singh Umesh Kumar (2004). Knowledge management and academic libraries. *ILA Bulletin* 42(1), pp. 27-31.
5. Natarajan,Ganesh & Shekhar, Sandhya (2000). Knowledge Management : enabling business growth. New Delhi :Tata McGraw-Hill

❑❑❑

Chapter – 28

Web 2.0 for Enhancement of Library and Information Services : Focus on Weblog

Shalini R Lihitkar and Ramdas Lihitkar

INTRODUCTION

For centuries, social and technological changes have been affecting every profession. During the last two decades rapid technological development has affected library services as well. Specifically for the last five years, Web 2.0 technologies have significant impact on the higher education sector as well on the libraries all over world. Tim O'Reilly invented the term Web 2.0 in 2004

DEFINITIONS

- "**Web 2.0**" refers to web development and web design that facilitates interactive information sharing, interoperability, user-centered design and collaboration on the World Wide Web. Examples of Web 2.0 include web-based communities, hosted services, web applications, social-networking sites, video-sharing sites, wikis, blogs, mashups and folksonomies.
- It is a second generation of services available on the web that lets people collaborate and share information online
- A Web 2.0 site allows its users to interact with other users or to change website content, in contrast to non-interactive websites where users

are limited to the passive viewing of information that is provided to them.

NEED OF WEB 2.0 IN LIBRARIES

- Way of Communication, interaction, sharing of knowledge.
- Continuously changing : Impact of ICT on Users Environment.
- Libraries have to integrate several technologies in their services in order to attract the users.
- Now users are not information consumers but are content creators

TRANSFORMATION TO WEB 2.0 TO LIBRARY 2.0

- Web 2.0+ Library = Library 2.0
- Web 2.0 + Librarian = Librarian 2.0

Web 1.0	**Versus**	**Web 2.o**
E-mail	→	IM
Double Click	→	Google Ad Sense
Ofoto	→	Flicker
Akamail	→	Bit Torrent
Mp3.com	→	Napster
Britannica Online	→	Wikipedia
Personal websites	→	Blogging
Evite	→	Upcoming.organdEVDB
Domain name speculation	→	Search engine optimization
Page views	→	Cost per click
Screen scraping	→	Web services
Publishing	→	Participation
Content management systems	→	Wikis
Directories (taxonomy)	→	Tagging("folksonomy")
stickiness	→	syndication

Library Transformation

Library 1.0	**Versus**	**Library 2.0**
Closed stacks	→	Open stacks
Collection development	→	Library suggestion box
Reorganized Integrated Library Services	→	User tagging
Walk-in-services	→	Globally available services
"Read-only" Catalogue	→	Amazon-style comments

Contd.

Print newsletter mailed out	→	Team –built blog
Easy= dumb users	→	Easy= smart systems
Limited service options	→	Broad range of options
Information as commodity	→	Information as conversation

TOOLS FOR WEB 2.0

- Blogs : A blog is a website where library users can enter their thoughts, ideas, suggestions and comments
- Wikis : A wiki is a webpage or set of WebPages that can be easily edited by anyone who is allowed access.
- RSS : It is a family of web feed formats used to published frequently updated work such as blog entries, news headlines, audio and video in a standardized format.
- IM : it is a collection of technologies that create the possibility of real-time text-based communication between two or more participants over the internet.
- Social Networking : It is a service which focus on building online communities of people who share interests or activities.
- Pod casting : A podcast is a series of audio and video digital media which is distributed over the internet by syndicated download, through webfeeds, to portable media playsers and personal computers.
- You Tube : Allows users to upload, tag, watch, rate, review, view and even create play lists.
- Tagging : A tag is a keyword that is added to a digital object to describe it.

APPLICATION OF WEB 2.0 IN LIS

Blog

- Serve as a platform where the users can file their concern, quires and suggestions regarding the services and activities of the library.
- As a form of publication
- As a collection development tool where the users request the resources.
- Marketing of library and information services
- As a discussion forum.

Wikis

- Social interaction and discussions among the librarians and users.

- Can also be used by users to share information and enhance the content and a record of these transactions is archived for future reference.
- As a Ref. resources to built for FAQ
- For creating subject guides, subject gateways etc.

RSS

- Announcement of the availability of new books and other resources in a given subject area.
- We can subscribe to RSS from the sources for compiling their customized alerts.
- Enhance library instruction programmes
- Promote events organized in the library
- Announce availability of new research and learning opportunities in various academic/research departments.
- Integrating library services through RSS feeds.

Instant Messaging

- Instant clarifications for the questions from users and vice versa.
- Reference librarians can also send text, video and audio files
- Online meetings
- For providing virtual reference services

Social Networking

- Librarians can create a page to approach new users.
- It can be used to interact, share and exchange resources dynamically in an electronic medium.
- For building network among the interested group in discussing the common interest.
- Content can be added to the library catalogue, including users book reviews or other comments.

Podcasting

- Podcasting promotional recordings about the library's services and programs
- It can be used for highlighting about new resources.
- Podcasts enable librarians to share information with anyone at any time.

- It can be a publishing tool for users and librarians' oral presentations.

You Tube

- It can be used as publishing tool for marketing of library and library products.

Tagging

- It can be applied to the LIS for editing the subject headings from the user point of view and thereby enhancing the indexing and relevancy of the searches, making the collection more dynamic

Celebrities........... have their weblogs ,Why not Teachers/ Librarians??? Focus on Weblog

- Weblog is a new tool for information sharing and dissemination.
- A Weblog is an applicant that contains reverse chronologically ordered posts on a common webpage.
- The term Weblog was coined by Jorn Bergers in December 1997. The First Weblog was built by Tim- Burner – Lee at CERN, The European particle physics laboratory,
- Weblog, originally a simple web browser based system for updating websites, has developed into powerful webbased content management system capable of acting as a platform for learning.

What is it?

Blog / Weblog is

- A web page containing brief entries arranged chronologically.
- Can be a journal or diary, 'What's New' page or links to other web sites.
- A Weblog is just a website organized by time.
- A Weblog is an online diary or frequently updated personal webpage.
- A frequent chronological publication of personal thoughts and web links.

There are two views regarding weblog.

- Light Weight Content Management Tool
- Community& Knowledge Sharing Tool

ADVANTAGES OF WEBLOGS

- No need to know HTML, FTP
- Add / edit content anywhere, anytime
- Dynamic, Quick and easy to develop
- Easy to publish
- No need to download software
- Open Source and open Access feeling
- No Rules

WEBLOG FUNCTIONS

- RSS Newsfeeds
- Individual or Collaborative
- Personal diaries, commentaries, news updates
- Add Categories by using tags
- Archives
- Able to add comments
- Tempelets+ Easy to create & edit
- Updated with any Frequency

USE OF WEBLOG

- Communicating
- Easy to distribute the content
- Interactive
- Open Access feeling
- For information seeking
- For giving current knowledge
- Promote College/centre events
- Support Our Dedicated Users
- Engage Our Students Community
- Announcement

WEBLOG IN EDUCATION

It can be used as Personal Journaling Space and discussion Space.

BLOGGING AS A TEACHING TOOL

- Feedback for revising the course, change of teaching strategies etc.
- An online course management tool
- A weekly topic is posted
- Post articles
- Students post their thoughts
- Class discussions
- Writing assignments and homework exercises.
- Exchange information
- Posts comments, questions and advice.
- Students post their thoughts on what they are learning.
- Students use the blog as a writing portfolio.
- Students read each other's rough drafts of writing assignments and give feedback.
- Discuss news related to the courses subject.
- Students discuss class activities.
- Online students can get to know each other by reading and commenting on each others blog entries.
- Posts class times, rules governing classes, suggested readings, and exercises etc.
- Provide links to Internet items
- Organize class seminars.

SUGGESTIONS

- High speed wireless network (Wi-Fi).
- Or one personal computer along with high speed internet is a must in every library.
- One must respect others ideas and comments.
- One must be encouraged to express views openly without hurting others.
- Encouraged to read each others blogs and respond as early as possible giving their suggestions and comments.
- The sender is expected to edit his entry properly before posting it.

- Each entry must be considered as a serious piece of writing, written with care and deep thinking.
- A class blog can be maintained by each student, where he is free to express his ideas and feelings without interference from any body including his instructor. This will give special feeling to him, feeling it as his own space. In the long run, this will serve as his journal that he can continue even after he has passed the course.

Creation of Weblog

1. Log on to https://www.blogger.com

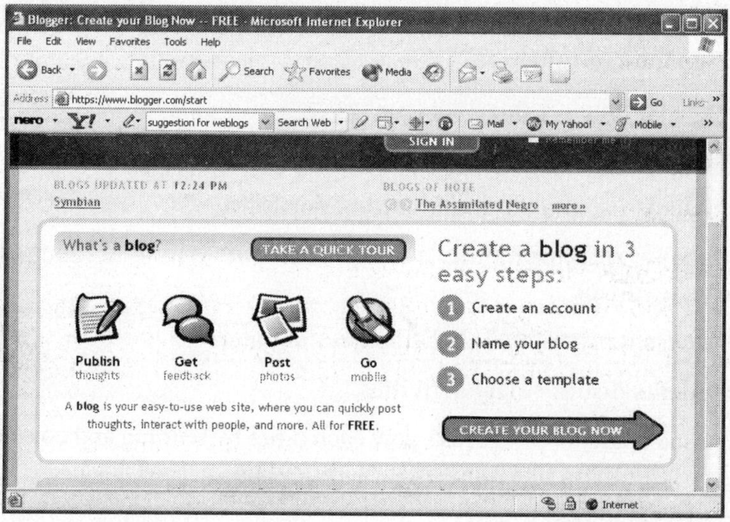

2. CA lick on Create an Account

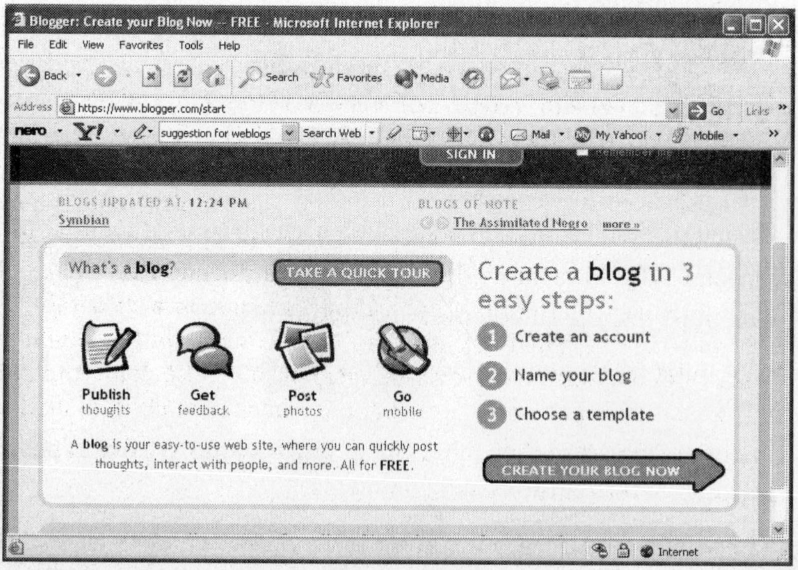

3. Name for your Weblog

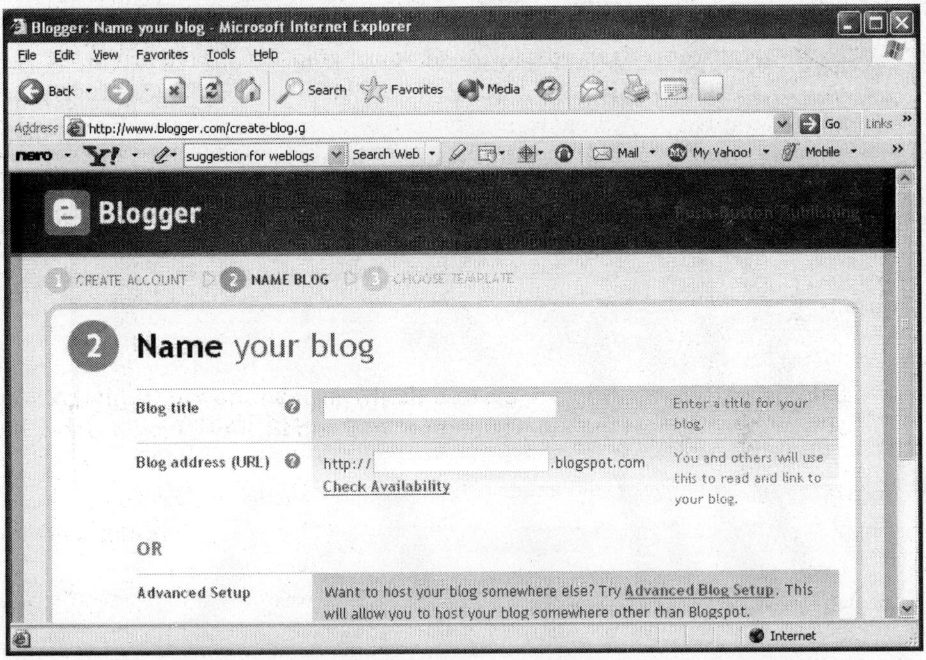

4. Choose a desired template

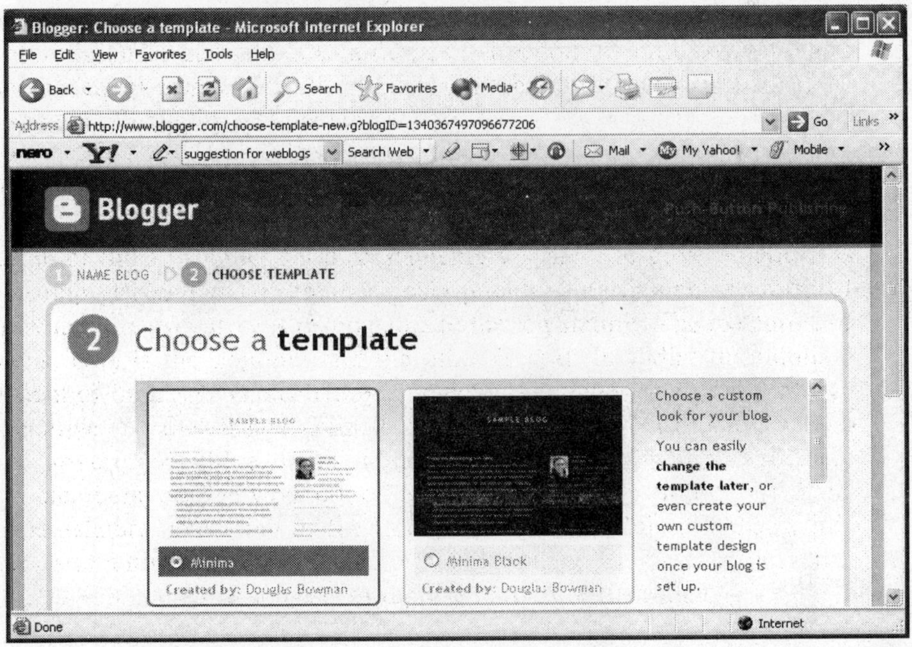

5. Creation of weblog

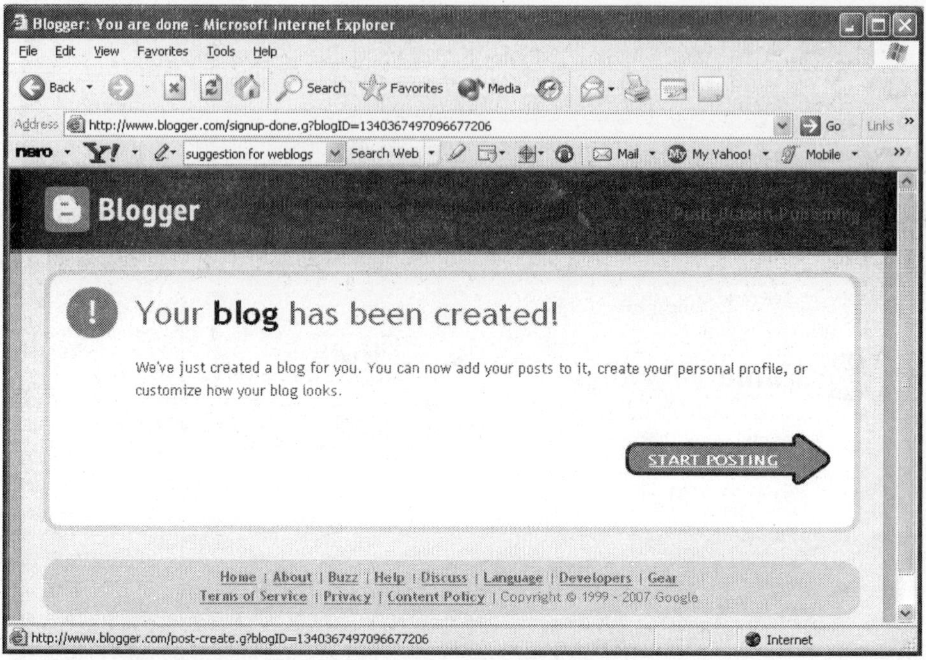

6. Posting of Entries

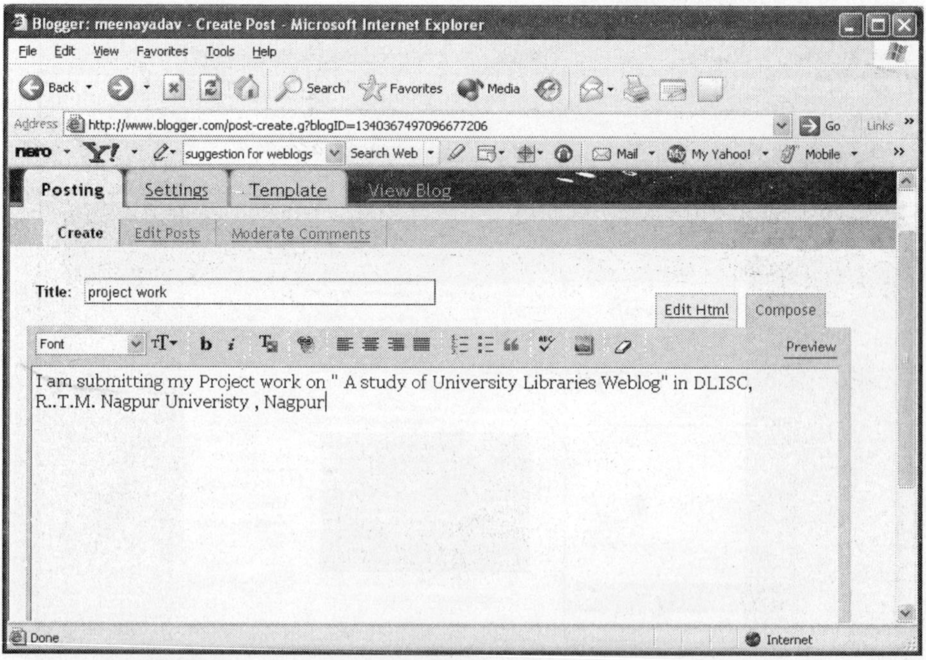

7. Display Screen of Posted Entry

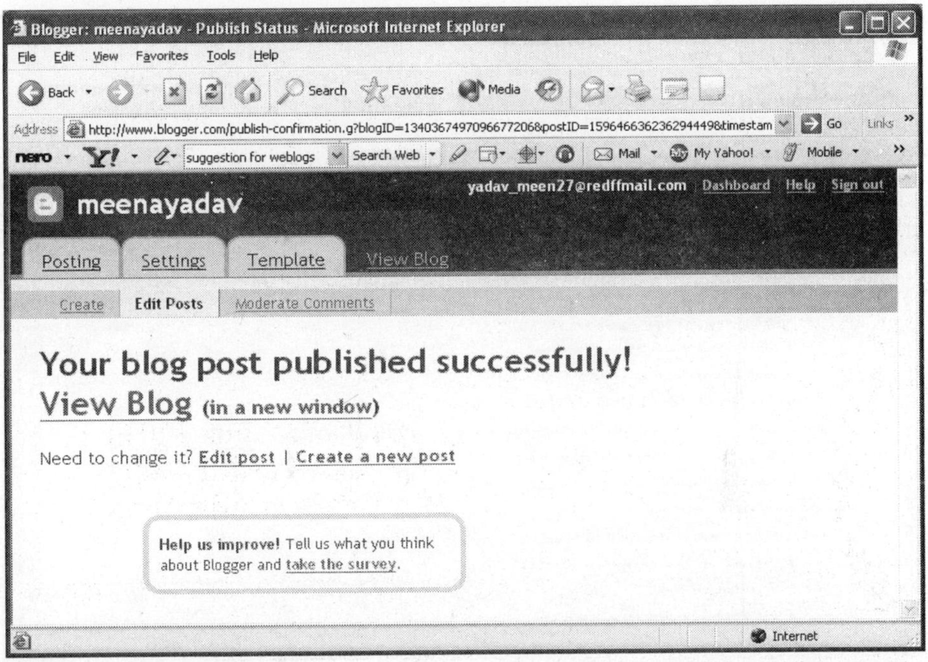

Viewing entries

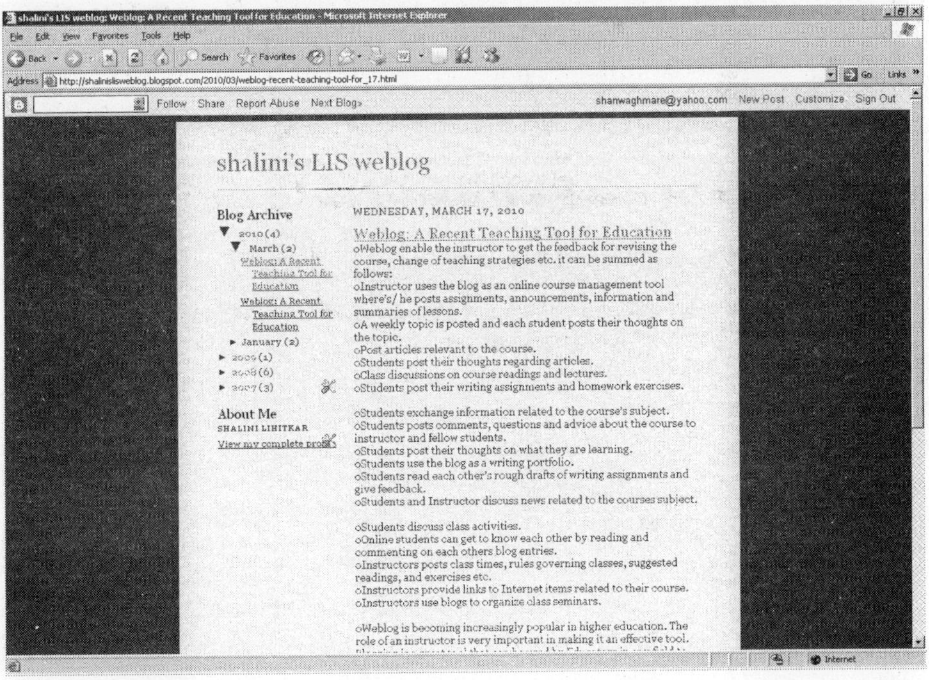

List Posted Entries

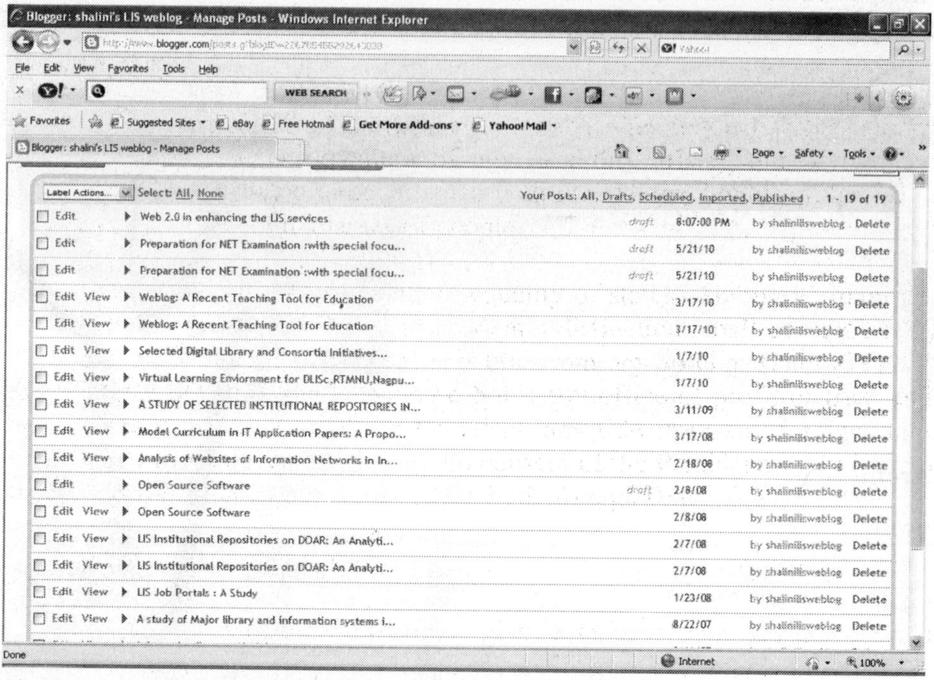

Posted

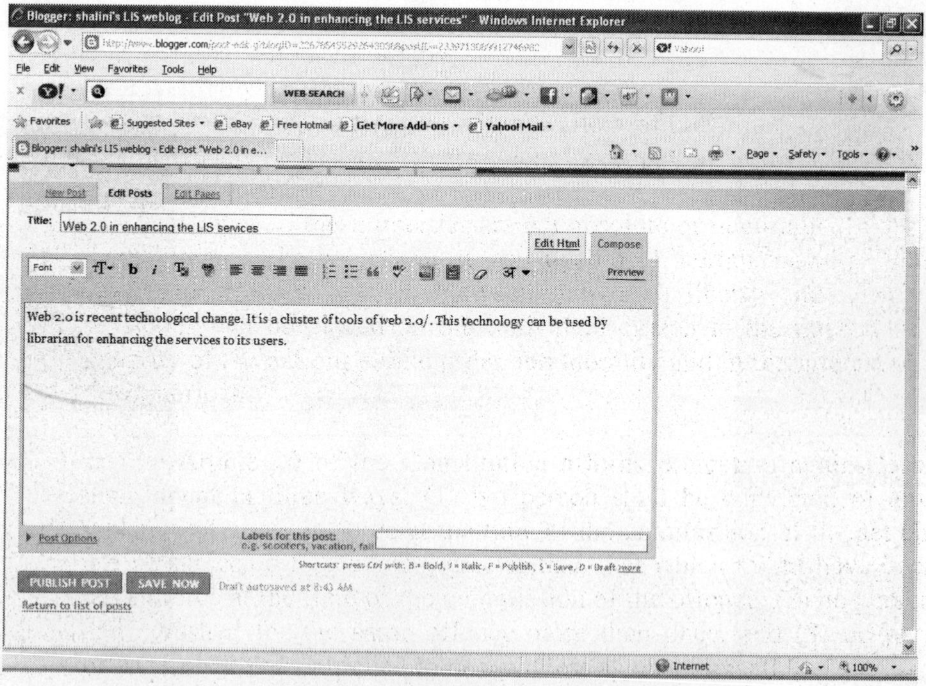

Viewing.

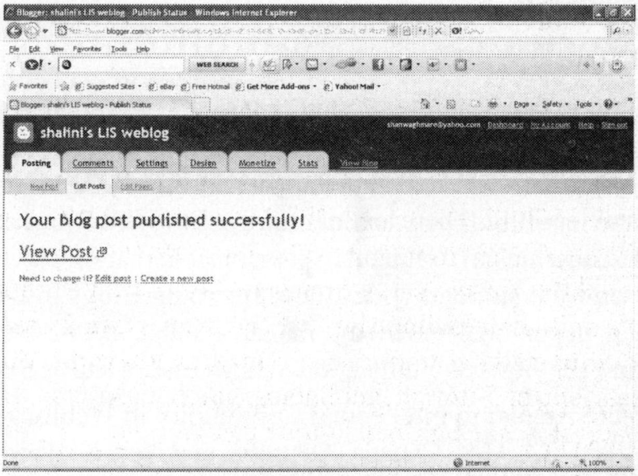

Archieve

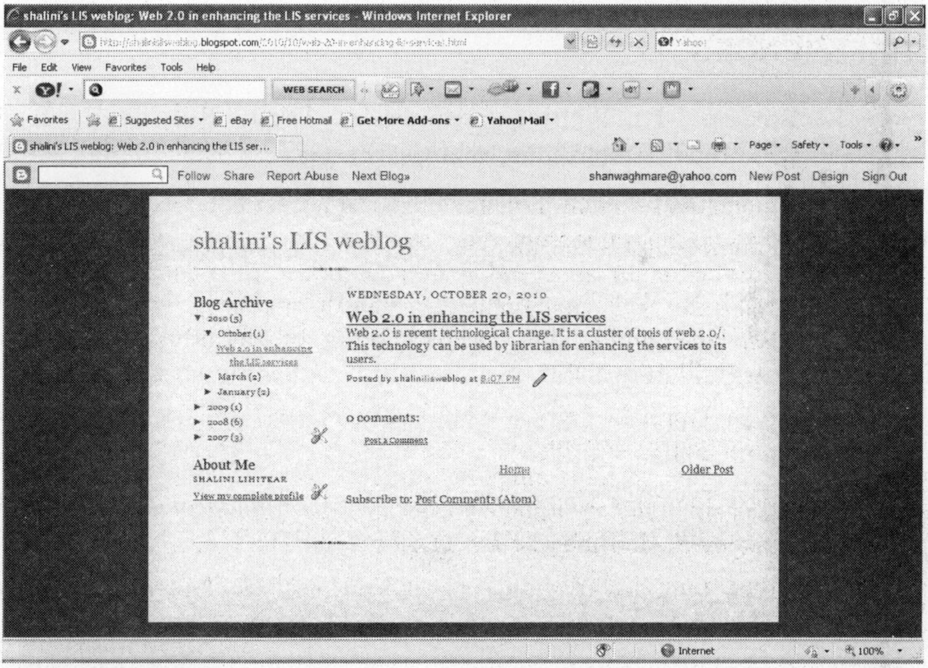

CONCLUSION

One of the basic requirements for education in the 21st century will be to prepare students for participation in a knowledge-based economy. Teachers in India need to be prepared for imparting the new age education. Hence teacher education program in India should integrate ICT component in such a way that teachers are enabled to face the new demands in the profession. Most of us are habituated for lecture-based and other direct methods of teaching. e- Learning is now the global scenario and we should not avoid that. It is very hard to change new training system but it is not impossible. Lots of issues and challenges are involved with this task but as soon as we put forward we will overcome all those problems.

Weblog is becoming increasingly popular in higher education. The role of an instructor is very important in making it an effective tool. Blogging is a great tool that can be used by educators in any field to enhance quality of teaching and learning. There are many ways in which Blogs and RSS feeds can be used in academic environment to promote and market services and resources to faculty and the students. Librarians are using Blogs in unique and diverse ways for e.g. in personal knowledge management, class announcements, posting student work for viewing, publication of tutor essays and as a community forum.

Humble Appeal to Intellectual Community in Weblogs are found only in countries like USA, U.K, Canada, Australia, and New Zealand. However checks of search engines and websites of weblogs are not found in India. Indian Institutions/teachers/Librarians should maintain their weblogs.

REFERENCES

1. Barger, J. Weblog resources FAQ Retrieved from www.robotwisdom.com/ weblogs. (Last access date:-20 May 2008).
2. Blogger-http://www.blogger.com (Last access date:-21 Feb 2008).
3. Bloglines-http://www.bloglines.com (Last access date:-2 March2008).
4. Blood, R. Weblogs: A history and Perspective, Retrieved from www.rebeccablood.net /essasy/weblog_history.html. (Last access Date: - 20 May 2007).
5. Clyde, laurel A. Library Weblogs. In *Library Management,* Vol.25, No.4/5,2004.p.183-189.
6. Clyde, Laurel A. Library Weblogs. *Library Management,* 2005 .22(4/5), 183-89. (Last access date:-21 May 2007).
7. Clyde, Laurel A. Weblogs_are you serious? *The Electronic Library,* 2004, 22(5), 390-402. (Last access date:-20 May 2008).
8. Garrod, Penny. Weblogs: Do they belong in libraries? Retrieved from www.ariadne.ac.in.uk/issued40/publiclibraries /intro.html. (Last access date :-22 May 2007).
9. Gupta , Sangeeta; Singh, Gurudev and Gopal, Krishan 2006). Blog : A Recent Online Tools of Information Sharing and Dissemination. *ILA Bulletin* 42 (2), pp.5-9. (Last access date:-22 May 2007).
10. http://blog-bib-liblogs.blogspot.com(Last Access Date : 4th Jan 2008).

11. http://search.blogger.com (Last access date :-22 March 2008).

12. http://www.blogger.com(Last Access Date: 2 Jan 2008).

13. http://www.libdex.com/weblogs(Last Access Date : 4th Jan 2008).

14. http://www.weblogs.com (Last Access Date : 3rd Jan 2007).

15. http://www.wikipedia.org/wiki/blog(Last Access Date: 1-Jan 2007).

16. Kumar, K. and Sharma, J (2008). Blogging: A Teaching Tool in Library Education. *In*. Dynamics in Digital Information Systems Ed. A. Amudavalli, New Delhi : Ess-Ess Publication..

❑❑❑

Chapter – 29

E-Learning and Web Based Library and Information Services: An Overview

Prabhu B. Gaddimani and Satish Kanamadi

INTRODUCTION

The phenomenal growth and reach of World Wide Web (www) has been one of the most significant developments in the last few years. It has rapidly gained popularity and has become most widely used application of the Internet. Today, the World Wide Web has emerged as the most powerful medium for information publishing and access. A plethora of information sources.

The user friendly interface and hypertext features of Web have been attracting a significant number of users as well as information providers. The web-based e-services are increasingly being used by research communities as a viable means to access to a plethora of digital resources in networked information environment. Concomitantly, utilization of such electronic methods and means is expanding substantially throughout the chain of e-research and scientific knowledge production.

RELATED LITERATURE

One aspect of higher education that got influenced by internet and its applications has been the emergence of electronic resources. Because of its utility in increasing the learning support, lot of literature is available on the aspect of e-resources, web based services of libraries, etc. Whilst information dissemination within networked library environment has been the subject of much scrutiny, there is a paucity of scholarly works considering research use of the web for support virtual researchers. The definition of Internet-base current awareness extended to cover a selection of one or more w-ICT systems to provide current notification of the existence of relevant new research information entities added to the databases e.g. alert of e-journal's table of contents (e-TOCs), and forthcoming meetings. The context of scholarly uses of the web-based communicating tools such as email among the faculty, scientists, researchers, and students within the so-called *invisible* or *virtual college* has been focused by many researchers.

CURRENT LIBRARY USER INFORMATION SERVICES

It's a practice to divide library user services into two categories: library public user services and library technical user services. Library public user services refer to circulation, bibliographic instruction, distance learning, government documentation, reference, special collections, and so on. Library technical user services focus on procedures and operations of maintaining, developing, and supporting library collections and services behind the scene, such as acquisition, cataloging and classification, interlibrary loan and document delivery, serials, systems, and so on.

Over the years, libraries have come to accept and use internet as the primary platform to build and deliver information resources, services, and instructions. Current library user information services, also called library user public services, have been evolving into two sections: traditional library user information services; and electronic library user information services. In the digital age, the most common library user information services still start from the personal oral or written communications between librarians and library users.

Traditional library user information services have the following two major features:

- Face-to-face: traditional library user information services usually are being processed by face-to-face personal communication, including eye contact, facial expression, oral communication, and written communication.
- On-site: traditional library user information services include, but are not limited to, on-site bibliographic instruction, campus outreach coordination and collaboration, classroom instruction, consultation, library tour, ready reference, user technical support, virtual reference, and so on.

On the platform of the internet and the world wide web (WWW), electronic library user information services range from bibliographic instructions computerized library catalogs, digital libraries, distance learning services e-databases, instant messaging services, interlibrary loan and document services, ready references, virtual classrooms, virtual references, and so on.

E-LEARNING

With the emergence of World Wide Web (WWW) in 1970s, the world of teaching and learning has adopted it as one of its main innovations. However, in spite of extensive use of web in education, varieties of terminologies are used to depict this new field of knowledge. Some of the terms mostly used interchangeably are as follows:

a) **Web-based Instruction**: It is a "hypermedia based instructional programme which utilizes the attributes and resources of the World Wide Web to create a meaningful learning environment where learning is fostered and supported". (Khan, 1997).

b) **Virtual Learning**: "The educational process of learning over the Internet without having face-to-face contact is known as virtual learning" (French, Hale, Johnson and Farr, 1999). However, some virtual learning may also include tele-learning.

c) **Online Learning**: It is synonymous to web-based learning where learning is fostered via the WWW only, in an Intranet or Internet. Mishra (2001) calls it as the new generation in the evolutionary growth of open, flexible and distance learning.

d) **E-Learning**: "The term e-learning covers a wide set of applications and processes including computer-based learning, web-based learning, virtual classroom, and digital collaboration" (WR Hambrecht + Co, 2000, p8). However, the term e-learning is becoming widely accepted as a substitute for online learning and web-based learning.

The web today is used in three different ways by educational institutions:

- Web integrated in the classroom teaching, that works as supplement to the face-to-face teaching;
- Web used as a 'mixed mode' approach to complement face-to-face teaching, normally called 'blended e-learning'; and
- Web used independently for teaching and learning as replacement for face-to-face teaching (Mitra, 1999; Berge, Collins and Dougherty, 2000; Bates, 2001).

The rapid spread of Internet and the World Wide Web (WWW) during the 1980's and 1990's has opened up new opportunities to make databases accessible via the web. Several advantages are seen for web-enabled databases:-

1. Global access to data that is in public domain, e.g.:-bibliographic, statistical, full text, image and multimedia databases;

2. Platform-independent access to data and information.
3. Dynamic updating of data ensuring that live data is available globally for use by decision makers, customers, vendors, etc. This is becoming particularly important in the rapidly growing e-commerce sectors.
4. The fact that a single interface, viz., Internet Browser is all that is needed on the client machine to access databases across the Internet,
5. The possibility for developing and delivering interactive solutions and for the collection of valuable feedback, reactions, analyses, and user preferences for use in business and other decisions.

EXPANDING ROLE OF LIBRARIES IN THE PRESENT WEB BASED – LEARNING AGE

Learning resources and the information services provided by a library are indispensable to any academic institution as a primary knowledge resource for study, teaching and research. Library adopts new information systems and services with the emergence of new and better information technologies. In the changing scenario, the faculty and instructors have begun to adopt e-learning strategies as a part of their teaching programmes and the library has a positive role to play to collect, organize, and disseminate learning web resources to complement the teaching and learning process. Following are some of the prominent factors that have given rise to a need for the web based library and information services.

a) Globalization of education demands that teachers and students be brought together at the same time, irrespective of the geographical location. This is possible through e-learning.

b) To enhance the competitiveness among the students by training them.

c) To provide access to greater level of resources and information services to students and teachers to enhance their learning opportunities.

d) Library and information services are expected to be like internet banking. A 24X7 information service, convenience of access at their desk top.

LIBRARY HOMEPAGE FOR INFORMATION DISSEMINATION

A good number of faculty and researchers regularly use this service and make effective use of their academic and research interests. Timely and wider dissemination made effective use and recognition of Library & Information Services and number of logs to library website increased. To allow the users remote access to the library and feel acquainted with the services of the library and to get satisfactory answers to their queries from the remote access. This will enable the user to familiarize with the library activities and access the library catalogues through the remote access. User can also renew/reserve books, access the content pages of his formal journals and ask for a copy of the article to be delivered to him at his work place.

Powerful tool that links all the electronic resources for easy access. Has the usual features of OPAC, Facilitates the operations such as downloading records and sending results and messages electronically reinforces the usefulness of the catalogue. It becomes another search engine. Referred as 'Web Cats' and as well a type of 'Information Gateways'. Some include information on the screens such as login id, username or password in boxes and users can see when they access the catalogue.

An Institutional Repository (IR) is an online locus for collecting, preserving and disseminating in digital form, the intellectual output of an institution, particularly a research institution. For a university, this would include materials such as research journal articles, before (preprints) and after (post prints) undergoing peer review, and digital versions of these and dissertations, but it might also include other digital assets generated by normal academic life, such as administrative documents, course notes or learning objects.

LIBRARY TRANSACTIONS AND THE WEB

Users were asked for an explanation as to what are the library transactions they wish to carry out at their convenience through the web.

- to search the books database
- to know the availability of a particular document
- to search books using all approaches
- to reserve a book
- to access current awareness bulletins
- to pay library dues
- to pay for fee based library services
- to know more about services rendered by library

CONCLUSION

Present day learning process is internet driven to a large extent. However, to utilize the resources of Internet to its maximum, it is necessary to make the users (faculty and research scholars) well-versed in the surfing and browsing on the Net. Access to resources on the Net cannot be achieved unless and until short-term courses or workshops and training programmes are conducted. This will help users to know various developments and searching techniques for accessing the desired information.

Information and Communication Technology based promotional services supplemented by the traditional practices will enhance the activities of promoting web resources and services in the libraries. The library web pages are playing good role in promoting the web resources. If few more web interfaces are added in the library websites for enhanced functionalities, it will be encouraging to the end-users and also the ultimate goal of investment on web resources could be achieved.

REFERENCES

1. Li, Lili (2006). Leveraging quality web-based library user services in the digital age. *Library Management,* 27 (6/7), pp. 390-399
2. Srivastava, Deepak K and Bajpai, Naval (2005). E-learning: A New Way of Education; University News, 43(26).
3. Haravu, L. J (2000). Web-Enabled Databases: An Overview of Technology and Problems. *Information Today and Tomorrow;* 19(1), pp. 7-11.
4. Huda Khan, Badrul (1997). Web-Based Instruction. Education Technology, New Jercy, p-480
5. Mishra, Sanjaya (2001). Designing online learning web 2.0 and online learning resources. UNESCO, p. 250
6. Mounissamy, P and Kaliammal, A (2006). Promoting Effective Use of Electronic Resources Using Library Websites by IITs and NITs : A Comparative Study; *IASLIC Bulletin,* 51(4) pp. 213-220.
7. Naushad Ali, P.M. and Hasan, Md. Ehsan (2003). The Use of Electronic Services of IIT Library Delhi: A Study of Users Opinion. *IASLIC Bulletin,* 48(2), pp .70-82.
8. Romesh Verma (2007). E-learning strategies in Teacher Education. *Univesity News,* 45(18), pp. 10-14.
9. Jayaprakash, Kannappanavar B.U. and Chidanand Swamy (2008). Web Resources and Services In. *International Conference on Knowledge for All : Role of libraries and Information Centers.*

❑❑❑

Chapter – 30

Web Credibility of Selected National Library Websites: A Study

R. Jeyshankar

INTRODUCTION

The World Wide has become one of the most important media for sharing information resources, digital documents, images, movies and various other types of resources. The research results, new findings, and opinions can also be put on the web from any where at any time. Owing to the dynamic nature of web information, the contents of many websites and their web pages are constantly being updated to reflect the latest changes.

The Web has also freed the user's dependence on library resources for finding information related to address and contact details of a person/institution, contents pages of books, journals, etc. Looking at the web has become an innovative trend in the reference service to complement dated print sources. At present many academic institutes in India have their own website and present all kinds of information about themselves. Information content is, however, one thing; Web site design and organisation is quite another matter. The existing institutions of Web sites are as different as are the institutions because even a high-quality institution may have a low-quality Web site that turns users off. Obviously, different institutions have a wide range of target groups, level of service, resources etc. Stover (1997) has outlined the different types of Web sites that academic, public and special libraries have created.

WEB CREDIBILITY: AN OVERVIEW

Fogg and Tseng (1999)[1] Web Credibility is a perceived quality which does not reside in an object, a person, or a piece of information. Therefore, in discussing the credibility of a computer product, one is always discussing the perception of credibility.

Fogg (2001)[2] studied that Web credibility is about making our website in such a way that, it comes across as trustworthy and knowledgeable. Many scholars agree that credibility perceptions result from evaluating multiple dimensions simultaneously. Although the literature varies on how many dimensions contribute to credibility evaluation, the vast majority of researchers identify two key components of credibility (i) Trustworthiness and (ii) Expertise. A person makes an assessment of both trustworthiness and expertise to arrive at an overall credibility assessment. In nutshell, web credibility is a perceived quality of a web site by a user, whereas web evaluation is the process of web credibility.

NEED AND IMPORTANCE OF THE STUDY

For research scholars, information seekers and many users, the World Wide Web is the main access point for library research. Libraries need to find venue for the virtual references by the library web home page as reference tool.

Now days a library aims at having its own homepage or websites in order to present its services to the user who increasingly prefer to interact electronically with the information resources available. This is the great boon to the user for accessing and exploring the information resources available. The structure, information and graphic design may facilitate or impede use.

Well-arranged and logically constructed home pages with relevant, nascent and timely information in pleasant and inviting graphics provide a positive experience and possibly stimulate the user into future use.

Thus designing and hosting library web page occupies a significant role in disseminating information to the society at large.

METHODOLOGY OF WEB CREDIBILITY

Credibility of a web site is no different than evaluating any other instructional tool. The expert usability website evaluation was carried out by Web credible's highly skilled in-house usability specialists Chandran and Ramesh Babu, 2008[3]. It is a comprehensive usability framework for any website and can specifically address the following areas:

Authority: As author for a book, so also a web builder or designer for a web page, who self identifies, acknowledges accountability for a site. One needs to check its credentials, sufficient authority to speak on the subject, authenticity of information and whether the site is accurate and permission sought to use photographs etc.

Accuracy of web documents: Accuracy of the web page means authenticity of the information on the website. The information in the website should be accurate and reliable.

Objectivity: The objectivity of the websites should encompass the question does the content reflect a bias explicit or hidden. We can say that objectivity maintain if websites dedicated to intended purpose.

Update: The information on the web page should be up to date, last update and the date information was created and the date last update. URLs change all the time so as an occasional broken links is forgivable.

Coverage: Coverage refers to the contents of the websites. A good library website should cover all aspect of the library activities such as total library collection, online public library catalogue, timings of the library, on going activities of the library, etc.

Design consideration: A good library website should use convenient design for its websites. There should not be too much of links, overdone styles, too much of graphics etc.

Lay out considerations: Lay out is the internal arrangement of library website. The structure of the website should be such way that a user can easily navigate through the website.

Graphics: A good library website uses minimum graphic design for its website. It should attract the already existing user as well as new user.

OBJECTIVES OF THE STUDY

The present study has the following objectives:

1. To evaluate the national library websites for the following details:
   - Authority information
   - Scope of the websites
   - Accuracy of the websites
   - Objectivity of the websites
   - Correctness of the websites
   - Website design and layout
   - Help information
   - Interactive search tools
2. To point out good library websites which could be a model for other national library websites.
3. To bring out suitable criteria for evaluation of national library websites.

HYPOTHESES

The following are the hypotheses framed for this study:

- A majority of the National Libraries have hosted web sites on the Internet.
- The National Libraries websites are heterogeneous in the structure and contents.
- Most of the web sites did not confirm to the established guidelines.

RELATED RESEARCH

Karp and Karp (1997)[4] offers guidelines about the web designing. Though it is not directly related to web credibility, adopting those guidelines will help to improve the website to its best. The article explains intelligent use of graphic elements and design can add greatly to the attractiveness of a web page. Fogg (2003)[5] proposes a theory that users notice and interpret various web site elements to arrive at an overall credibility assessment. Mangala Hirwade (2006)[6] evaluated the web sites of Indian universities with special reference to Library web pages. 273 Indian Universities were selected for this study, out of these universities, 91(59.87%) have included information about their libraries in the web site. Major findings and suggestions were presented and Directory of Indian University Web Sites was created as a by-product of the study. Jasek (2007)[7] offers a short set of simple-to-implement guidelines in his pamphlet - How to Design Library Web sites to Maximize Usability to help librarians to design usable library web sites. The guidelines are based on a survey of literature on library website design and usability testing; results of usability reviews conducted by Elsevier for library customers and established best practices in website usability.

METHODOLOGY

These library websites were evaluated according to the website evaluation criteria and using web page evaluation work sheet suggested and proposed by Nancy[8] Nielson, 2004[9] and Narendra Kumar, 2007[10]. For the evaluation of these websites, evaluation sheet was prepared containing points like authority information of the library, scope feature that could be present in the library website, online catalogue or search tool, overall structure of the website, graphic considerations, etc.

ANALYSES AND INTERPRETATION OF THE DATA

For this study, 30 National Library websites were identified from USA, UK, India, Germany, Italy and France and data was collected. For this study, we have decided to use two different criteria's compare and evaluated library websites.

- Criteria for library website comparison and Designing a Check List Nielson(2004)[10]
- Web evaluation worksheet given by Nancy[9]

After evaluating above 30 websites according to these two criteria sets the results obtained by both are then compared each other.

Table 1 Features Present in the Library Website Homepages

Sl. No	Features	Number of Libraries	%
1	Library hours	28	93.33
2	Information services and function	24	80.00
3	Events and other actives	24	80.00
4	Collection information	16	53.33
5	Users comments	15	50.00
6	Library news	8	26.67
7	Access to online materials	6	20.00
8	Facilities of the library	3	10.00

It can be seen from Table 1 that 93.33% i.e. 28 library homepage provide information on library hours, the next feature that is present is 80% of the website provide information about services and functions of the library and events and other ongoing activities of the library. 53.33%, i.e. 16 libraries provide collection information and 50%i.e. 15 libraries asked for user's comments in their websites. 26.67%, i.e. 8 library websites provide library news feature and 20% i.e.6 access to online materials from their websites. 10% of the libraries i.e. only 3 libraries give information about facilities that are provided in the libraries.

Table 2 Library-wise distribution of Features present in the National library Websites

Sl. No	Libraries having no.of features	Total no. ofLibraries	Percentage
1	6 Features	3	10.00
2	5 Features	6	20.00
3	4 Features	11	36.67
4	3 Features	7	23.33
5	2 Features	3	10.00
Total		**30**	**100.00**

It can be seen from Table 2 that only 3 libraries have covered 6 features of the 8 features listed by the researcher, that is 10% of the libraries 7 libraries i.e. 20%of the libraries have covered 5 features and 36.67% (11) websites have 4 features and 23.33% i.e. 7, 10% (3) libraries have covered only 3 and 2 features each respectively in their websites. This is presented explicitly in the graph below.

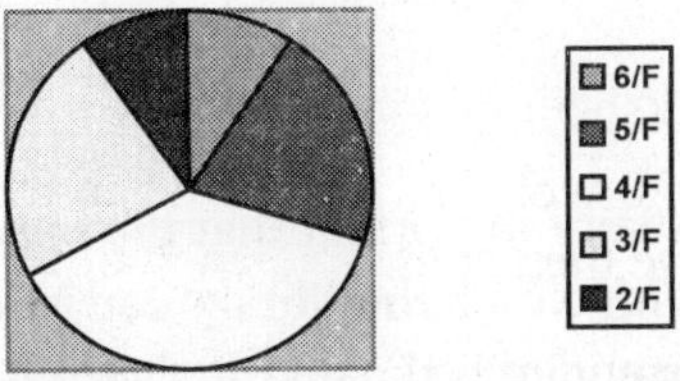

Fig. 1. Library Wise distributions of Features present in the Library Websites

Structure of the Library Homepages

The structure of the library home page is the arrangement of the contents of the websites. This should be arranged in such a way that a user can easily identify different services, functions, collections information, library hours, updated information etc. The structure should be clear uncluttered, without too many confusing links. At the same time, it should be provide all the information in an organized form. On the basis of these criteria, the library websites have been evaluated to have excellent, good, or satisfactory structure. This is based on the judgment of the researcher.

Table 3 Grades for the structure of Library Homepages

Sl. No	Grade	No. of Libraries	Percentage
1	Excellent Count	4	13.33
2	Good Count	15	50.00
3	Satisfactory Count	11	36.67
	Total	**30**	**100.00**

From Table 3 it can be seen that not all library websites have a good structure for their library home page. Only 4 libraries (13%) have been graded as excellent, while 15 library (50%) and 11 (36.67%) library websites have been graded as good and satisfactory, respectively.

Update of Information

A library website should be dynamic in the sense that it has to be constantly updated to reflect the changes and activities that are taken place in the library. An ideal library website should give information about when it was last updated or modified to give the user an idea about the information provided in the home page.

The home page should also carry information about the date of creation, date last modified and what information was updated and when it is going to be updated next.

From the analysis it was seen that 16 out of the 30 library websites have mentioned the updated date and the remaining 14 library websites did not mention the updated information. None of the websites have mentioned what is updated in the website and when it is going to be updated next.

Contact Information

For library website, it is very important that the users are provided with details of the various means with which the library can be contacted. The main contact information usually provided is the mailing address, E-mail, telephone and fax number, name and designation of the contact person.

Table 4 Type of contact information in library websites

Sl. No	Type of contact Information	Number of Libraries	Percentage
1	E-mail	30	100
2	Telephone	30	100
3	Fax	30	100
4	Postal address	30	100

From the Table 4 we can seen that all library websites have provided contact information such as e-mail, phone number, fax number, postal address.

Help Information

Help information plays a very important role in the library websites. An user often will be browsing a library website in a remote location at his own timings and therefore may have a problem while browsing. They can not approach the library staff; more over in a public library, all categories of users could be browsing the website. Therefore the user should be provided with general help, but help is provided only in searching interactive catalogue or database. The analysis reveals that most of the librarie's websites have not provided help facility. This can be considered as one of major drawback of the library websites analyzed in the study.

Comments and Suggestions

A good library website should be sensitive to comments and suggestions given by the users. This will enable a library to refine and modify its services in response to the user's needs and demands. A library website should adequately provide for any comments and suggestions for library users. A majority of the library websites are not sensitive to the user's suggestions and comments. The analysis shows that only 14 library websites (53 %) have provided for comments and suggestions.

Search Tools in Library Websites

One of the most important facilities of library web page are the search tools and online forms. This facility allows the users to access, search, and browse a library databases, catalogue, bibliography etc. without stepping into the library building from any where, any time convenient to the users. User's online forms allow the users to place orders, reservations for library documents.

Table 5 Different types of search tools used by different libraries

Sl. No.	Library Name	Collection type	Search feature
1.	Swiss National Library	Obituary search	Interactive
2.	The British Library, UK	Catalogue	Interactive and Advanced
3.	Library of Congress, USA	Catalogue	Interactive and advanced
4.	National Library of Thailand	Catalogue	Interactive and advanced
5.	National Library of Romania	Catalogue	Interactive and advanced
6.	National Library of Portugal	Search our interne	Interactive
7.	National Library of Poland	Catalogue	Interactive
8.	National Library of Namibia	Catalogue	Interactive
9.	National Library of Libya	Catalogue	Interactive
10.	National Library of South Korea	Catalogue	Interactive
11.	Jordan National Library,	Catalogue	Interactive and advanced
12.	National Library of Ireland	Catalogue	Interactive and advanced
13.	National Library of Iran	Catalogue	Interactive and advanced
14.	German National Library	Catalogue	Interactive and advanced
15.	National Library of Australia	Catalogue	Interactive and advanced
16.	National Library of Bangladesh	Catalogue	Interactive and advanced
17.	National Library of Canada	Union catalogue	Interactive and advanced
18.	National Library of China	Catalogue	Interactive
19.	National Library of France	Catalogue	Interactive and advanced
20	National Library of India	Catalogue	Interactive

Advance search features in interactive search tools

The library websites that have interactive search features in them can be analyzed from different points of view. They are

1. Search features/search options
2. Access points/approach points
3. Limiting features
4. Additional features like sorting, number search, inter library loan request, expert search etc.

Search features

The search features provided are search by word, phrase search, natural language search, Boolean search and truncation. A detailed help is also provided in some websites.

Table 6 Search features presented in the Interactive Search tools

Sl. No	Search Features	Yes		No	
		Number	%	Number	%
1	Help	13	65.00	7	35.00
2	Word	17	85.00	3	15.00
3	Phrase	15	75.00	5	25.00
4	Natural language	6	30.00	14	70.00
5	Boolean	11	55.00	9	45.00
6	Truncation	2	10.00	18	90.00

Table 6 reviews the most common type of search feature. Word search is offered by the 85% i.e.17 library websites Phrase search is offered by 75% and Boolean 55% followed by natural language search by 30% and truncation option by 10% with 15,11,6 and two library websites respectively, 13 library websites provide help in their interactive search tool.

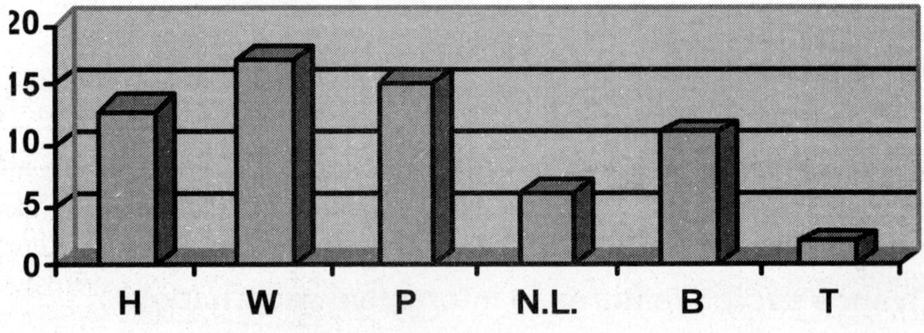

Fig 2 : Search Features in Interactive Search tools

Access points: (searchable fields)

The different searchable fields provided by the library websites are author, title, subject, ISBN, and Call number. Table 8 gives the access points in interactive search tools.

Table 7 Access points in Interactive Search Tools

Sl. No	Access Points	Yes		No	
		Number	%	Number	%
1	Author	18	90.00	2	10.00
2	Title	18	90.00	2	10.00
3	Subject	17	85.00	3	15.00
4	ISBN	6	30.00	14	70.00
5	call	10	50.00	10	50.00

From the Table 7 we can see that 90% of the websites provide author and title as access points. Subject follows this as access point with 85%. Only 50% provide call number as an access point and 30% ISBN as an access point. Graph below makes this data very clear.

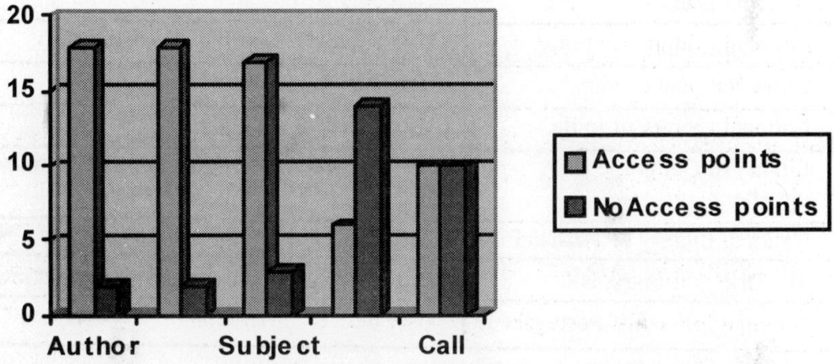

Fig 3 : Access points in Interactive Search Tools

Limiting Features

Many library websites also offer limit options in their interactive searches. These limit options are language, format, year of publication (Table 8). The search results can also be sorted according to different criteria. Among library websites analyzed that have interactive search tools 40% provide limiting options by language, 30% provide by format and 25% by year of publication and also 25% have sort options in their interactive search tools.

Table 8 Presence of Limiting Features in Interactive Search Tool

Sl. No	Limiting Features	Yes		No	
		Number	%	Number	%
1	Language	8	40	12	60
2	Format	6	30	14	70
3	Year of publication	5	25	15	75
4	Sort field	5	25	15	75

Additional features

Apart from these features there are also some additional features. Eight library websites provide the options of searching the database by diving user details; 2 library expert search facilities and 2 library databases can be through journal title. Other than this some other search features offered by the libraries are number search, inter library loan request loan request, ISBN, OCLC number etc. Table 9 gives the list of libraries and the additional search features.

Table 9 Additional Features in Interactive Search Tool

Sl. No	Name of library	Additional Search Features
1	National Library of Australia	Number search, interlibrary loan request
2	National Library of Bangladesh	User details, expert search
3	National Library of Canada	User details, journal title
4	National Library of China	User details
5	National Library of France	User details
6	Swiss National Library	User details
7	National Library of India	User details
8	Library of Congress, USA	Limiting features by audio books, periodicals, and cds.
9	National Library of Thailand	User details
10	The British Library, UK	ISBN, ISSN, OCLC Number, journal Title
11	National Library of Portugal	User details

Multimedia feature: The purpose of library website is not only to provide information for existing users but also act as an advertisement or as a global brochure to the library. Hence the website should be designed to be attractive using graphics, images, animation and other multimedia features wherever necessary. It is seen that all library websites analyzed in this study have used graphics and images and only 3 library websites have used animation and other multimedia facilities.

Analysis of Library Websites Using Check- Lists Suggested By Nancy Everhart

The library websites were also analyzed using a checklist suggested by Nancy Everhart. These checklists consist of 8 features under which different questions are posed. Each main section is allocated certain points. The checklist for 100 marks. Depending upon the answers to the questions, grade is allocated to the library website. Based on these grades the library websites have been ranked (Table 10). The main features for which evaluation is done are Update, content, authority, navigation, experience, multimedia, and miscellaneous.

Table 10 Top 5 Ranks according to Nancy Everhart Criteria

Sl. No	Library name	Total points	Rank
1	Library of Congress, USA	69	I
2	National Library of Russia	69	I
3	The British Library, UK	68	II
4	National Library of Australia	68	II
5	National Library of India	67	III
6	National Library of China	67	III
7	National Library of France	65	IV
8	Swiss National Library	65	IV
9	National Library of Canada	64	V
10	National Library of Portugal	64	V

When the top 10 library websites ranked according to Nancy Everhart and Elisabeth Tom Mathews criteria where compared, it is seen that the top 10 library websites are getting top rank in both methods of analysis , showing that there is lot of co-relation with the result of analysis according to both the criteria.

Table 11 Rank Comparison between Elizabeth Thom Mathews and Nancy Ever Hart Evaluation Methods

Sl. No	Rank a ccording to Nancy Everhart	Name of the Library	Rank according to Nielson
1	I	The British Library, UK	II
2	I	Library of Congress, USA	II
3	II	National Library of Canada	III
4	II	National Library of China	IV
5	III	National Library of France	II
6	III	National Library of India	IV
7	IV	National Library Board-Singapore	III
8	IV	National Library of Malaysia	IV
9	V	National Diet Library	I
10	IV	National Library of New Zealand	IV
11	VII	German National Library	V
12	VII	National Library of South Africa	V
13	VII	National Library and Documentation Center, Srilanka	VI
14	VII	National Library of Iran	VI
15	IX	Swiss National Library	VI
16	X	National Library of Pakistan	IX

MAJOR FINDINGS OF THE ANALYSIS

1. Almost all national library websites provide information about library hours, information services and function and events and activities of the library in their websites. Other features like collection information, access to online materials, library news is not covered in the majority of the websites.
2. The structure of the library websites is for large majority good.
3. It is surprising to note that, national library websites do not give update information which is one of very important criteria for library website. A library should not only mention when a particular database or website has been updated but also mention what exactly has been updated and when the next update will be.
4. All national library websites have provided adequate contact information with giving E-mail address telephone and fax number in addition to postal and contact names. However none of the library websites have provided helps information. This is a crucial feature that has to be present especially in a public library website. Only 50% of the national library websites have provided for user's comments and suggestions.
5. 67% of the national library websites analyzed are providing OPAC facilities. The search features of OPAC are quite advanced with the provision to search a word, phrase, natural language search, Boolean search and truncation. They provide various access points like author, title, subject, ISBN, and call number.
6. The top 10 national library websites, which could be model, are Library of Congress, USA, National Library of Russia, The British Library, UK, National Library of Australia, National Library of India, National Library of China, National Library of France, Swiss National Library, National Library of Canada and National Library of Portugal. As a result of this study, it was possible to point out a criteria for evaluation of the library website which are listed below:
   - Authority information
   - Objectivity of the website
   - Accuracy of the information
   - Update of the information
   - Content
   - Navigation/ arrangement and format
   - Design consideration

- Layout consideration.
- Experience
- Multimedia/j graphics
- Access
- OPAC facility
- Help information

CONCLUSION

It is observed that most of the public library websites studied are very slow to open. The one reason for this could be that library servers are not upgraded. Some library websites do not leave forwarding information after they change URLs. Library websites especially national library websites have to take care of this aspect whenever they change their URLs. Library websites do not update very frequently when compared to other commercial websites. It is also seen that many library homepages, specifically in European and American countries, are developed in their national languages without having English versions. Multimedia features are not exploited to the full. National librarie's websites not only serve as excellent media for publishing the library activities, programmes, resources and services, but also help to bring to the notice of the users all the significant information which they must know in developing and using their library in due course of time. National librarie's web site and their library pages need to be evaluated periodically by using established criteria like web design, accessibility, arrangement, navigation, quality of content etc. It is also suggested to conduct periodic user studies on web usability. This will help to improve their web sites according to the user needs.

APPENDIX - A

List of 30 National Libraries and its Websites

Sl. No	Name of the Library	URLs
1	National Library of Australia	www.nla.gov.au
2	National Library of Bangladesh	www.nanl.gov.bd
3	National Library of Canada	www.banq.qc.ca
4	National Library of China	www.nlc.gov.cn
5	National Library of France	www.bnf.fr
6	National Library of India	www.nlindia.org
7	National Diet Library	www.ndl.go.jp
8	National Library of Malaysia	www.pnm.my
9	Nepal National Library	www.nnl.gov.np
10	National Library of New Zealand	www.natlib.govt.nz
11	National Library of Nigeria	www.nlbn.org

Contd.

12	National Library of Pakistan	www.nlp.gov.pk
13	National Library of Greece	www.nlg.gr
14	National Library Board-Singapore	www.nlb.gov.sg
15	National Library of South Africa	www.nlsa.ac.za
16	National Library and Documentation Center, Srilanka	www.natlib.lk
17	Swiss National Library	www.nb.admin.ch
18	The British Library, UK	www.bl.uk
19	Library of Congress, USA	http://lcweb.loc.gov
20	National Library of Thailand	www.nlt.go.th
21	National Library of Romania	www.bibnat.ro
22	National Library of Portugal	www.bn.pt
23	National Library of Poland	www.bn.org.pl
24	National Library of Namibia	www.nln.gov.na
25	National Library of Libya	www.nllnet.net
26	National Library of South Korea	www.nl.go.kr
27	Jordan National Library,	www.nl.gov.jo
28	National Library of Ireland	www.nli.ie
29	National Library of Iran	www.nli.ir
30	German National Library	www.d-nb.de

REFERENCES

1. Stover, M (1997). Library web sites: mission and function in the networked organization. *Computers in Libraries*, 17(10), 55-57.
2. Fogg, B.J and Tseng, H (1999). The elements of computer credibility, *Proceedings of the SIGCHI Conference on Human Factors in Computing Systems: the CHI Is the Limit, Pittsburgh, PA, 15-20 May,* pp. 80-87.
3. Chandran, D and Ramesh Babu, B (2008). Web Resources: Access and Evaluation. *In: Library Resources and Services in the Digital Era,* (pp127-135) edited by B. Ramesh Babu et al. 2008. Kattangulathur: SRM University.
4. Karp, T and Karp,M (1997). Art and the Zen of Web Sites.Retrieved from http://www.tlc-systems.com.
5. Fogg, B. J (2003). Prominence-Interpretation Theory: Explaining How People Assess Credibility Online. Retrieved from portal.acm.org/citation.cfm?id=765951.
6. Mangala, Anil Hirwade (2006). Websites of Indian Universities: An evaluation. Bombay: Himalaya Publishing House.
7. Jasek, Chris (2007). How to Design Library Websites to Maximize

Usability. Retrieved from http://libraryconnect.elsevier.com/lcp/0502/lcp0502.pdf.

8. Jeyshankar, R; Ramesh Babu, B; Narendra Kumar, A. M and Nageswara Rao, P. (2010). Web Credibility of Engineering College Web Sites Affiliated to Anna University, Tirunelveli (Tamil Nadu, India), Sixth International Conference on Webometrics, Informetrics and Scientometrics & Eleventh COLLNET Meeting, October 19 – 22, 2010, University of Mysore, Pp.788-804.

9. Nancy Everhart, St. John's University, Division of Library and Information Science, 8000 Utopia Parkway, Jamaica, NY11439(718) 990-1457.

10. Nielson, Jakob (2004). Designing Web Usability. New Riders, California USA. World Best Enterprises. Quality Criteria for Website Excellence: World Best Website Awards. Retrieved from http://www.worldbestwebsites.com/ criteria.htm.

11. Narendra Kumar, A. M (2007). Users' Expectations from the Web Sites. *Conference Proceedings of the National Seminar on-Library Users' Expectations in Information and Communication Technology (ICT) Environment edited by P. Manohar and S. Gopalakrishnan. 7-8 September 2007.* Chennai: MIT, Anna University.

12. Nageswara Rao, P; Narendra Kumar, A. M and Ramesh Babu, B. (2009). Web Credibility of Autonomous College Websites in Tamil Nadu: A Study. *Library Herald.* 47 (3):194 -216.

❑❑❑

Chapter - 31

Open Source Software in Development of ICTs: Issues and Challenges

Y. Uma Devi, T. Sreenivasa Rao and V. Shailaja

INTRODUCTION

The term open source describes the practices in production and development that promote access to the end product's source materials. Open Source Software (OSS) came into existence with the development of ICTs. The services and the collections of the libraries and information centres are becoming global due to the application of Information Communication Technologies. Information can now be accessed from even the remote places with the help of internet. The term "open source" refers to software that includes the original source code, used to create it so that users can modify it writing to their requirements.

It also includes the right of redistribution; therefore, there may be products that are based on other open source products. While the software may be free, a developer or distributor may charge for services such as special programming, installation, training and technical support, etc. In general, the source code of OSS is widely accessible, freely available and reusable. Now the institutions especially the academic institutions are starting to build their own repository to serve their community locally and globally.

FEATURES OF THE OSS

- Open source software is normally created and maintained by developers crossing institutional and national boundaries, collaborating by using internet-based communication and development tools.
- The concept relies on peer review to find and eliminate bugs in the program code, a process which commercially developed and packaged programmes do not utilize.
- Products are typically a kind of "free", often through a license that specifies that applications and source code are free to use, modify, and redistribute as long as all uses, modifications, and redistributions are similarly licensed.
- Successful applications are tend to be developed more quickly and with better responsiveness to the needs of users who can readily use and evaluate these applications because they are free.
- Open source programs are typically created as a collaborative effort in which programmers offer the user a flexibility of use and share the changes within the community.
- Quality, not profit, drives the open source developers who take personal pride in seeing their working solutions adopted.
- Intellectual property rights to open source software belong to everyone who helps build it or simply uses it, not just the vendor or institution that created the software.

ADVANTAGES OF OSS

OSS has many advantages, the important ones are:

- The availability of the source code and the right to modify it.
- The rights to redistribute modifications and improvements to the code and to use the software in any way.
- There is no one with the power to restrict in a unilateral way how the software is used, even in a retroactive way.
- No denial to an individual or to a group to access source code of the software.
- There is no single entity on which the future of the software depends.
- There are fewer conflicting priorities due to marketing pressures.
- It provides a new forum for democratic action.

- Licensed software can not place restriction on other software that is distributed with it.
- Distribution of License should not be specific to a product and License should be technology-neutral, etc.

SOME OF THE POPULAR OSS FOR LIBRARY INFORMATION CENTERS

Koha is the first open-source Integrated Library System (ILS) in use worldwide. Its development is steered by a growing community of libraries collaborating to achieve their technology goals. Koha's impressive feature set continues to evolve and expand to meet the needs of its user base. Koha includes modules for circulation, cataloging, acquisitions, serials, reserves, patron management, branch relationships, and more. Koha uses a dual database design that utilizes the strengths of the two major industry-standard database types (text-based and RDBMS). Koha is built using library standards and protocols that ensure interoperability between Koha and other systems and technologies, while supporting existing workflows and tools. Koha is distributed under the open-source General Public License (GPL). Its new features include a new user interface design, more advanced search functions, better multibranch capabilities, user tagging and many generic enhancements.

DSpace is one of the first OSS platforms to store, manage and distribute the collections in digital format. DSpace is the choicest software for academic, nonprofit and commercial organizations, building open digital repositories. DSpace preserves and enables easy and open access to all types of digital contents including text, images, moving images, mpegs, data sets, etc. And with an ever-growing community of developers, committed to continuously expanding and improving the software, each new DSpace installation benefits from the previous. It is a groundbreaking digital repository system that captures, stores, indexes, preserves and distributes digital research material. As much of the world's contents are now being developed and disseminated in digital format, the software supports next generation digital archiving which is more permanent and shareable than current analog archives.

Greenstone is a suite of software for building and distributing digital library collections. It provides a new way of organizing information and publishing it on the Internet or on CD-ROM. It is a multilingual software, issued under the terms of the GNU General Public License. The aim of the Greenstone software is to empower users, particularly in universities, libraries, and other public service institutions, to build their own digital libraries. Digital libraries are radically reforming how information is disseminated and acquired in UNESCO's partner communities and institutions in the fields of education, science and culture around the world, and particularly in developing countries. It knows how to create collections from "standard" file formats such as HTML files, email messages, PDF documents, JPEG and GIF images, Word documents as well as plain text files.

NewGenLib is an Integrated Library Management System, now freely available as an open source under the most widely used free software license, GNU General Public License (GNU GPL). Before becoming an open source product at the end of 2007, it was already in use in 122 libraries, mainly in India and in Syria, Sudan, Cambodia, etc. Its important features include: completely web based, complies with international metadata and interoperability standards like MARC-21, MARC-XML, z39.50, SRU/W, OAI-PMH, uses chiefly open source components - scalable, manageable and efficient, OS independent - Windows and Linux flavors available, z39.50 Client for federated searching, Internationalized application (I18N)-Unicode 3.0 compliant, easily extensible to support other languages, data entry, storage, retrieval in any (Unicode 3.0) language, RFID integration, networking, automated email/instant messaging integrated into different functions of the software, form letters are configurable and use XML based Open Office templates, extensive use of set up parameters enabling easy configuration of the software to suit specific needs.

Fedora Flexible Extensible Digital Object and Repository Architecture (FEDORA) is an RPM-based, general purpose collection of software, including an operating system based on the Linux kernel, developed by the community-supported Fedora Project and sponsored by Red Hat. The Fedora Project's mission is to lead the advancement of free and open source software and content as a collaborative community. One of Fedora's main objectives is not only to contain software distributed under a free and open source license, but also to be on the cutting edge of such technologies. It can be used to develop institutional repositories and other interoperable web-based digital libraries and the system implements the Fedora architecture, adding utilities that facilitate repository management. It has been developed by the University of Virginia and Cornell University.

CDS/ISIS for Windows is the most widely used software for Indian libraries, available freely from the UNESCO website. It has all the features of a complete Integrated Library Management Software and the support for this software is available locally as a number of professionals are trained in its use. It also has a very strong base for international discussion forum. Most of the libraries in India started computerizing their cataloguing activities with this software and later on shifted to other commercially available software and OSS.

ISSUES AND CHALLENGES OF OSS

The two critical issues driving the establishments for adopting OSS is that, the establishments use OSS to become more independent from pricing and licensing policies of large software companies, and the establishments are using this software because they want to support the open source community.

The main issue of open source software development is peer production by bartering and collaboration, with the end-product, source-material, "blueprints," and documentation available at no cost to the public. The library database should be published on Internet, i.e. all modules should be web based and network centric. Members can see the things from home or remote location. Library staff can make data entry from remote and different locations in India. If libraries are maintaining their database and dynamic website on LAN or single machine (unless mandatory), they are lagging behind others. In case of open source, the library will have to work hard to get it published through its ISP. A majority of the libraries in India are maintaining their databases on LAN or local single PC. It is not the proper automated switching software. Many libraries simply do not have the in-house expertise to support open-source software development.

OSS IN PUBLIC SECTOR

Many governments are avoiding using proprietary software because it is relatively easy to hack into, and then the governments have to depend on programmers of the commercial software to fix the problem. Governments also like OSS because by using it, they will not be locked into a contract as they would be with a company like Microsoft. It is difficult to draw an exact picture of the usage of OSS in the public sector because there are huge differences in the implementation of OSS between country to country and also within a single country. Software implementation and usage is normally part of the responsibility of the single governmental institutions themselves.

Due to the lack of political policy directives in the context of OSS, IT managers in public institutions are normally within their budgets free to buy and install the software they consider to be the most appropriate for their situation. The terms free software and open source software refers to two different software perspectives and none of them is without shortcomings. Free software is seen as anti-commercial while open source is supporting commercial initiatives.

CONCLUSION

OSS has much potential for libraries and information centers, and there are numerous projects, including Koha, NewGenLib, Greenstone, DSpace, Ganesha, etc. that demonstrate its viability in this context. It gives library staff an option to be actively involved in development projects, and this involvement can take many forms, such as reporting bugs, suggesting enhancements and testing new versions. Currently available OSS projects cover application areas ranging from the traditional library management systems to innovations like Greenstone and DSpace, which complement traditional systems. Open Source essentially empowers less privileged communities though it does not follow that it is meant only for them. There is no denying the fact that OSS enables bridging the digital divide in more ways than one.

Libraries in the developing countries are able to support electronic access, digital libraries, and resource sharing because they are able to use OSS. Even libraries in well developed countries are becoming more inclined towards OSS to improve their services. The Dspace is fairly powerful software. The major advantage of the software is that it allows submission of digital documents by its members. DSpace, EPrints, Greenstone and KOHA are among the top OSS which are widely used in India and world over because of their flexible searching, browsing, phrases and almost zero maintenance features.

REFERENCES

1. Biswas G, Paul D (2008). "NewGenLib, The First Indian Open Source Software: a Study of Its Features and Comparison With Other Software", 23rd National Seminar of IASLIC held at Bose Institute on Library Profession in Search of a New Paradigm, Kolkata, pp. 10-13.
2. Perspectives on Free and Open Source Software Edited by Joseph Feller, Brian Fitzgerald, Scott A. Hissam and Karim R. Lakhani.
3. Producing Open Source Software: How to Run a Successful Free Software Project by Karl Fogel.
4. http://www.dspace.org
5. http://www.koha.org
6. http://www.fedora.info/documentation/
7. http://software.eprints.org/
8. en.wikipedia.org/wiki/Open_source
9. en.wikipedia.org/wiki/Open-source_software
10. www.public-software.in/node/533

❑❑❑

Chapter – 32

Library Science : A New Dimension of Information Industry Yet To Open

Arun Modak and (Smt) Sonal Singh

RISE OF INFORMATION INDUSTRY

Market place created by the convergence of computers, telecommunication and microelectronics. The whole business is depend on marketing, therefore marketing of any product is the whole business seen from the point to point of view of its final result, that is from the customers point of view. Thus marketing means art of selling of working with market to actualize potential exchanges for the purpose of satisfying human needs and wants. It is the systematic gathering, recording and analysis of data about problems relating to the marketing of goods and services.

GLITCH IN INFORMATION INDUSTRY

Today information industry is a buss word every day user vista is opening. Some companies believe there are no new opportunities. They believe this information industry in mature that they are selling a commodity. But there is no such thing as a mature market or a commodity. It's only getting in the way of imagination. Starbucks didn't see the coffee market as mature.

Lateral marketing is to think of product in relation to another product service or idea. Through the thinking across two products rather than cereals plus a snack. Instead of putting loose cereal in a box, they use the cereal in the from of a snack bar that can be carried and eaten any time. This health bar suddenly people are able to consume cereal any time of the day in a conrenient form.

Marketing Guru Philips Kotler defines marketing as the analysis, planning implementation and control of carefully formulated programmes, designed to bring about voluntary exchanges of values with targets, markets for the purpose of achieving on designing the organization offering in terms of target markets need and desired on using effective pricing communication and distribution to inform, motivate and service the markets. Marketing brings in an element of competition. This will result in providing better services.

MARKETING OF INFORMATION INDUSTRY PRODUCTS AND SERVICE

Today, information is the power and libraries and information centers are the reservoir of this information libraries are non-profit service industries and information is their key product. the possible products and services offered by a library or information centers may be as mentioned below.

- Physical information products / services such as books journals, bibliographics, database etc.
- Electronic information product / services such as CD- ROMs etc.
- Online information product / services such as MEDLINE, PRAWESS etc.

Marketing of information products and services is fairly a new concept. As results of the complex and multidimensional activities of the society, the demand for information products and services, is steadily expanding. In addition, the factors such as rising cost, change in information demand, increasing threat from the emerging information industry etc. necessible the use of the marketing techniques in libraries. To survive in the modern completive world, libraries must rise up to the situation to provide the right information to the right user at right time and in required manner. For this, libraries have to use modern techniques used in other business organization.

Marketing of information products and services means transference of information to potential inevitable due to limited budget in all libraries irrespective of size and region. Marketing of information product and services offers a great potential to survive and grow their services. The core of marketing concept is user oriented therefore, marketing and its techniques if applied to library and information service can help in vital to fulfill the expected need of information seekers.

By applying marketing concept, the library and information centers to disseminate their product and services to satisfy users, needs through predetermined well-defined coordinated plan and activities. Thus marketing of information product and services helps is increasing users for their satisfaction.

The information industry has grown dramatically in services revenue and conference over the last decades. It has now emerged as an important area for libraries and information center. Libraries and information centers have begun to realize that marketing of information products and services in an integral part of administration, especially as a means for improving user satisfaction and promoting the user of services by current and potential users.

There main factors namely the information explosion the technology revolution and escalating library cost are responsible for encouraging the library profession to develop a marketing approach in its operation and services marketing has become an essential factor for survival. The information industry mainly focuses on marketing of information and product.

Methods of Marketing

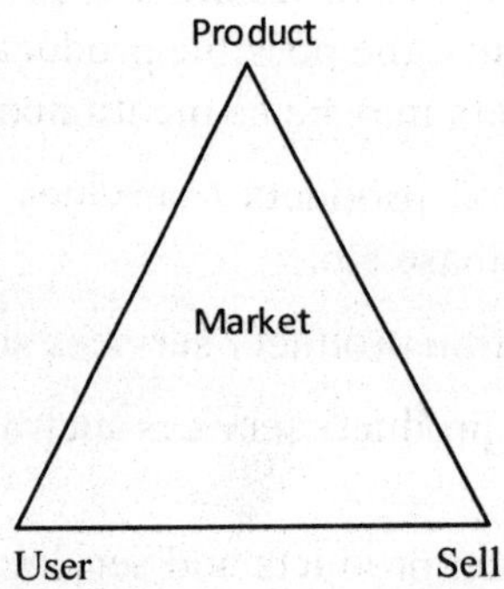

1. Initiation to user
2. Advertising or publishing
   a) Display
   b) Distribution
   c) Organizing exhibition
3. User education programme
4. Bibliographical instruction
5. CAS (Current Awareness Services)
6. SDI (Selective Dissemination of Information)
7. Knowledge of different information system
8. User education about technological development
9. Seminar lecture and Group discussion.

HOW INFORMATION INDUSTRY AND PRODUCT VIABLE IN LIBRARIES?

Every day, there is a continuous increase in industry of every field. In order to minimize the expenditure, cheap cost, more useful increase in production, the research and development are in progress. It has become essential to establish information center in the library to there jobs. The industrial libraries provide the information services very satisfactory.

Thus in order to ensure a balanced growth, the governments, particularly in the developing countries, must develop adequate information policies and information infrastructures. To create information awareness and promote its use, efforts must be made to spread information literacy. It means, people in all walks of life must be aware to find, retrieve, and use information strategically information can affect the stake of people positively or negatively. If knowledge is power information is instant power because it can be used instantly. Keeping in view the power of information, it must be managed and used strategically. Such as producing below -

Generic group definition

Each organization recognized the value of planning broad definition on their products. For example. The publishing company its basic product as information not books.

Target group

Each product is basically produced to target different kinds of customers depending upon the types of products.

Differential Marketing

When a business organization sets out to serve more than one target groups it will be maximally effective by differencing its product offering an communication.

Customer behavior

In order to satisfy the customer it is significant important to analyse the behavior of customers on account of the utility of the information product.

Differential advantage

In order to reaching the target groups an organization in advised to think in terms of seeking differential advantage of the product.

Marketing tool

The modern organization depends upon a multitude of tools to sell their products that is improvement consumer and dealers, advertising, sells promotion etc.

Integrating marketing planning

In order to sells their information product an organization should have overall co-ordination of their different activity being performed by the same the tools of marketing do not worked at cross purpose.

Continuous marketing feedback

In order to get the positive response about their product a continuous, marketing feedback is needed.

Marketing Audit

To understand the overall benefit as well as the loss of the product a continuous marketing audit is necessary for an organization to remain viable its management must provide for audit of its objectives, resources and opportunities.

INFORMATION CENTERS

The information centers in India are given below :

- Indian Institute in Management Ahmedabad
- Social Science, H.M.L. in Baroda
- Economic and social studies in Hyderabad.
- Ecological and Science Studies in Development Alternatives, Calcutta.
- Institute of Development Studies, Madras.
- National Institute of Social Defence in New Delhi.
- G.B. Pant Social Science Institute, Allahabad.
- IICSc, Bangalore
- Social Science & Arts SNDT, Women's University in Bombay.

We should remain very careful while choosing the information industry product and services. Therefore, if marketing techniques applied to library and information services, which will help into, fulfill the expected need of information seekers. So all I can say that marketing of information product and services helps to users for their information seeking behavior satisfaction.

REFERENCES

1. Agrawal, S. P (1987). Social Science information and documentation, New Delhi.
2. Kotler, Phillips (2007). Marketing Management. New Delhi : PHI.

3. Malhotra, Naresh K (2007). Marketing Research An applied orientation; New Delhi.

4. Nargundkar, Rajendra (2006). Services Marketing; New Delhi.

5. Tripathi, S.M. and Kumar, K (2002). Terminology for library and information science, New Delhi. ESS ESS Publication.

❑❑❑

Chapter – 33

Revamping of The School Libraries: A Requirement to Fulfil the Right to Education Act - 2009

V. Nireekshan Babu and M. R. Murali Prasad

INTRODUCTION

'Library is to Education' as 'Soul is to Body'. Library has always been central to education and self-improvement. Library is like an ocean of knowledge. One can find information in a library in almost all areas, be it history, politics, economics, geography, science, fiction, computers, or technology a library has it all. A library is like the whole world encompassed in one room. It is very essential to the education and school system. Libraries are an integral part of the education system and one is incomplete without the other. Francis Bacon quoted that *Libraries are the shrines where all the relics of the ancient saints, full of true virtue without delusion or imposture, are preserved and reposed.*

EDUCATION SYSTEM IN INDIA

India consists of 28 states, 6 union territories and a national capital territory having a rich and diverse culture spanning many years. The Constitution of India distributed the powers between the Union and the States in three lists such as Union list, State list and Concurrent list. Education is in the Concurrent List. Under the State list, state governments are exclusively responsible for education in their respective states. Union government is responsible for maintaining national and integrative character of education under the Union list. But both state and central government share responsibility for education in case of partnership under the Concurrent list.

Article 45, in the Directive Principle of Constitution of India provides free and compulsory education for children. The later added Article 21A namely the Right to Education says that the state has to provide free and compulsory education for all until the age of 14 years. Also, the Parliament passed an Act with 86th Amendment in 2002 that makes elementary education a Fundamental Right for children in the age group 6-14 years.

In India, there are two categories in providing education such as Public (Government) education, which is the major provider of education and Private education. The pre-university school education has different levels, the names given by the state governments, might differ:

Nursery	: Pre-nursery, Lower Kindergarten, Upper Kindergarten
Primary	: From 1st class to 5th class
Upper Primary	: From 6th class to 7th class
Secondary	: From 8th class to 10th class
Higher Secondary	: From 11th class to 12th class

The National Council of Educational Research and Training (NCERT) is the higher body for school education in India. The NCERT provides support and technical assistance to a number of schools in India on many aspects of enforcement of education policies. In India, the various curriculum bodies governing school education system are:

- The state government boards as Secondary School Certificate (SSC)/ Secondary School Leaving Certificate (SSLC)
- The Central Board of Secondary Education (CBSE) board.
- The Council for the Indian School Certificate Examinations (CISCE) board.
- The National Institute of Open Schooling (NIOS) board.
- International schools affiliated to the International Baccalaureate Programme and/or the Cambridge International Examinations.
- Islamic Madrasas schools, whose boards are controlled by local state governments, or autonomous, or affiliated with Darul Uloom Deoband.

SCHOOLS, ENROLMENTS AND DROP OUTS IN SCHOOL EDUCATION

According to the report of Seventh All India School Education Survey

(AIES), it has been found that the total number of schools in the different stages (primary, upper primary, secondary and higher secondary school stage) is 1031367. Out of this, 853457 schools recorded in rural areas whereas 177910 schools in urban areas with different stages of schooling.

From the same report, it has also been found that there had been substantial expansion in the number of schools during the period of 6th AIES and 7th AIES. And the growth in the total enrolment in the school has increased by 32.31% in both rural and urban areas. Because of these initiatives taken by the States and Centre, education system in India has expanded exponentially over the past five decades, but its current achievements are grossly inadequate for the nation to realize its potential greatness.

At the same time, the dropout rate was 34.9 per cent at the primary level, 52.9 per cent at the upper primary level and 62.6 percent at High school level in 2002-2003 (Selected Educational Statistics 2002-03, 2005). These high drop-out rates from both primary and secondary school, combined with low enrolment rates at the higher levels deprive tens of millions of children of their full rights as citizens.

Further, less than 7 per cent of the children ever pass the 10th standard public examination. Apart from addressing the needs of a large illiterate population, India's knowledge strategy must also develop innovative approaches to enhance knowledge acquisition among the large community of school drop-outs. Unless something is done to drastically reduce drop-out rates, by the year 2016 there will be approximately 500 million people in the country with less than five years of schooling, and another 300 million that will not have completed high school. In other words, about two-thirds of the population will lack the minimum level of education needed to keep pace with and take advantage of the social changes occurring within the country and worldwide (Garry Jacobs Vision 2020).

LIBRARY FACILITIES IN SCHOOLS

As per the Fifth All India Education Survey (1992) there are 7, 35,771 schools in all, out of which only 2, 93,427 (i.e. 39.88%) have libraries. Level wise analysis indicates that 26.18% primary schools, 66.97% upper primary schools, 90.12% secondary schools and 94.08% higher secondary schools have libraries. In the same survey, it was reported that only.15% of rural schools and 8.28% of urban schools have full-time librarians at the secondary school level. At the higher secondary school level only 29.58% rural schools and 46.10% urban schools have full-time librarians. However, the average of trained librarians is about 65% only in all schools. There are 1441 full time trained librarians. Others include from a teacher in-charge to a clerk or even personal assistant of the Principal of the school. The trained librarians have either a Diploma in Library Science or a Bachelor's degree in Library & Information Science. The statistics about the collection of books are quite revealing. 17.8%

schools have less than 100 books, 9.6% have 100-249 books, 5.3% 250-499 books, 3.64% have 500-599 books, 2.55 % have 1000-1999 books, about 2% has 2000-3999 books, and 1.5% has 4000-4999 books. The medium of instruction in government schools in India is mostly Hindi and the State/regional languages as India is a composite culture having a multiplicity of languages. In Public schools it is English. Majority of the schools are using more than one language as the medium of instruction.

As per the Seventh All India Education Survey (2002):

Table 1 Number Of Schools Having Library, Trained Librarian and Number Of Books With Them

A. Secondary Schools

Area	No. of Schools	No. of schools having library	No. of school having librarians				Schools with no. of books in Library		
			Full time		Part time		Up to 500	501 to 5000	> 5000
			A	B	A	B			
Rural	63576	47040 (73.99%)	2971	1927	1104	2531	23326	22698	1016
Urban	27165	23050 (84.85%)	3606	1999	1200	2224	9289	12077	1684
Total	90741	70090 (77.24%)	6577	3926	2304	4755	32615	34775	2700

A - Trained, B - Untrained

Table 2 number of schools having library, trained librarian and number of books with them

B. Higher Secondary

Area	No. of Schools	No. of schools having library	No. of school having librarians				Schools with no. of books in Library		
			Full time		Part time		Up to 500	501 to 5000	> 5000
			A	B	A	B			
Rural	22847	19925 (87.21%)	4946	1548	1123	1228	5528	11788	2609
Urban	21022	19376 (92.17%)	7699	1933	879	1678	3941	10854	4581
Total	43869	39301 (89.58%)	12645	3481	2002	2906	9469	22642	7190

A - Trained, B- Untrained

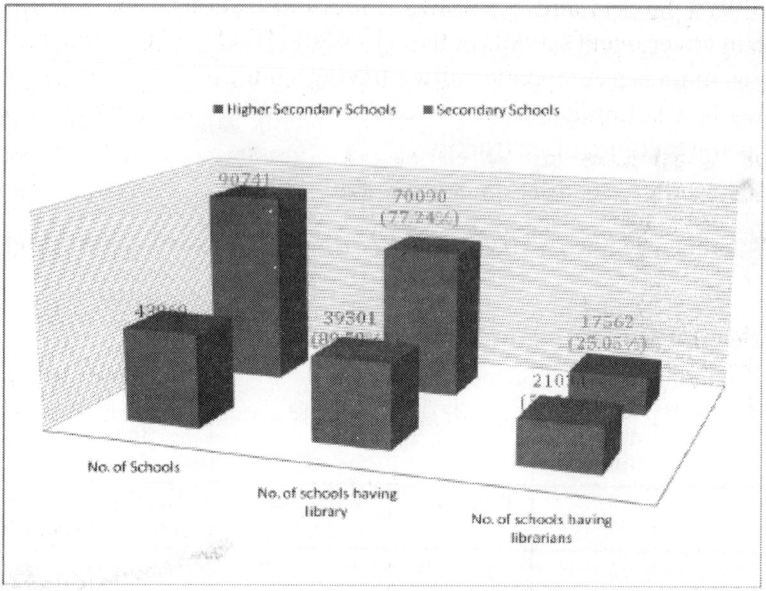

Figure 1 : Comparision status of higher secondary school and libraries

It is clear from the above illustrations (Table 1, Table 2 and Figure 1) that:

- 70,090 (77.24%) secondary schools and 39,301 (89.59%) higher secondary schools are having library facility whereas in 6th Survey out of 65564 secondary the percentages for secondary and higher secondary schools were 80.65% and 90.21% respectively.
- 73.99% of rural secondary schools are having library facility, whereas 84.85% of urban secondary schools are having library facility. Similarly, 87.21% of rural higher secondary schools are having library facility as against 92.17% of urban higher secondary schools.
- In secondary and higher secondary schools having library facility a proportion of 14.98% secondary schools and 41.03% higher secondary schools are having full time librarian. Only 10.07% secondary schools and 12.49% higher secondary schools are having part-time librarian.
- In secondary schools having library facility, the largest proportion of schools, i.e. 32,615 (46.53%) schools are having book strength of up to 500 books. Only 2,700 (3.85%) schools are having book strength of more than 5,000 books. Among higher secondary schools having library facility, the largest proportion of schools, i.e. 10,126 (25.77%) schools are having book strength of 2,001 to 5,000 books. Only 7,190 (18.29%) schools are having book strength of more than 5,000 books.

ROLE OF LIBRARIES IN SCHOOLS

The library enables the individual student to obtain intellectual, inspirational, and recreational activity through reading and nurture the personality of a student, right from the childhood. Enrollment in school is not a measure; sustaining a student and giving a quality education to the student is an important task. A library and its services are essential to any education system and that will help to develop a habit of continuous reading even after classes are completed. This reading habit will improve the learning levels of the student and its leads to take higher education in nature.

Emphasizing the role of the library in school, Dr. S.R. Ranganathan the Father of Library Science in India stated that the school libraries should act as laboratories for students and the librarians should function as guides to help the students in learning and using the books for improvement of knowledge and scholarship.

Also, the IFLA/UNESCO School Library Manifesto mentioned that the school library provides information and ideas that are fundamental to functioning successfully in today's information and knowledge-based society. The school library equips students with life-long learning skills and develops the imagination enabling them to live as responsible citizens.

Libraries support the curriculum, promote literacy development, and foster lifelong reading habits among children through the collection of library such as books, magazines, activity charts, maps, toys, etc. In addition, Libraries provide:

- The library strengthens the school in its vision and mission to educate and teach.
- The library makes books and other learning materials available in order to facilitate a self-sufficient action, the creation of student's own thinking and the awareness of the importance of his/her activities and hobbies.
- The library is useful for students and teachers as an information center, both for learning and recreation.
- The library gives equitable access to learning material to all students without social groups, creed, and income levels.
- The library is a location that encourages individual study, group discussions, groups collaboration and group presentations.

NEED OF REVAMP THE SCHOOL LIBRARIES

As per 2001 Census of India, 65% Indians are literate and almost every child has an access to school with around 95% of our rural education having a primary school within one kilometer of their home. The National Policy on

Education 1986 states that the investment on education be gradually increased to reach a level of 6% of the national income as early as possible. In spite of the resource constraints, the budgetary allocation on education has increased over the years. As part of the mid-term Strategic Plan and the Millennium Development Goals priorities, UNICEF India is also committed to ensuring quality education for all children.

Right to Education Act came into force in India from Thursday, 1st April 2010 and is one of the flagship programmes in the 100 day agenda of the UPA government. By implementing this Act, children would get the fundamental right to free and compulsory education. The new law will ensure that quality education is provided to children aged between 6 and 14 years of all communities, including minorities and backward classes and ensures reservation of 25% seats in private schools for children from poor families.

National Knowledge Commission of India (NKC), also address the Right to Education as:

- There is a need for a central legislation affirming the Right to Education.
- This must entail a financial provision requiring the central government to provide the bulk of the additional funds needed for realizing the Right to Education.
- The legislation should also lay down minimum standards of quality in school education and for it to be effective, the responsibility of the Government, at different levels, must be recognized and made justifiable.

All the acts and commissions believe that providing universal access to quality school education is a cornerstone of development and a minimum essential condition towards making India a knowledge society.

Library is a knowledge access point. Without a library a school will not be complete. Libraries are interconnected with education system and one is incomplete without the other.

Established libraries in the schools are a neglected lot in India. Moreover, the situation in rural areas is worse than the urban areas. The number of the librarians or skilled librarians working in the schools is still less in number as per number of libraries. Although the central government has made libraries a priority to help raise the literacy rate, yet these are not receiving the right attention as revealed by the 6th All India School Education Survey of 1993. Their resources in terms of staff and funds are scarce, as these have received the least priority. The budget allocation is also very poor in education in India (only 3.7% on GDP) when compared to the developed countries as UK (5.9%), USA (5.5%) and Canada (5.2%). The school libraries neither have good collection nor sufficient space because of the financial constraints. The libraries of private schools are slightly better than government schools. The situation is worst in case of libraries of government primary and middle schools. As a result, the school libraries are neither able to inculcate the reading interests among the children nor do they help in achieving information literacy. Although the number of school libraries in primary, secondary and the higher education is growing, yet there are many problems to overcome.

With the importance of libraries in schools, the NKC submitted its recommendations on School Education to the Government of India to:

- Set up a National Commission on Libraries
- Prepare a National Census of all Libraries
- Revamp Library Information Science (LIS) Education, Training and Research facilities
- Re-assess staffing of libraries
- Set up a Central Library Fund
- Modernize library management, encourage greater community participation in library management
- Promote Information and Communication Technology (ICT) applications in all libraries
- Facilitate donation and maintenance of private collections
- Encourage Public Private Partnerships in LIS development

This is the time to revamp the libraries in schools all over the India through the Right to Education Act, 2010. According to the Act, Section 19 that no school shall be established, or recognized unless it fulfills the norms and standards specified in the schedule. The schedule mention that a library shall be in each school providing newspapers, magazines and books on all subjects, including story books.

CONCLUSION

There is a dire need to revamp the school libraries in India. A school library should be exciting and welcoming, a place for children to delight in stories and a sign that the school is making its environment fit for learning. To enhance the literacy rate, quality of education and reading habits of the students, the status of the school libraries has to be improved. To achieve this, the Government of India, State Governments, the School Management, Librarians and teachers have as to work cooperatively.

Firstly, The Government of India must establish a Council for libraries in India such as All India Council Technical Education, Indian Council for Medical Research, etc. For this purpose, library legislation should be passed in the Parliament. In this legislation they have to clearly mention the rules and regulations to improve the libraries right from the school libraries to higher education libraries.

Secondly, the School Libraries Association should be established such as in USA, UK, Australia and else where in the world. The association has to frame the rules, standards and regulations according to the school needs as per Indian situations, represent to the government or higher authorities when ever required. In addition, the association should conduct conferences, workshops, hands-on-experience to emerging technologies in Library and Information Science. The association has to promote the Library and Information Science literature to the professionals through publications.

Thirdly, the government has to take steps to interlink public libraries and school libraries to enhance reading habits both in students, parents and family members. Raja Rammohanroy Library Foundation (RRLF) has taken steps to support school libraries towards development of library collection. Families have been targeted because illiteracy seems to be passed from one generation to the next: children whose parents are functionally illiterate are twice as likely as their peers to be functionally illiterate. Family literacy encourages the children reading habit and education as parent's role as the child's first teacher.

Fourthly, the school libraries/librarians consortia should be established to share information, to conduct career enhancement programmes, to exchange professional knowledge etc.

Lastly, the school librarians must play a vital and positive role in providing services to their users. Librarian must support the teachers and students to find information for their needs at the right time. Librarians must implement/apply Information Communication Technologies to library development activities time to time. School librarians have to follow the day to day technology developments and to learn through attending professional conferences/workshops and meetings frequently.

REFERENCES

1. IFLA. Quotations about Libraries and Librarians: Subject List, http://archive.ifla.org/I/humour/subj.htm
2. http://www.dnaindia.com/india/report_right-to-education-act-implemented-challenges-still-remain_1366189
3. Talan, Carole (1990).. Family Literacy: Libraries doing what libraries do best. *Wilson Library Bullitin* 65(3), pp. 30-32, 158.
4. National knowledge commission: Recommendation on school education, New Delhi, 2007. http://www.knowledgecommission.gove.in/downloads/documents/booklet_student.pdf
5. Special Facilities in Secondary and Higher Secondary Schools, 7th All India Educational Survey. http://www.ncert.nic.in/html/pdf/

Publication/Journal2008/Survey_reports2007/Specific_%20Facilities/Specific_Facilities.pdf

6. http://www.ifla.org/V11/s11/pubs/manifesto.htm
7. Preeti Mahajan (2010). School libraries in India: Present-day scenario, Library Philosophy and Practice, June, 2010. http://findarticles.com/p/articles/mi_7005/is_2010 _june/ai_n5461912/pg_5 ?tag=content; coll
8. Garry Jacobs Vision 2020. Towards a Knowledge Society. Paper prepared for New Delhi: Planning Commission
9. Government of India 2005. Selected Educational Statistics 2002-03. New Delhi: Ministry of Human Resource Development, Statistics Division.
10. National Council of Education Research and Training 2002, Seventh All India School Education Survey: Guidelines for Survey Officers. New Delhi: Department of Educational Surveys and Data Processing.
11. Vishal D. Pajankar and Pranali V. Pajankar (2010). Development of School Education Status in India. *Journal of Social Science* 22 (1), pp. 15-23.
12. Government of India: Ministry of Law and Justice. The Right of Children to Free and Compulsory Education Act-2009, No.35. New Delhi.

❑❑❑

Chapter – 34

Public Libraries in the Service of Society

Md. Nurul Islam

INTRODUCTION

'Society', this word is derived from the Latin word 'socius' which literally means a companion. Society is complex organism constituted by persons bound in willing allegiance to some common standards of psychological approach and outward behavior [10]. The story of libraries reflects the social, economical, cultural and educational needs to which libraries have responded. In preliterate society, human beings depended on live memory and the spoken words. By 2700 BC, the Sumerians had established private and government libraries for preserving their varied writings for use in the form of clay tablets. Ancient Egypt, from where writing was developed, produced some libraries which were composed of papyrus rolls [11]. So we can see, from the very initial stage of the society; books, papers, manuscripts, drawings, copper plates and other articles were being presented to it by various sources. We know that there is close relation between books and society. Healthy society is the creation of sound mind by books. Without sound mind, social progress can not be achieved properly. Every significant book may reflect distinct period of history. It is not essential to say that an author and his works can create new culture and lead to social changes. The books of authors of different countries in the world had / have a long influence on society [3].

In this present era, literature and knowledge is growing very fast and for their proper collection, preservation and to properly disseminate to people, we need public libraries. Society always depends on smooth growth and this growth is neither willful nor arbitrary[10]; it is consistent and systematic. For smooth and systemic growth of society, the government of different countries and states in the world have established schools, colleges and universities. No doubt, the government, different organizations, industrialists have to give priority to drinking water, sanitation and other conveniences. On the other hand, to remove illiteracy or to educate the citizens/nations and to introduce the human beings with phenomenal explosion of knowledge and information, government and other reputed agencies have established and also are establishing public libraries whose services play a vidal role in national progress and development.

SOCIAL DEVELOPMENT

Society is not static; it is dynamic, animated and vibrant. If society changes, the value system and culture necessarily gets changed. This change will be possible by proper education. Eucation is impartation of knowledge and training from the accumulated store of the human race and the impartation of skills necessary for meaningful, creative and adjusted living in society. It is the duty of global public libraries to inspire the public with new ideas for better living and better thinking.

The social changes are based on (10)

1. Curriculum and instructional strategy
2. Learning requirements and learning style
3. Free from duplication of information
4. Provision for validation and tryout
5. Maintenance and distribution, etc.

The role of public libraries in this present scenario of "social development" is very crucial and multifaceted. These facets may be children education, adult literacy, community information, citizenship education, international studies, exhibitions, health information, sports society, coaching and guidance, job information, carrier counseling, publications, etc.

Public library is a social institution. Which and develops in response to social conditions and needs for equipping the people with necessary proportion of accumulated knowledge and preparing them for co-operative social life. Knowledge society and citizenship education are two faces. The citizenship education is based on the acquisition of knowledge. Actually, citizenship education is one of the goals of public libraries across the globe. The citizenship education depends on national educational policy of that particular country. Hence, it is urgently required to have universal public library system, which integrates the component of global citizenship education.

The world in the 21st century is a knowledge based society with multiple opportunities [9]. Knowledge and information are effective apparatus in society, which can play vital role in improving the quality of life of human beings. Now a days, information is one of the most important weapons, which analyzes past, present and future and predict in solving problem and decision-making and play a crucial role in the community for its socio-economic development. Public library gives information relating to different aspects to the people, which are very needful for community development. The new idea of Community Information Service (CIS) [3] has been added in public library services.

Public libraries should provide opportunities and take necessary steps for developing the personality of the readers so that they may achieve their full potential and involving them in different nation building activities on the one side, and broad basing of sports and achieving excellence at national and international level on the other. It is indispensable that government or sponsoring authority should formulate principles and proper guidelines which will assist to make sports society of public libraries in that state.

In the 21st century, the challenging danger of the earth's environment scenario is climate change and global warming, due to excessive usage of fossil fuels [9]. A great number of people in our modern world are still uninterested, indifferent and ignorant on the issue of global warming [8]. The public libraries can arrange seminars, discussions, about the most complex issue of climate change and playa crucial role to increase public awareness on climate change and global warming.

A public library is a cultural, recreational and educational institution and is need of the community. It is one of the important media for mass-communication which is essential not only for the continuance of the existing democratic institutions but also to encourage their growth and development in future. A public library can rightly be called an index to the human development [7] in the field of humanities, social, physical and biological activities. In fact, personal, social and emotional development of the human being can be a success by establishing public libraries.

In September1948, the international seminar was organized by UNESCO in co-operation with IFLA in Manchester and London. The basic theme was public libraries with emphasis on their services to popular education and the promotion of international understanding [4].

The UNESCO public library Manifesto 1994 state the following key missions which relates to information, literacy, education and culture and should be at the core of public library services [6]:

1. Creating and strengthening reading habits in children at an early age
2. Supporting both individual and self conducted education as well formal education at all level

3. Providing opportunities for personal creative development
4. Stimulating the imagination and creativity of children and young people
5. Promoting awareness of cultural heritage, appreciation of the arts
6. Supporting both individual and self conducted education as well as formal education at all level
7. Providing opportunities for personal creative development
8. Supporting the oral tradition
9. Ensuring access for citizens to all sorts of community information
10. Providing adequate information services to local enterprises, associations and interest groups
11. Facilitating the development of information and computer literacy skills
12. Supporting and participating in literacy activities and programs for all age groups and initiating such activities if necessary

The UNESCO public library manifesto of 1994 (2nd revision) [6] also encourages growth of literacy through different programmes such as National Education Programme, National Literacy Mission, Total Literacy Campaign, Education for All Programme, etc. The decision of the Member states of UNESCO to authorize the institution or organization to undertake a programme of public library development is of great significance.

ROLE OF LIBRARY ASSOCIATIONS

Promotion and enlargement of public libraries and its services and duties is an important aspect of national advancement. In Western Europe and North America, public library system is an integral part of the social structure [4]. Every association has a vital role in their respective subject field. The subject intellectuals and library professionals are supporting public library movement and the society gets benefits to developing socio-economical, socio- educational, socio-cultural life. The library associations of different countries have a unique role in education, research, literacy programmes and awareness programmes. The associations should support more schemes/ projects of NGOs, providing rural public library services. Many associations have started publishing journals, newsletters, bulletins for their members. The state level associations are really active in public libraries' growth and movement in their respective states.

The objectives of the library associations are also in the direction of growth and progress of public libraries. Some of them are listed below: [1],[5]

1. Promotion of library movement and to interact with the society
2. Promotion of library and information science education, research, new ideas of the subject

3. To encourage library professionals to participate in workshops, seminars, conferences and symposia
4. Bring out publication in the form of journals, newsletters, books, etc
5. Establishment of libraries, documentation and information centers and to assist in their function and activities
6. Maintain liaison with state and other libraries associations and co-operation with international organizations with similar aims
7. Coordinate the activities and to assist amongst the different libraries, scientific and research institutions, learned societies, business and industrial organizations, etc.

CONCLUSION

The public library is an integral portion of present society and perform a very crucial role in the community. It should be regarded as a social force which can greatly influence the modern society. It aims at securing for the citizen of nation; justice, liberty and equality. It is establishing new horizon of social structure. It is to be considered as an instrument of social change. It is difficult to visualize a prosperous country without establishment, enlargement, development and advancement of public libraries. Therefore, it is the duty of government of national, state and local to establish and maintain public library system under the clear mandate of laws and regulations and also extend support and give priority to promote research for this purpose.

REFERENCES

1. Raman, M (2009). Establishing relationship with wider society: Role of media relation unit in university. *University News* 47 (32), pp.18-21.
2. Rao, K.S. (2010). Union budget: A serious concern toward economic growth. *Kurukshetra* 58 (6), pp. 19-23.
3. Mukherji, B (2009). Books, libraries and culture. *IASLIC Bulletin* 54(1), pp.3-8.
4. Sardana, J. L (2002). Libraries and information studies in retrospect and prospect. New Delhi : Concept Publishing, pp.338-347.
5. Kishan Kumar (2003). Library Organization. New Delhi : Vikas Publishing House, pp.201-219.
6. http://www.unesco.org/webworld/libraries/manifesto/libraman.html
7. Bottomore, T. B (1972). Sociology : A guide to problems and literature. 1972. Bombay : George Allen & Unwin, pp.113-133.

8. Nayak, J (2010). An investigation into the awareness, knowledge and attitude of students, teachers toward climate change. *University News* 48 (27), pp.8-12.

9. Abdul Kalam, APJ (2010). Technology is the foundation for the sustained development of the nation. *University News* 48(2), pp.24-28.

10. Bhatnagar, C. P (1971). The crisis in Indian society. Delhi : National publishing, pp.1-17.

11. Sengupta, B and Chakborty, B (1981). Library, Library science and Librarianship. Kolkata : World Press, pp.29-40

❑❑❑